HOLLYWOOD
Vampires

HOLLYWOOD
Vampires

JOHNNY DEPP, AMBER HEARD,
and the Celebrity Exploitation Machine

KELLY LOUDENBERG
MAKIKO WHOLEY

DEYST.

An Imprint of WILLIAM MORROW

DEYST.

HarperCollins books may be purchased for educational, business, or sales promotional use. For information, please email the Special Markets Department at SPsales@harpercollins.com.

FIRST EDITION

Designed by Renata De Oliveira

Library of Congress Cataloging-in-Publication Data has been applied for.

ISBN 978-0-06-333381-9

25 26 27 28 29 LBC 5 4 3 2 1

If you would be a real seeker after truth, it is necessary that at least once in your life you doubt, as far as possible, all things.

—RENÉ DESCARTES

Contents

PART III

PART IV

Authors' Note

Hollywood Vampires is based on more than three years of reporting. This book started as a documentary in March 2021 about the defamation battle between Amber Heard and her ex-husband, Johnny Depp. In June 2022, after the jury ruled in favor of Johnny Depp and the highly publicized trial came to a close, we realized that this story demanded the kind of careful narration, discussion of context, and nuance that could only be achieved in a book.

The reporting is drawn from several hours of our own documentary footage inside Amber Heard's home, with Johnny Depp's legal team in their War Room, and outside the Fairfax County Circuit Courthouse in Virginia. We also referenced hours of exclusive footage given to us by Amber's former girlfriend Bianca Butti, as Amber and her legal team prepared for *Depp vs News Group Newspapers Ltd*, a separate defamation trial brought by Johnny against a UK tabloid in 2020. In addition to footage, we spent two years interviewing more than a hundred people about the doomed marriage between Johnny and Amber and its aftermath. From trial spectators and fans to civil rights lawyers and academics to close friends of Amber and Johnny, we considered a range of perspectives for the reporting of this book. In addition to hours of extensive interviews, we reviewed court materials for both the UK and US defamation trials, including raw courtroom footage, daily transcripts, witness statements, journal entries, therapy notes, audio and video evidence, deposition video, and photos. We also referenced a bounty of legacy media stories, books, and tabloid articles, and we analyzed content and commentary on social-media platforms like Twitter, Instagram, Facebook, and TikTok. The book has been professionally fact-checked.

Most of our sources are named, but some people asked us to use pseudonyms for fear of being sued for defamation themselves. Because Amber didn't participate in this project after it turned from a documentary into a book, perspectives from her side during and after the *Depp vs Heard* trial are not reflected as thoroughly as Johnny's, whose team gave us continued access. We did our best to be fair and balanced.

This book contains descriptions, some of them graphic, of physical, verbal, and sexual abuse that may be disturbing or triggering to some readers.

Timeline

1963 — June 9: Johnny Depp born

1983 — Johnny moves to Hollywood

1986 — April 22: Amber Heard born

2003 — Amber moves to Hollywood

2008 — Johnny and Amber meet during casting for *The Rum Diary*

2012 — Johnny and Vanessa Paradis split

2013 — Johnny proposes to Amber

2015 — February 3: Johnny and Amber marry in a civil ceremony in LA

2016 — May 21: Police are called to Johnny and Amber's downtown LA penthouse

May 23: Amber files for divorce and requests a temporary restraining order, citing incidents of domestic violence

June 1: *People* magazine hits newsstands with a cover photo of Amber's injured face

2018   April 27: UK tabloid *The Sun* publishes article calling Johnny a "wifebeater"

June 1: Johnny sues *The Sun* publisher News Group Newspapers Ltd for defamation

December 18: Amber publishes *Washington Post* op-ed calling herself "a public figure representing domestic abuse"

December 20: Johnny "unofficially" dropped from the Pirates of the Caribbean franchise

2019   March 1: Johnny sues Amber for defamation (complaint filed in the circuit court of Fairfax County, Virginia)

2020   July 7: *Depp vs News Group Newspapers Ltd* (UK defamation trial) begins

November 2: *Depp vs News Group Newspapers Ltd* ruling announced

2022   April 11: *Depp vs Heard* (US defamation trial) begins

June 1: *Depp vs Heard* verdict announced

Cast of Characters

THE CELEBRITIES
Johnny Depp

Amber Heard

THE INNER CIRCLE
Christi Dembrowski

Johnny's sister and business partner

Whitney Heard

Amber's sister

Bruce Witkin

Johnny's childhood friend, bandmate, and former business partner

Sam Sarkar

Johnny's 21 Jump Street castmate and later colleague

Jason Forman

VP of Infinitum Nihil, Johnny's production company

Stephen Deuters

CEO of IN.2, Johnny's European production company

iO Tillett Wright

Amber's friend

Bianca Butti

cinematographer and Amber's former girlfriend

Beechy Colclough

Johnny's celebrity therapist

Raquel "Rocky" Pennington

witness and ex–best friend to Amber

Malcolm Connolly

Johnny's bodyguard

Jerry Judge

Johnny's chief of security and father figure

Nathan Holmes

Johnny's longtime assistant

THE STAFF
Jack Whigham

Johnny's manager

Ben King

Johnny's butler and house manager

Russell Borrill

Johnny's personal chef

Kevin Murphy

Johnny's LA house manager

Sara Nelson

Amber's former assistant

Dr. David Kipper

Johnny's concierge doctor and Hollywood addiction specialist

Debbie Lloyd

Johnny's personal nurse

Erin Falati

Amber's personal nurse

THE LAWYERS
Adam Waldman

Johnny's Svengali-like lawyer

Samantha Spector

Amber's divorce lawyer

Laura Wasser

Johnny's divorce lawyer

Eric George
celebrity attorney and adviser to Amber

Roberta Kaplan
founder of Time's Up Legal Defense Fund

Jen Robinson
Amber's UK lawyer

Elaine Bredehoft
Amber's lead counsel in Depp vs Heard

Benjamin Rottenborn
Amber's co-counsel in Depp vs Heard

The Black Pearl (Johnny's legal team)
including Benjamin Chew, Camille Vasquez, Jessica Meyers, and Samuel Moniz

Kathleen Zellner
wrongful conviction attorney

THE AGENTS
Christian Carino
CAA

Tracey Jacobs
UTA

EXTRAS
Paul Barresi
Hollywood fixer, Amber's former private investigator

Elon Musk
Amber's former boyfriend

SanDee Edwards
Fairfax local and Johnny Depp supporter

Molly Golightly
Pennsylvanian life coach and YouTuber

Yvonne de Boer
ex-costume designer and Johnny's self-proclaimed number one fan

HOLLYWOOD
Vampires

Prologue

Worldly fame is but a breath of wind that blows
now this way, and now that, and changes name as it
changes direction.
—DANTE ALIGHIERI

The Hollywood sign looms large above the grimy avenues of "the town" below—a world of taquerias, smog-check stations, drugstores, dentist offices, and hamburger stands. Woven throughout this utilitarian southwestern city is a unique network of movie studios, producers, talent managers, agents, writers, makeup artists, creature designers, and actors. Most people who pack up their aspirations and arrive in Hollywood are met only by unabating failure. But it may be those who "make it" who face the biggest challenge to sanity and soul: fame. Barred in and unable to interact with the world of the nobody, A-listers reside in a land of smoke and mirrors, easily lost among the sycophants and people-pleasers, beguiled by drugs aplenty, and fed upon by the hungry vampires collecting commissions.

Fame is a Faustian bargain. A-list Hollywood celebrities are canonized, showered in riches, and woven into history, our society's ultimate form of attention and reward. But in the eyes of corporate studios, divorce lawyers, talent agents, business managers, and concierge doctors, celebrities are living commodities. To the public, they're objects to covet, idolize, and exploit—sometimes in the form of tiny plastic facsimiles.

They're also ideological pawns of the cultural zeitgeist. Such was the case for actors Johnny Depp and Amber Heard, who were both sucked deep into the Hollywood star system—a hall of mirrors built on image, power, and money—and whose short-lived love story and bitter divorce became deeply entangled in the ideologies and heated politics of the moment. Their ensuing legal battles—which culminated in the infamous defamation trial *Depp vs Heard*—unfolded against, and were witnessed through, the #MeToo movement, the first Trump presidency, the COVID-19 pandemic, and the overturning of *Roe vs Wade*.

Celebrity trials have always captured the public's imagination, playing out like soap operas in the media. For as long as there have been TVs, the question of whether to televise these trials has been debated. In 1993, a new television station called Court TV broadcast the Menendez brothers' double-murder trial live from the courtroom, an emergent form of "reality TV," and millions of viewers tuned in to watch. True-crime TV was born. Two years later, the genre soared as the O. J. Simpson trial consumed America. When the not-guilty verdict was announced, 150 million people were watching. Cell phone providers noticed a 60 percent drop in usage during the broadcast, as people stayed glued to their TVs. One year later, Judge Judy came to CBS. High-profile trials become surrogates for the public's deepest hopes and fears, like anxieties around race relations and police corruption in the O.J. Simpson trial or intensified fear of "stranger danger" during the Ted Bundy trial. Like folklore, they reveal our shared beliefs and values. Prosecutors and defense attorneys know this better than anyone and use it to their advantage in the courtroom. The high-stakes drama of the court makes for good television.

With *Depp vs Heard*—which was watched by millions of people worldwide—what began as a salacious celebrity divorce grew into a national occupation, one that created a cultural schism and raised controversial questions about freedom of speech, the slippery nature of truth and fact, the boundaries of domestic abuse, the impact of social media and social justice movements on the legal process, and the ability of celebrities to represent complex social problems. Was *Depp vs Heard* a #MeToo case from which to draw grand, societal conclusions? Or was it a he-said/she-said scenario warped by money, greed, and fame?

Far from a forensic rehashing of the trial, the story we tell in this book broadens the lens to unravel a much more complex narrative—about fame, fandom, and contemporary feminism, and how the celebrity industrial complex capitalized on a viral social moment. We were journalists and filmmakers on the ground for the six-week trial in Fairfax, Virginia, but our investigation of the story began two years prior, when we met Amber Heard in the Hollywood Hills. Before, during, and after trial proceedings, we interviewed and filmed dozens of people closely associated with the lawsuit, including close friends of Johnny and Amber, as well as their lawyers, agents, business associates, publicists, assistants, and personal staff. We spoke extensively with Johnny's PR team in Fairfax and embedded with his attorneys in their "War Room" at the Ritz-Carlton. We spent time with the influencers who became famous covering the trial on YouTube, Twitter, and Instagram, and who steered public debate about the case. And we spent hours with Johnny and Amber themselves, who granted us unprecedented access into their private worlds.

This book probes the psyches, motivations, and backgrounds

of the key figures in the drama, as well as the ecosystem of fans, influencers, and media that arose around it. In telling this story, our goal is to complicate simplistic narratives and convenient assumptions that have come to surround the *Depp vs Heard* controversy—and by extension the #MeToo movement—as well as to reframe, as this story did for us, some of the most contentious debates today. Who can be an abuser and who can be a victim? When is it acceptable to question a woman's story? How much and what type of evidence is needed to come forward and be heard without prejudice? Can our society make space for imperfect victims? Should celebrities be the spokespeople for social justice movements? And what does it mean to do justice—for victims and alleged abusers alike—in a post-#MeToo world?

Walter Benjamin once said, "The cult of the movie star, fostered by the money of the film industry, preserves not the unique aura of the person but the 'spell of the personality,' the phony spell of a commodity." The price of fame is to be reduced to a product to be bought, sold, exploited, and ultimately discarded like yesterday's news. This fame cycle doesn't exist in a vacuum. It's an elaborate, interlocked system hinging on those who are idols and those who idolize. We, as authors, are writing the story for consumption yet again, and we recognize we are part of the system too. At its core, this book shows that the Hollywood system is vampiric, a teeming network of people feeding off one another's vitality and humanity for their own gain.

PART I

PART 1

CHAPTER 1

Going Gonzo

I n March 2009, Johnny Depp's luxury megayacht set sail from his private Bahamian island, Little Halls Pond Cay. The trip to Vega Baja, Puerto Rico, would take a week. Johnny would be there for a two-and-a-half-month stint to film *The Rum Diary*, the first movie by his production company, Infinitum Nihil. His yacht, the *Vajoliroja*, was named after his long-term partner, Vanessa Paradis; himself; his daughter, Lily-Rose; and his son, Jack, using the first two letters of each of their names. The teak-paneled, Turkish-made vessel rivaled lavish celebrity boats owned by Sir Elton John and Tiger Woods. A behemoth at 156-feet long, and outfitted with multiple sprawling decks and cinema, its lacquered pirate-ship-shaped exterior gleamed in the sun. Working with LA-based interior designer LM Pagano, Johnny had purchased and redesigned the boat for a reported $30 million to feel like "the Orient Express on the ocean." It had five bedrooms, each with en suite bathrooms, designed with opium-den interiors of maroon-hued velvet, wood-paneling, antique furniture, and silk textiles.

A crew of eight tended to Johnny and his guests. Inside the living room, Johnny joked and told stories with his two British assistants, Stephen Deuters and Nathan Holmes, his film sound technician Keenan Wyatt, and the writer Douglas Brinkley, who was writing a piece about Johnny for *Vanity Fair*. Douglas also happened to be the literary executor of Johnny's hero, the gonzo journalist Hunter S. Thompson. This wasn't a typical interview setup. The five men watched *Tropic Thunder* and YouTube clips of James Brown and Dean Martin roasts, eating meals prepared by an onboard chef consisting of grilled beef-and-cheese sandwiches, fresh seafood, salads, and Chicago-style pepperoni pizza. To wash it all down was Red Bull and booze. Lots of booze. Johnny repeated an old adage for Douglas: "Money doesn't buy you happiness. But it buys you a big enough yacht to sail right up to it."

Money is what Johnny had at that time. He was among the highest-paid actors in the world, reportedly making north of $50 million a year. The yacht was a sign of just how much Johnny's lifestyle had changed since he landed in Los Angeles in December 1983 to play guitar in a rock band. When he arrived in Hollywood, he was broke. One of his first jobs was hustling personalized ballpoint pens over the phone. Back then, he and his best friend Bruce Witkin would take telemarketer jobs for a week, pick up the pay, then quit when it became commission-based.

Johnny was the antithesis of Hollywood, a grungy, bohemian poor kid from Kentucky. He chain-smoked during interviews, telling a reporter once that he wished he could have another mouth grafted on so he could smoke six packs a day. He was covered in tattoos and self-inflicted scars that marked momentous occasions ("My body is my journal," he said. "It's a journal of skin."). He collected freaky clown paintings, rare guns, and insect specimens. Part of Johnny's appeal was that he seemed like an artist who happened to land in Hollywood. People often compared him to James Dean or Marlon Brando. Tim Burton described Johnny as "a great character actor in a leading man's body."

Throughout the 1990s, Johnny mostly acted in low-paying, critically respected indie films like *Dead Man* and *What's Eating Gilbert Grape*. Back then, Johnny was known to choose his roles based on his personal connection to the story and the characters, who were often outsiders. "My career was never about commercial success," Johnny told a reporter in 2004. "I never wanted to be remembered for being a star. It wasn't that I was rejecting Hollywood; I was rejecting the idea of being a product." Even after he achieved A-list celebrity status, he still didn't seem particularly interested in stardom.

Then Mickey Mouse came calling.

Playing Captain Jack Sparrow in the Disney franchise Pirates of the Caribbean transformed Johnny from an indie darling to a mainstream folk hero. Johnny's self-styled Jack Sparrow character was a swaggering outlaw he modeled after his friend Keith Richards and cartoon skunk Pepé Le Pew. Johnny had already charmed the world with his raw portrayal of Edward Scissorhands, and in Jack Sparrow he created a different type of lovable misfit.

Critics called Johnny's initial performance as Captain Sparrow "one of the most dazzling characters of the decade." He'd managed to insert an artful character into a product of pure commerce. By 2007, after starring in three installments of the Pirates franchise, the gold-toothed, dreadlocked Captain Jack Sparrow had evolved into a Disney icon, folded into the same universe as Donald Duck, Buzz Lightyear, and the talking cars from *Cars*. Jack Sparrow had boundless capitalist potential, including franchising deals in toys, clothing, action figures, and a playable character across several video games. The Pirates of the Caribbean theme park rides at Disneyland (built in 1967) and Disney World (added in 1973), on which the movies were based, were redesigned to feature swaggering animatronic replicas of Johnny's character.

Photos of Johnny as Jack Sparrow were printed on packaging for M&M's, Kellogg's cereal, and fruit snacks. He was miniaturized as a McDonald's Happy Meal plush toy.

By 2011, Pirates-related merchandise would make Disney $1.6 billion. By 2017, the five Pirates films would make Disney a combined $4.5 billion at the box office. Johnny would eventually be paid a reported $265 million by Disney for five Pirates films. With more commercial roles, Johnny realized he was making a deal with the devil, but he kept his focus on the artistic sandbox he could make within those roles. When it came to more corporate projects, Stephen described Johnny's philosophy as: "My job is the character and there is no difference in my approach whether it's an indie western or a huge Disney franchise."

His lifestyle grew to match his paychecks. The same guy who said money "reveals" people and told reporters he's "still exactly the guy that used to pump gas" now traveled by private jet, black car, and megayacht. With global fame came a loss of anonymity and a higher cost of existence. Johnny, Vanessa, and their children could no longer roam free without security and private drivers.

Even before Pirates, Johnny dealt with intense stalkers. One of them showed up on the set of the 1997 film *Donnie Brasco* while he was shooting a scene with Al Pacino. They were filming in lower Manhattan, sitting inside the picture car when Johnny spotted his stalker down the street, recognizing him from previous run-ins. The way Johnny remembered it, the look in his eyes was as if he was there to kill. But when the man approached, all he said was, "Hi, Johnny." The next time he saw the stalker, the man dumped all of his personal belongings, including his cats, in front of Johnny's Hollywood club, the Viper Room.

Another time he and his assistant Stephen snuck out of a hotel on the Left Bank in Paris without telling Johnny's security.

Stephen said they were walking to a local bookstore and within minutes, "it was like *A Hard Day's Night*" and they were swarmed by fans. Once they got inside the store, the owner locked the door and Stephen called security to come rescue them. "Johnny, who normally had a sense of humor about these things, was quite shocked at the volume of attention."

While he's always been a sex symbol, Johnny has also been a folk hero to his fanbase, more accessible and relatable than other stars like Brad Pitt or Tom Cruise. Johnny wore old rumpled T-shirts and jeans, would talk to anyone on the street, gave his money away in droves, took gifts from fans—and was seen actually wearing the gifts—and generally tended to decry the bullshit and unfairness of the world. He appealed to everyday people.

Now that he was a global superstar, it wasn't one-off oddballs that Johnny lamented but the paparazzi helicopters circling his house. He told his friends that he "lived his life behind windows." On his yacht, Johnny found freedom on the open sea.

After a week at sea, the *Vajoliroja*, flying its Jolly Roger flag, anchored in the crystal-blue waters of Puerto Rico. Johnny was both producing and starring in *The Rum Diary*, which was adapted from a Hunter S. Thompson novel written in 1959. The lost manuscript had sat unpublished at Hunter's house until Johnny himself "discovered" it while doing field research for his role in Terry Gilliam's 1998 film, *Fear and Loathing in Las Vegas*. Hunter had welcomed Johnny into his world with unlimited access. His "fortified compound" Owl Farm was in Woody Creek, Colorado, a rural area a few hundred miles west of Denver, where Hunter raised peacocks, shot guns, and kept a pet wolverine. Johnny took his field research with Hunter seriously, saying, "We were good friends, but I had a job to do. I was there to sponge, to steal, thieve, and/or pilfer as much of his soul as I could . . . He continued to give, and I continued to take . . . Simply staying with Hunter was never an option. You had to *live*." And live he did, for several months, spending his days and nights with Hunter in a booze- and drug-fueled dream state. Johnny described one of Hunter's early "tests" for him: handing him a twelve-gauge shotgun and directing him to shoot a propane tank with nitroglycerin taped to the side, resulting in an eighty-foot fireball in the backyard.

Across the hallway from the bedroom where Johnny slept, with a keg of gunpowder as a bedside table, was a storage room known as the War Room. Here, Johnny came across an old cardboard box of papers. Inside, he spotted a "folder with a rubber band around it." Scribbled on the front page in Hunter's handwriting was *The Rum Diary*.

Johnny and Hunter sat on the floor cross-legged, reading. *The Rum Diary* followed a hard-drinking journalist named Paul Kemp who moves to Puerto Rico to work as a local newspaper reporter, searching for a story among a bevy of lost souls. Hunter had written the novel based on his experience as a vagabond freelance journalist in Puerto Rico in his early twenties. "*The Rum Diary* was simply too good to remain lost," Johnny determined. Lynn Nesbit, Hunter's literary agent, later insisted the manuscript was never lost; Hunter just didn't think it was that good. But Hunter was okay with Johnny resurrecting it because he needed money. According to Johnny, Hunter wanted to make the book into a film and Johnny would star in it. Hunter told him: "Hot damn . . . yessir, let's you and I produce this fucking caper together, Colonel! We'll have Hollywood groveling at our feet!"

Benicio del Toro, Johnny's costar in *Fear and Loathing in Las Vegas*, was set to direct *The Rum Diary*, but the project languished and Johnny and Hunter eventually set their sights on someone else: Bruce Robinson, director of the 1987 cult British comedy classic, *Withnail and I*. Johnny had tried to attach Bruce to *Fear and Loathing*, but by then Bruce had left filmmaking behind "by choice" after his first foray into Hollywood had ended terribly.

Jennifer 8, his serial killer film released in the early '90s, had been compromised by studio interference: "There were four different heads of studio on that movie, they all wanted different things," Bruce said. "I had no aspiration to be a film director ever again in my life—I made a promise, in fact, to myself that I would never do it again. I kept the promise for seventeen years and then I was on vacation in Spain and I got a phone call and it was Depp." Surprised and confused by how Johnny found him in Seville, Bruce agreed to read a copy of *The Rum Diary*. Then he agreed to write the script—but he was adamant he was not going to direct. He was done with Hollywood. But Johnny persisted for years, and eventually resorted to begging. In 2005, Bruce finally gave in.

Johnny was ecstatic, but he couldn't share the good news with Hunter. He'd shot himself at Owl Farm earlier that year. The police report stated that a piece of paper was found inside Hunter's typewriter with a single word typed: "counselor." Johnny funded Hunter's funeral, a $5 million affair attended by 250 people. Per his wishes, Hunter's ashes were shot out of a cannon placed atop a 150-foot tower formed in the shape of a fist clutching a peyote button, while red, white, green, and blue fireworks exploded in the background. Hunter's death encouraged Johnny to keep trying to get *The Rum Diary* made. "[I] sure as fuck wasn't going to give up now," he said.

A year earlier, *Variety* magazine had reported that Graham King, a producer known for blockbuster films like *The Aviator* and *Traffic*, would finance and co-produce films with Johnny's new production company, Infinitum Nihil (IN), the name of which was "Infinite Nothing" translated into Latin. Graham King would also cover the overhead costs for IN and provide money for project development. Actors were increasingly spearheading their own production companies as a way to make more money, influence cinema, wrest control from studios, and create roles that inspired them. Brad Pitt and Jennifer Aniston started Plan B Entertainment in 2001, Leonardo DiCaprio headed Appian Way Productions, and Adam Sandler had Happy Madison Productions. Six major conglomerates—Disney, GE, News Corporation, Sony, Time Warner, and Viacom—controlled all the major movie studios and networks. They were moving toward IP-driven, A-list-focused content. Johnny wanted to make indies with unknown actors, using obscure source material. His company employed three people: Johnny as CEO; his sister, Christi Dembrowski, Johnny's assistant since the early '90s, as president; and his long-time friend Sam Sarkar as head of development.

Among indie filmmakers, IN gained a reputation as a company with a lot of false stops and starts, buying up book options and not following through on producing them. "More like . . . infinite zero," said one inside source we'll call "Elena," a primary crew member behind the making of *The Rum Diary*. "It's the place where projects go to die. They will buy the rights, and nothing will come out on the other end." Elena's personal friend was "razmatazzed" by IN for two years before it became apparent that they didn't have the energy to get projects off the ground. Elena described the company as a poorly managed "cult" with a kind of unquestioning loyalty to Johnny.

"Johnny is so spacey and mystical, you have these conversations and then he leaves and you are like, 'this is going to be amazing, namaste,'" Elena said. "It's a bunch of hipster gobbledygook and then he's gone and you don't see him." Johnny's method for selecting which films to produce was also mercurial. Once, he asked the artist and filmmaker Julian Schnabel, who directed Johnny in the movie *Before Night Falls*, to pick one of five books that Johnny had optioned.

"I picked [Nick Tosches's] *In the Hand of Dante*," Julian said. Johnny had reportedly agreed to purchase the Tosches archives for $1.2 million late one night at London's Dorchester hotel. He'd made the agreement on hotel stationery, sealing it with his signature and what appeared to be drops of blood.

"I don't know what happened, but we haven't talked for years," Julian continued. He insisted there wasn't a fight, but that Johnny just disappeared on him after that. One time, Julian was talking on the phone to a film contact, who happened to be riding in a car with Johnny. "I said, 'Why don't you put him on the phone?' but he didn't want to talk. I said, 'Well, tell him I love him.' And he said, 'Tell him I love him too, but I'm riding another wave now.' I said, 'What the fuck does that mean?'" Julian seemed offended by the brush-off. He'd spent time with Johnny's family and taught him how to paint. Julian made the movie anyway with Oscar Isaac as the lead.

Despite his reputation for capriciousness, by 2009 Johnny was still one of the hottest stars in town and people were clamoring to work with him. His films had collectively earned more than $3 billion and he'd been nominated for three Oscars. That year, he'd be named *People* magazine's "Sexiest Man Alive" for the second time.

The pieces were also finally falling into place for *The Rum Diary*. But in order to start filming, he'd need a cast.

The most important role to cast was Johnny's love interest. The character of Chenault was a free-spirited, flirtatious beauty from Connecticut who had a torrid affair with Johnny's character Kemp. Johnny had a casting call at the Infinitum Nihil office on

Melrose. Keira Knightley was up for the part, as was Scarlett Johansson. But a captivating twenty-two-year-old blond newcomer from Texas beat them both out. Amber Heard was a relative unknown with a slew of supporting roles under her belt in films like *Pineapple Express* and *Zombieland*, in which she played the love interests, as well as lead roles in lesser-known horror and action films like *All the Boys Love Mandy Lane* and *Never Back Down*.

Amber's lack of show business connections was no match for her ambition. After a successful first year in the industry, she said in an interview, "If this whole thing hadn't worked out I would have killed myself or gone back to school. The latter would have been the last option."

As badly as Johnny wanted to bring Hunter's novel to life, Amber wanted to star in it. She auditioned for the part several times, remarking that it was a long process, a grueling one. She wrote handwritten letters to the film's producers and director. Like Johnny, Amber was a huge fan of Thompson. She insisted she was perfect for the role of Chenault. Notably, the film's script left out the more unsavory aspects of the novel, namely the chronic racial slurs, as well as parts of Chenault's story, like Kemp's violent rape fantasies about her, verbal and physical abuse, and a climactic scene where she's brutally gang raped.

When Johnny first met Amber at his office, he said he took one look at her and thought, "Yep . . . That's the one . . . she could definitely kill me. That's what Hunter wants."

After Johnny and his crew arrived in Vega Baja, Puerto Rico, Amber showed up to set with her girlfriend Tasya van Ree, a willowy, dark-haired Hawaiian artist and model. The pair had been together for a year but wouldn't go public until the following year, when

Amber openly acknowledged her bisexuality during a 2010 event for GLAAD. According to a source on set, Amber also brought two small dogs, which she described as service dogs for her narcolepsy. She said their constant yapping would "bark her awake," the source recalled.

Amber greeted director Bruce Robinson in the production office, introducing Tasya as her "wife." (In March 2008, Amber had petitioned a California court to change her last name to van Ree, after the couple entered into a domestic partnership.) As an assistant escorted Amber and Tasya to their apartment, Bruce looked over at Johnny and a few other crew members inside the office. Panicked and flapping his arms like a bird, worried that the co-stars wouldn't have chemistry, he exclaimed, "She's gay?!"

Johnny tugged on his cigarette and replied to Bruce, "Don't worry, no leading lady of mine stays gay for very long."

Though he projected an air of a playboy, Johnny was in a committed long-term relationship with the Parisian singer, actress, and mother to his two kids, Vanessa Paradis. In 1998, they'd met at the opulent Hôtel Costes when Johnny was filming Roman Polanski's *The Ninth Gate* in Paris. "She was wearing a dress with an exposed back and I saw that back and that neck, and then she turned around and I saw those eyes, and—boom! My life as a single man was done." The pair were notoriously private, but in a 2004 interview with Oprah, Johnny said, "I mean Vanessa and my kids gave me life. Just, I mean, put me in a whole other arena."

Before Vanessa, Johnny dated Kate Moss for three years after meeting her at Café Tabac in the East Village in 1994. They were the "It" couple of the '90s, a thrilling public merger of fame and beauty. Bret Easton Ellis's novel satirizing that decade's celebrity culture, *Glamorama*, contains several references to Johnny and Kate as a type of revered entity. Before Kate, Johnny had been one half of a celebrity couple with his *Edward Scissorhands* costar Winona Ryder, a relationship that had also infatuated the public. But the relationship with Vanessa was different, something he seemed more driven to protect from the spotlight.

It was Johnny's own bad-boy persona that drew the kind of attention he was now so determined to deflect. That image had been cemented in 1994, when he was arrested for criminal mischief after trashing a hotel room in New York City, resulting in a nearly $10,000 fine. Afterward, Johnny said it had been a bad day, that he felt sick of people putting him on display and only talking about "the work" and the money when it came to him. His star only rose further. "Criminal movie star is a really good look for Johnny," director John Waters said of the ordeal.

Five years later, in 1999, Johnny got in trouble with the law again as he was leaving Marco Pierre White's restaurant Mirabelle in London with Vanessa Paradis. By then, Vanessa was several months' pregnant with their first child, Lily-Rose. When paparazzi started closing in on them, Johnny asked them for some space. When they ignored him, he picked up a wooden plank and began swinging at the photographers, warning them to stay away. No one was hurt, but Johnny was arrested and put in jail for several hours. When Lily-Rose was born in Neuilly-sur-Seine, an urban commune just west of Paris, photographers lined up outside of Vanessa's hospital room window and snapped photos of Johnny each time he stepped out for a cigarette while he hid behind an umbrella. "Now, that's no way to live. That's a sick thing to have mixed in with the most beautiful memories of your life. It's like a jail," he said.

Becoming a family man signaled a transformation for Johnny. Three years after Lily-Rose was born, Vanessa gave birth to a son, Jack. The family of four settled down on a farm in the South of France. Johnny settled into a sedate domesticity, telling reporters he was happiest playing with the kids in the garden and going swimming at the beach with the family. He credited Vanessa with turning his life around, stating that she insisted he exercise, eat healthy, and cut down on drinking and smoking. His family life consisted of a glass of wine or two before dinner and watching the sunset as his kids played nearby.

Johnny's childhood friend Bruce Witkin remembers this period of Johnny's life fondly. Vanessa was an accomplished singer with several hit songs and collaborations with Serge Gainsbourg and her ex-boyfriend Lenny Kravitz. She also recorded music with Johnny, who cowrote two tracks on her fourth album, *Bliss*. Bruce Witkin tagged along with the couple as they toured the world. Even Hunter Thompson had noticed Johnny had changed his ways. "Johnny seems happy with his new gentrification," he said in 1999. Still, Thompson sensed something amiss. "He's too smart to be really happy."

Bruce Witkin said Johnny never talked to him about his mounting relationship issues with Vanessa, but as the years passed, and Johnny's fame soared to new heights in the 2000s, Bruce also sensed Johnny's growing unease. According to him, Johnny drank moderately and didn't do drugs, maybe dabbling in a little weed, while he and Vanessa were together, but as they started to drift, Johnny's drinking and drug use picked up. "I think every marriage has a point, that hump I call it, that you have to work through. And when you're not handling your day-to-day stuff, how do you work through that?" Bruce said. "Why it didn't work out I don't know, but suddenly there was Amber."

The night before the first day of production in Puerto Rico, Johnny, Douglas Brinkley, and Bruce Robinson held a dinner. Johnny led a toast, calling for a successful shoot in honor of Hunter S. Thompson. "Here's to Hunter, here's to rum," he said. The next morning, Johnny polished off his last glass of a bottle of $2,000 1989 Haut-Brion wine, rallying himself to get to set. "The time has come to start channeling Hunter."

Johnny and Bruce Robinson set up an empty director's chair for Hunter, so he was "always there," with a pack of Dunhill cigarettes and a bottle of Chivas Regal whiskey in his seat. Every morning they'd dip their fingers into the bottle and dab whiskey behind their ears like perfume. "This was for him," they said of their daily ritual.

Amber said good-bye to Tasya, who went back to LA, and filming for *The Rum Diary* began. This is when, as one crew member recalled, Johnny and Amber became "locked into that death dance." Everyone on set, from the director, to the gaffers, to the PAs, witnessed Johnny and Amber's mutual infatuation unfold in real time. In a now infamous scene from the film, they stood under the stream of a shower as they kissed with passion, running their hands through each other's hair. "That moment . . . felt like something; it felt like something I should not be feeling," Johnny later said. At first, Amber played it cool. "I grew up watching his movies, so it was a little surreal, but I very much become my character while I'm working. I'm not Amber Heard making out with Johnny Depp in the shower." Later, she admitted there was more to it. "It didn't feel like a normal scene. It felt real," she said.

A source close to production described *The Rum Diary* as an imitation of a film set. The infrastructure and crew were in place, but no one wanted to do the work and no one had a clear vision of what the final product should be. They'd forgo getting certain shots needed for continuity, doing the absolute minimum they could. Even though the film was the debut from his new production company and had been years in the making, this source said Johnny didn't seem to have the discipline and made the process "torturous."

According to Elena, once filming started, Johnny effectively abandoned Bruce Robinson in the filmmaking process. He locked himself away in his trailer and checked out, leaving Bruce alone at the helm, who was now doing the two things he promised to never do again: direct a Hollywood movie and drink. Johnny's assistant Stephen's recollection was different: "It was long days and long hours, but it was quite thrilling because it was our project, something Infinitum Nihil had put together."

After nearly two and a half months, production wrapped and Johnny took a long vacation on his yacht with Vanessa and the kids. Amber returned to LA, where Johnny sent her a wrap gift, a dress she'd worn in the movie with a note that read "Happy Wrapping." This was in addition to a bicycle, expensive collectible books, and the guitar he'd already gifted her.

Johnny continued spending like a king. Even though he'd booked big-budget movies like Tim Burton's *Dark Shadows* and Gore Verbinski's *The Lone Ranger*, he was digging himself into debt. He was especially fond of real estate, and properties were piling up. By 2009, he owned a 1931 replica Bavarian castle in West Hollywood called "Sweetzer" on a private four-acre cul-de-sac; a forty-one-acre horse farm in Kentucky called "Betty Sue's Family Farm," named after his mother; a forty-five-acre private island in the Bahamas; and a sprawling estate in Southern France with a twelve-bedroom main house, a chapel, a bar and restaurant, two swimming pools, a skate park, and a Pirates of the Caribbean–themed wine cave decorated with skulls and scarves.

In October of that year, his sister and assistant, Christi, spoke on the phone with Joel Mandel, who'd been Johnny's business manager at The Management Group (TMG) for a decade. They were worried. Christi told Joel that Johnny didn't want to talk about his financial situation, and that Joel needed to do whatever it took to shore up Johnny's accounts. The following month, Joel sent Christi an email encouraging her to have Johnny sign paperwork for a line of credit in the amount of $6 million. But Christi couldn't get Johnny alone long enough to sign.

Joel asked Johnny to take it easy on holiday spending and be conservative at the upcoming John Dillinger auction. Even before playing him in the 2009 film *Public Enemies,* Johnny had been obsessed with the Depression-era bank robber. Now, he wanted the dead man's stuff. Joel also needed to talk with Johnny about paying back the existing loans they'd taken out and to "look realistically at income and expenses and work together on how to make sure these are back in balance." Johnny told Joel he was doing his best to curb his Christmas spending, but insisted he had to keep flying private jets because a commercial flight with paparazzi would be a "fucking nightmare of monumental proportions." He tried to allay Joel's fears by detailing all the paychecks coming down the pipeline: $20 million for *The Tourist,* $35 million for Pirates 4, and $20 million for *Dark Shadows.* "Other than that, i got bikes, cars, property, books, paintings and some semblance of a soul left, where would you like me to start???" he offered over email.

By the end of January 2010, Johnny still hadn't signed the loan document paperwork. He was $4 million overdrawn from the bank.

The Rum Diary opened in October 2011 to mixed reviews. Commercially, the film flopped, making $30 million worldwide against its $45 million budget.

In the two years since filming in Puerto Rico, Amber and Tasya had been regularly snapped together by the paparazzi in Los Angeles, shopping, eating at Joan's on Third, and cruising around in Amber's blue 1968 Ford Mustang. Together, they'd become part of the mainstream Hollywood scene in LA, attending brand launches, movie premieres, charity events, and after-parties. Tasya described Amber as her muse: "Gala is to Salvador Dalí, Kiki de Montparnasse is to Man Ray, Beatrice is to Dante Alighieri."

Meanwhile, Johnny's mounting struggles with alcohol were hastening the demise of his fourteen-year partnership with Vanessa. In February 2012, Johnny wrote in an email to his friend Mathias Bouchin, "I know now that I was not happy . . . I have been living in a state of constant poison for years. This cannot continue. I need peace. Vanessa needs peace and deserves to be happy." The following month, Johnny sent Elton John, his buddy in sobriety, an email with the subject line "100 days." In the email Johnny told Elton he'd been sober for a hundred days and thanked him for his "love, understanding and complete dedication to the curing of my poisoned wet brain and liver resembling Mrs. Thatcher . . . I would have been swallowed up by the monster were it not for you. That is a simple fact."

In June 2012, Johnny and Vanessa announced their separation. Stephen, Johnny's assistant and friend, said that it was a sad time for Johnny and that it appeared he felt enormous guilt with regards to his kids, because they were still young. Even though they'd never married, Johnny reportedly gave Vanessa $100 million in the separation.

That same month, Johnny gifted Amber a $6,500 Palomino horse named Peaches and Creme. Amber renamed the horse Arrow. There were tabloid reports of Amber regularly visiting Johnny on the set of *The Lone Ranger* in New Mexico. For his forty-ninth birthday, Amber gifted Johnny a foot-long turquoise-handled knife, the blade inscribed with "hasta la muerta," meaning "until death." Less than a week later, Amber and Tasya announced their split.

Johnny and Amber claimed they didn't have sex until after they'd ended their respective relationships with Vanessa and Tasya. But, a decade later, Amber would tell a courtroom that she recalled they'd started dating in October 2011. During the press tour for *The Rum Diary*, Johnny had invited Amber, through his publicist, into his hotel room in London. "It felt like there was electricity to the room . . . I got up and left, and as I went to leave, he grabbed both sides of my face, similar to what he did in Puerto Rico when we were filming that scene and he kissed me and I kissed him back."

Johnny, twenty-two years older than Amber, was very much her type. The year before she met Johnny, she'd told a reporter, "All the guys I date are older than me. It's actually a sickness, like an addiction." She'd dated Mexican filmmaker Alejandro Monteverde, nine years her senior, when she was eighteen living in her hometown of Austin, Texas, and then continued seeing him when she moved to LA, where he helped her meet people in the industry. Then she dated Mexican telenovela actor Valentino Lanús, eleven years her senior, for a stretch of months. Amber had also been romantically linked to the actor Crispin Glover, twenty-two years her senior.

Bruce Witkin was stunned that Johnny was jumping straight into another relationship. He thought Amber represented the aspiring, ambitious side of Hollywood that Johnny had always run from. But Johnny insisted they were a perfect match. "We connect on a lot of levels, but the first thing that really got me was she's an aficionado of the blues," Johnny said. "I would play a song, some old obscure blues song, and she knew what it was." He continued, "She's very, very literate. She's a voracious reader as I have been, so we connected on that as well, and she's kind of brilliant and beautiful."

"I don't know, man," Bruce told Johnny. "Why do you have to dive into another relationship? You just stopped one that was fourteen years." He encouraged him to enjoy being a bachelor and "Go Clooney it up."

But Johnny was a serial monogamist. Before his long-term relationships with Vanessa and Kate Moss, he'd been engaged four times, first to makeup artist Lori Allison and then actress Sherilyn Fenn, followed by Jennifer Grey, then Winona Ryder, whom he dated for three years, famously tattooing "Winona Forever" on his arm (later changed to "Wino Forever"). Their breakup happened shortly after the filming of *What's Eating Gilbert Grape*, and Johnny told an interviewer in 1994 that he abused alcohol to deal with the heartbreak. "The shoot was four months. During that time, I poisoned myself regularly. At the time I was trying to escape from my own brain, so I was drinking a lot."

"He's always looking for the right girl, and when he finds her, he goes all in and gets obsessed," Bruce said. "There's not many women he's gone public with, so when he does commit, he commits."

But Amber and Johnny didn't seem ready to commit just yet. Throughout 2012, they weren't exclusive, dating on and off. Amber had also started seeing Marie de Villepin, the artist, model, singer, socialite, and daughter of former prime minister of France, while also being pursued by Elon Musk, whom she'd nearly met on the set of *Machete Kills*, in which he made a cameo. "If there is a party or event with Amber, I'd be interested in meeting her just out of curiosity. Allegedly she is a fan of George Orwell and Ayn

Rand . . . most unusual," Elon wrote the film's production team. The film's director arranged a dinner, but Amber stood Elon up. Elon tried again to get lunch with Amber in LA. He insisted he wasn't angling for a date—she just seemed like an interesting person.

But Johnny vowed not to let a girl like Amber "slip through his fingers." In early 2012, Amber spent time with Johnny at his private Bahamian island for a romantic getaway. For the entire month of September, he sent her a handwritten poem and a bouquet of roses every day. As a Christmas gift, he renamed "Vanessa's Beach" "Amber's Cove." Not long after, Amber returned to the island and was met with a surprise: Johnny had built a $3 million beach bar, which he'd named "Cafe Cabrones" (*cabrones* being the Spanish equivalent of "bastards"), that was an exact replica of the one from the set of *The Rum Diary*. The set designer from the movie created the plans, and, according to the project manager, the build-out "required construction of a temporary ramp on an environmentally sensitive beach to bring equipment and materials ashore." It was an extravagant romantic gesture. Amber was smitten.

There was no turning back now. They would forever be linked in name. Johnny Depp and Amber Heard. Amber Heard and Johnny Depp.

CHAPTER 2

Fish-Hooked

As Amber and Johnny's relationship grew more serious, Johnny drifted further away from his small and trusted network of family, friends, and staff. "All of a sudden his world became that world," Bruce Witkin said.

On a warm Friday afternoon in late May 2013, a few weeks before Johnny's fiftieth birthday, a small group of Amber's friends drove two hours east from Los Angeles to meet at the Hicksville Trailer Palace. Set on two and a half acres of fenced land in Joshua Tree, Hicksville's eleven themed trailers are arranged in a circle around a small saltwater pool and firepit. Arriving ahead of her and Johnny, Amber's friends settled into vintage patio chairs faded by the desert sun, waiting for the guests of honor to arrive.

Amber's younger sister, Whitney, picked up a paddle from the Ping-Pong table, a large Pabst Blue Ribbon sign above her head. Amber and Whitney, a year and a half apart in age, had always been close. Amber helped Whitney make the move to Los Angeles, where she worked as Amber's assistant while chasing her own dreams of stardom. Whitney enjoyed the Hollywood lifestyle as much as Amber did and frequently tagged along for red-carpet events, but there were rumors that their relationship could be combative, beyond the normal highs and lows of sisterly love. Soon after arriving in California, Whitney was cast in a low-budget reality show called *Detroit Street Diaries*, following a group of young, attractive women in LA living in a dreary downtown apartment complex on Detroit Street, south of Hollywood. "Whit," as she was called, gave off a "bad ass rocker" vibe in the title sequence of the show, wearing thick black eyeliner and flicking open a skull-shaped lighter for the camera. Midway through filming the series, Whitney came to set with visible bruises and scratches on her body. That day they were filming behind-the-scenes footage for the show's intro sequence. Three women in bikinis and over-sized sunglasses, Whitney included, lounged around the apartment complex's pool drinking margaritas. On camera, one of the cast members turned to Whitney, looking at her injured body, and stated, "I can't believe Amber beat your ass." Whitney laughed it off, pushed up her sunglasses, and said, "We're not gonna talk about it anymore." The other cast members continued to implore Whitney about the fight with her sister, but Whitney kept changing the subject. Lisa Raphael, the creator of the show, who was also a close friend of Whitney and Amber's at the time, said she saw the scratches and bruises on Whitney that day, and the scratches looked like they were from nails. Whitney told her they'd gotten into a little argument. "Whitney wanted to go back to Texas and not be Amber's assistant anymore, so they got into it," Lisa said.

Now, running late to join Whitney and friends in Hicksville, Amber and Johnny revved down the desert highway. A security guard and Johnny's assistant Nathan Holmes followed behind. The couple would be shacked up in the "New World" trailer, the largest on the property, which was decorated in a 1950s theme as an "homage to B movies." There were pink flamingo curtains and bunk beds inside, plus a queen-size bed in the back.

Amber's friends formed a receiving line to greet Johnny when they arrived. Soon, the steaks were off the grill along with sour cream baked potatoes and Doritos. For dessert: drugs. As the sun sank, Amber and Johnny's guests refilled their drinks and talked about which drugs they'd be taking that night. Some people wanted to stick to coke, others preferred to "hippie flip" and take both mushrooms and ecstasy (MDMA). Amber's new friend Kelly Sue Milano, whom she'd met through her best friend from Texas, Raquel "Rocky" Pennington, had never taken drugs, but when Johnny offered her mushrooms, she thought, "Why not?" and popped a tiny bit into her mouth, hoping for the best.

Before long, Kelly Sue started to feel disoriented. Sitting next to the fire, an ember landed on her dress, but she didn't notice until it had burned a hole clean through. She'd taken a minuscule amount of mushrooms, but she felt extremely high. Friends talked and laughed around the fire, and Johnny played guitar with another friend of Amber's, the canopy of desert sky sparkling above.

Then, suddenly, the energy shifted. Amber and Kelly Sue were getting touchy-feely, and Johnny snapped at Kelly Sue. To Johnny, it looked like Kelly Sue was coming on to Amber. But according to Kelly Sue, it was the other way around. Amber was being flirtatious with *her*. In future legal filings, Amber would state that Johnny violently grabbed Kelly Sue's wrist in front of the whole group and asked her menacingly, "Do you know how many pounds of pressure it takes to break a wrist?" Kelly Sue would deny this ever happened. Johnny lashed out at her verbally, she'd attest, but he didn't touch her or physically threaten her. She was shaken and shocked by his outburst, especially because it was during her first psychedelic drug experience, but she was never afraid for her safety.

After his conflict with Kelly Sue, Johnny and Amber retreated to their trailer and a fight ensued—one that would later be cited as "violent incident 3" out of fourteen incidents of domestic violence detailed by Amber in legal filings. Johnny took his rage out on the trailer, Amber would allege, breaking a sconce and a glass cabinet, destroying the place in a blacked-out rage. She'd also claim he ripped off her dress and forced a "cavity search" on her body while hunting for his cocaine.

The next morning, Kelly Sue stumbled out of her trailer in a daze. The sun was already beating down on the AstroTurf. Kelly Sue said Amber seemed cheerful, sitting with her feet in the pool. "That couldn't have just been mushrooms I took," Kelly Sue told the group. "That was outrageous, there must have been something else going on."

As Kelly Sue recalled, one of Amber's friends laughed and said, "Maybe you got a cup of Amber's special wine." They joked that she'd been "fish-hooked," because Amber had mixed MDMA into some of the Solo cups. Amber laughed sheepishly.

Before leaving the Trailer Palace, Amber and her friends took a group picture, arms around one another wearing half-baked and hungover smiles, cans of Red Bull and empty water bottles littering the table in front of them. Johnny wasn't in the picture.

In the months that followed, it would become apparent to Amber and Johnny's inner circles that they were a match made in hell. Friends, family, employees, and acquaintances were brought into fights as participants and, later, as sworn witnesses.

It was a toxic roundabout of fighting and making up, and things would only get worse.

CHAPTER 3

Psychic Jiu-Jitsu

There's a saying in Hollywood that you remain whatever age you become famous at. For Johnny and Amber, fame arrived at the tail ends of turbulent childhoods marked by family dysfunction and substance abuse.

Born on the outskirts of Austin in 1986, Amber grew up in a modest two-story tan brick home with a small front yard. The house was part of a development of single-family homes in Manor, Texas, the same town where Johnny filmed *What's Eating Gilbert Grape* in 1992 and early 1993. Johnny's character Gilbert worked at the local grocery store, Manor Grocery, a nine-minute drive from Amber's childhood home.

On the surface, Amber was the picture of a normal American kid growing up in the 1990s. She read teen fashion magazines, wore Abercrombie & Fitch and Doc Martens, and, according to her father, David Heard, pinned Johnny Depp pictures to her bedroom walls. But sources close to Amber and Whitney said they both described growing up in a climate of chaos, abuse, and violence, and that they escaped by moving to Hollywood.

When asked about their childhood at trial, Whitney would describe it as "very normal," with "happy moments and less-than-happy moments." She said their father would occasionally enact "heavy discipline" on them, using belts and hands to strike them. Whitney said she never saw her father hit her mother, Paige, but recalled a time he pushed her into the refrigerator. While the girls were growing up, both Paige and David struggled with substance abuse. David would have periods of sobriety and then fall off the wagon. Whitney would later admit in a deposition that the physical beatings were linked to his alcohol abuse. Paige would drink steadily throughout the day but never appeared inebriated or unsteady on her feet. Bianca Butti, whom Amber later dated after divorcing Johnny, described the relationship between Amber and Johnny as reliving a lot of stuff from their childhood. Bianca said that Amber had described her father as "a hardcore alcoholic, a rageaholic . . . When he drank, he was a monster to her mom and to them."

A 1982 police report from four years before Amber was born cited Amber's father in connection with an illegal dog-fighting ring on a ten-acre plot of land in Midland County, Texas. On the property, listed as "under the charge and control" of David Heard, was an abandoned house, seven chained-up pit bulls, a fighting arena, and "instruments," including a poker used to commit animal cruelty. They also found narcotics. David pleaded "nolo contendere," meaning he didn't accept or deny responsibility for the animal cruelty charges but agreed to accept the punishment rendered: fifteen days in jail and a $250 fine.

After leaving Texas, Amber described her teenage self as precocious and cultured. In 2013, Amber told a reporter of her high school years: "I didn't have any concept of celebrities or Hollywood," and in 2017 she told *Vanity Fair*, "When I was growing up, my friends had 'NSync posters and I collected feminist propaganda from World War II." But according to a former classmate of hers at St. Michael's Prep, the upscale Catholic high school she attended, Amber wasn't into history, literature, or cinema. She was interested in being famous.

As a teen, Amber went around to small businesses in town to raise money for promotional material for the beauty pageants she'd compete in. In 2002, at age sixteen, Amber walked into one of the biggest modeling and acting agencies in Texas, Acclaim Talent, where she met the agency head, Jeffrey Nightbyrd, who saw something in her. "Amber was unlike the other girls," he said. "I felt she had real potential." Amber was smart and perceptive, and he admired her drive to get out of Austin and change her lot in life. "I dealt with her father a good number of times. I thought he was an okay guy," Jeff stated. "He had rough economic patches, and became an alcoholic."

Jeff put Amber up for the cute young girl roles—"The little waitress in the diner that has three or four lines. That's where you start," he said.

Amber also played the daughter from a teen pregnancy in a Kenny Chesney music video for the song "There Goes My Life." She embraced her youth and sexuality. "I basically didn't matter. All I did was pretty much take my top off, which is fine," she joked. "I knew that that was an opportunity, and I was not scared or shy of it."

Jeff was clear that the cliché, at least at that time, was true: sex sells in Hollywood. While Jeff gave Amber advice about the industry, the most important lesson he taught her was how to capture the attention of the press. Jeff came up in the counterculture movement of the '60s and '70s. His mentor was Allen Ginsberg, and Jeff was a member of the radical anti-establishment Youth International Party, called "Yippies," known for street theater, political pranks, and a pro-drugs stance. In the '70s, he'd cofounded the alternative newspaper *Austin Sun* and later edited at the *Los Angeles Free Press*. Jeff was friends with Jay Levin, founder of *LA Weekly*, which published influential writers like Jonathan Gold and entertainment reporter Nikki Finke, who'd go on to found *Deadline Hollywood*. "Writers need a good story with an angle. You have to be captivating," Jeff said.

Jeff taught Amber a concept borrowed from his Yippie days termed "psychic jiu-jitsu," a way to manage one's own public image. "I remember one day a *Daily Variety* reporter called me after he interviewed Amber and asked if she was *really* reading Tolstoy, Dostoevsky, and the Russian classics, because he knew she didn't go to college. 'Do you believe that?' he asked me. 'I really don't know,' I said, 'but you don't need to go to college to be smart and curious.' It didn't matter if she read it or not, that was her *angle*. The media doesn't want nonoffensive prattle, they want stories." Jeff recalled another incident at a preproduction movie party. "Most of our actors talked with other Austin actors who were, of course, of no career use. Amber asked me in quiet tones, 'Who should I be talking to?' I said, 'See that pudgy nerd standing alone by the bar. That's the guy. He's the film editor. Never hurts to make friends with the editor.' Beautiful Amber walked over, welcomed him to Texas, and ordered him a margarita. They enjoyed a half-hour conversation about film editing. And her scene made the final cut of the film."

Jeff told her about a big movie by a fancy Hollywood director, Peter Berg, that was coming to film in Austin called *Friday Night Lights*. Amber was cast in a small role as Maria, the teenage love interest—and she did have to take her top off. Peter was freshly divorced and twenty-two years older than Amber. "He helped her when she got to LA," Jeff said. There were rumors of a romance, and Amber's sister, Whitney, later confirmed in a deposition that they had a "relationship." Incidentally, one of Peter Berg's first acting roles was as a guest star on an episode of 21 *Jump Street* with Johnny Depp in 1988.

While working on *Friday Night Lights*, Amber also met her costar Garrett Hedlund's agent Megan Silverman. Megan introduced herself, saying she'd heard about Amber from another director and that she'd love to meet if Amber ever found herself in LA. "And then from that moment, I was just like, how do I get to LA?" Amber later said, describing her journey to Hollywood. "I need to just save as much money as a one-way ticket costs. I was able to afford it, I think, for the following week. I told my parents the day before that I was gonna head out to LA, and [they] were like, 'Tomorrow?' And I said, 'Yeah.' . . . My dad [said], like, 'That won't work. That's crazy. You know, many other pretty blonde girls go out to LA to try to be movie stars. This is a stupid idea, and you should stay in Texas.'" But Amber was set on getting out. "When I put my mind to something, I really do it . . . with scary determination."

Now retired from Acclaim Talent and living in Mexico, far from the Hollywood Walk of Fame, Jeff Nightbyrd described the teenage Amber as ambitious. "She'd say things like, 'I'll do anything for you, I'll do anything you want.' I said, 'Great offer, but I'm not in to it.' I'm not a prude or some goody-goody, but if you're going to have a real agency, you can't get slippery and slimy." He taught Amber how to control the media and her image, but he never stressed the importance of mastering the craft of acting. "You have about ten years where your looks can get you those roles. Once you hit your thirties, you better have talent. For women, it's very tough, you're not an object of desire to be consumed anymore." Jeff thought Amber had it right about Hollywood: you can use your sexuality to get what you want. "God bless her. She had a clear-eyed view of the world. Sexuality is the one thing that worked in Hollywood and she knew that."

Female sexuality—unfettered, unapologetic, all one's own—could be a form of power, and Amber embraced it. In *The Informers*, a Bret Easton Ellis adaptation, she played a teen drug addict who contracts AIDS. When an interviewer asked her if the numerous sex and nude scenes bothered her, she replied, "I think it's silly the way society puts a high price-tag on the body. It leaves a bad taste in my mouth. It's sad. Those remnants of religion. I don't appreciate people's conservative views on that. It's less intimidating than you think it is. It's beautiful. It's art."

Nearly all of Amber's early roles were as the "hot girl," or the "pretty girlfriend," but Amber fought hard to complicate that stereotype in the press, who often reduced her to an assemblage of body parts. "Looks can be deceiving," a 2007 *USA Today* interview with Amber began. "When twenty-one-year-old Amber Heard first sits down on the back patio of the Elixir coffeehouse in her super-skimpy green mini, flashing her long eyelashes and sipping iced tea with full glossy lips, an impressive intellect is not the first image that comes to mind." The interviewer expressed surprise when Amber "revealed herself to be a well-read young woman who despised television." Amber told the interviewer that she enjoyed salsa dancing and painting landscapes. The writer ended his piece describing a scene from a television series in which she wore a wet white negligee.

In many of her early-career interviews, Amber seemed to be employing elements of what Jeff Nightbyrd had taught her, injecting the conversation with as many compelling tidbits about herself as she could. She embraced being the hot girl, posing suggestively in lingerie for men's magazines like *FHM* and *Maxim*, but she wanted to be the hot girl who was also intelligent and surprising. Back then, Amber described herself as a guy's girl, into hunting, fishing, and riding horses. She was also a rock climber, loved bungee jumping, had "crazy" bowling skills, and liked to spend hours at the Beverly Hills Library reading about the death penalty. Amber told reporters she loved classic muscle cars and had owned several from the '60s, boasting that she'd never need roadside assistance from a man. "I hotwire my own cars." She was into guns too, telling one interviewer, "My baby is a .357 magnum," stating she owned several other types of guns and was a member of a local gun club. Back then, Amber said she always kept a gun near her bed for protection while sleeping.

In 2008, Amber told journalists she was reading Christopher Hitchens's *The Portable Atheist* and remarked, "What's better than casting an outspoken atheist, but a drug-using outspoken atheist!" In an *FHM* interview with Amber that the journalist called "bewildering," the psychic jiu-jitsu clearly worked. The journalist described Amber as having "a smart brain, lack of Hollywood diplomacy, and penchant for conversational hand grenades." Amber told him, "I piss people off more than I befriend them," and, on searching for love, she said, "It's about finding someone who pisses me off. I'm in it for the challenge." It's difficult not to think of what lay ahead when she stated, "It'll be a sad day when I care what a stranger thinks of me and I curb my thoughts to get further with my career. Someday all I'm going to have is my opinions and my loud mouth." In 2012, she told an Italian reporter that she reads almost four books a week.

Sometimes, Amber's stories bordered on the incredible. In the spring of 2010, she told a reporter that in the previous months, her hotel room had been broken into, her personal belongings had been stolen, and someone had rummaged through her trailer on set. She told a story of being "picked up in Eastern Europe, arrested, kidnapped, and mugged." Amber also said she was held at knifepoint in a taxi cab in Chile but fought off her attacker—while wearing high heels—and made it back in time for a cocktail at the hotel bar.

It was also widely known that Amber enjoyed drugs. A source who was close to Amber during her early years in Hollywood said she used cocaine "a lot." She said Amber had an anger problem, and using cocaine only made her rage worse. "If you have an anger problem, you have an anger problem. But sober is better." Years later, on the stand, Amber would testify that she tried coke a few times when she was eighteen or nineteen years old but stopped using any drugs, including cocaine, when she got with her ex-partner Tasya. The source said she watched Amber's live testimony and laughed out loud when Amber said this.

She became a successful "scream queen" in mediocre horror movies, but in interviews with the press, her life took on a stranger shape than any fictional roles she played.

While Amber became a master at using the Hollywood media to craft a compelling picture of herself, Johnny shied away from self-mythologizing. As one of the most sought-after and highly paid actors in the industry, he didn't need to give quippy sound bites; he had a slew of fans, agents, publicists, and executives to do that for him.

And tabloids.

Since there have been celebrities, there have been gossip magazines chronicling their every move. *Photoplay*, one of the first American film fan magazines, chronicled the Tinseltown exploits of silent movie stars starting in 1911. *Us Weekly* and *People* have documented the West Hollywood club hopping and leisurely strolling of stars like Ashton Kutcher and Paris Hilton since the 1970s. These grocery-store impulse-purchase rags have always worked in a symbiotic relationship with the celebs they chronicle, in part *creating* the celebrity.

The genesis of the "celebrity" dates back more than two hundred years, to the age of the Romantic poet Lord Byron. Described by his lover Lady Caroline Lamb as "mad, bad, and dangerous to know"—an epithet often used to describe Johnny's muse and friend Keith Richards—Byron was the most famous man in Europe during his lifetime. The public obsessed over his fad diets of vinegared potatoes, his sex scandals, and his concept of "wasted elegance," an idea Keith Richards and Johnny took to the extreme. Richards wrote in his memoir about the consequences of fame and being mythologized by fans. "I can't untie the threads of how much I played up to the part that was written for me," he said. "I mean the skull ring and the broken tooth and the kohl. Is it half and half? I think in a way your persona, your image, as it used to be known, is like a ball and chain. People think I'm still a goddamn junkie. It's thirty years since I gave up the dope! Image is like a long shadow. Even when the sun goes down, you can see it."

Johnny had acquired his own distinctive public persona, that of a charismatic leading man with the allure of a rock star. But many say his rise to fame, which has become Hollywood folklore, was almost accidental. Johnny was born in Owensboro, Kentucky, and lived in more than twenty different houses before the age of fifteen, mostly around Miramar, Florida, where his family moved in 1970. He didn't usually move far enough that he needed to change schools, but he often had to make new friends. He said his mom, Betty Sue, a waitress, liked moving often, for reasons Johnny didn't always understand. He shared a room with his brother who was ten years older and who listened to a lot of Bob Dylan and Van

Morrison. He tried his mother's "nerve pills" at eleven, started smoking at twelve, and lost his virginity at thirteen.

He described his childhood as "shell shocked;" if his mother walked past, he'd have to shield himself from her physical abuse. But it was the verbal abuse that got to him, the names "cock-eye" or "one-eye" that she called him because of his lazy eye. "The psychological abuse was almost worse than the beatings," he'd later reveal in trial testimony. "Because the beatings were just physical pain, and the physical pain you learn to deal with, you learn to accept it. But the psychological and emotional abuse, that's what kind of tore us up, I think." When his mom was raging on pills or booze, he'd simply run away until she calmed down. He also escaped through drugs, claiming to have done "every kind of drug there was" by the age of fourteen. Betty Sue married Johnny's dad, John, when she was twenty-five and he was twenty-one. John, a civil engineer, wasn't perfect either. A DUI in Florida in 2000 suggests he also had his own demons with alcohol.

Johnny's best friend, Bruce Witkin, was a slight, curly-haired musician and producer who met Johnny in Florida when he was eighteen and Johnny was seventeen, exactly a year and a day apart in age. They formed a band together, The Kids, and for several years Johnny lived in the "band house" formed by Bruce's mother before moving to LA in 1983 to try to make it big. In LA, Johnny, now twenty, met an agent through his new actor friend Nicolas "Nic" Cage. Nic had rented Johnny his old room at the Fontenoy building in Hollywood. One day, they were playing Monopoly together and Johnny was winning. Observing Johnny in the moment, Nic realized he had potential for acting. He sent Johnny to meet his agent, which led to an audition for *Nightmare on Elm Street*. Johnny landed the part that day and got swept into acting. Bruce stuck with music.

Johnny got his next major role on the television series 21 *Jump Street*. At the time, Fox was a brand-new network, and 21 *Jump Street* became one of the network's first big hits, along with *Married . . . with Children* and *The Simpsons*. Johnny was somewhat embarrassed to be up in Vancouver making this soapy TV show and not playing music with The Kids back in LA, but he was earning more money than he'd ever seen. Fox quickly made Johnny the face of the show, catapulting him to teen-heartthrob status. When Bruce went up to see him in Canada, Johnny expressed his frustration over becoming a novelty pinup. "I don't think he liked it, but it paid the bills, and he was learning to act."

A few years into filming 21 *Jump Street*, Johnny met Sam Sarkar, a background actor on the show. Sam was rangy with long black hair and tanned skin, resembling a young Damo Suzuki. Sam and Johnny would go on to be lifelong friends, and decades later Sam would take over development at Johnny's company, Infinitum Nihil. Sam described Johnny as an "extremely good-looking person with the spirit of a troll" and said they became friends because they were equally weird people. Johnny and Sam would order drinks by color: red, blue, and green. They both were heavy smokers; Sam even smoked in the shower. At the "Luv-a-Fair" punk club in Vancouver, a 1970s-era music venue where Sonic Youth and Killing Joke played, Johnny and Sam went on "99 cent" night, which they termed "99 drinks" night. They ordered "Slippery Nipples" and talked about the hard-drinking writers they admired, like Hunter S. Thompson and Charles Bukowski. For Sam, who was from Nova Scotia, where you brought a twelve-pack to a party and people wondered why you didn't bring any to share, drinking was a lifestyle.

One Sunday evening, an up-and-coming agent named Tracey Jacobs was at home channel-surfing when she paused on 21 *Jump Street*. Johnny captivated her: "My Lord, I'd never seen a guy like this before. He was making fun of everything. It was so subtle what he was doing, on a show that could have been so mundane." She told herself, "I have to represent this guy." Johnny stood Tracey up at least four times before they finally met. She wore a power suit and sported a strawberry-blond wig with drawn-on eyebrows, her lips outlined in pink pencil.

Tracey wasn't like other Hollywood agents, and Johnny liked this about her. "She could feel. She was a fuck-up," he said. He thought this made her deeper, more likable. He signed with Tracey in 1988.

Tracey pushed Tim Burton to cast Johnny as Edward in *Edward Scissorhands*. Johnny said he wept when he read the script for the first time. "It hit me so hard. Edward filled me with imagery, emotions, and memories." Tim was reluctant—he already had his eye on Tom Cruise. "There's no way he's going to see me as this character," Johnny lamented. "Right now, I'm a TV actor on a series. Fox used my head to promote *21 Jump Street*." He called Tracey and told her to cancel the meeting. "I'm not going," he said. Johnny thought Tim was never going to cast him because "everyone in Hollywood is after that part." Tracey asked him if he was fucking nuts and persuaded him to audition. Fox also wanted Tim to cast Tom Cruise, but Tim realized he wasn't right for the part. Tom kept interrupting his audition to ask technical questions, like how Edward was supposed to use the bathroom with scissors for hands.

Johnny got the part of Edward Scissorhands. After filming a final season of *21 Jump Street*, he planned to leave the show to begin work with Tim. One night after shooting an episode, Sam Sarkar came over for dinner at Johnny's bohemian one-bedroom apartment inside a historic hotel called the Sylvia on Vancouver's English Bay. The apartment was bare. Johnny stood inside the small kitchenette making dinner wearing gloves made of scissors and pantyhose. As he walked around his apartment, his fingers fidgeted. They settled in to eat dinner, and the clips of Johnny's blades became a soundtrack. Afterward, as they watched TV, Sam stared nervously as Johnny expertly lit the cigarette hanging from his lips.

Night after night, Johnny practiced maneuvering his new appendages. "I went to sleep with the hands on," he later remembered. "Woke up and one had been thrown across the room. I nicked myself a few times. After a while, it became second nature."

It was Johnny who developed Edward's classic idiosyncrasies and fleshed out the character. "For an early acting experience, that's pretty amazing art," Sam said.

Throughout the '90s, Tracey sent Johnny the scripts for *Speed*, *The Matrix*, and *Titanic*, but he mostly acted in critically acclaimed indie films like *Ed Wood*, *Dead Man*, and *Donnie Brasco*. "I read the first twelve pages of *Titanic* and I had to stop to smell the store where they sell Hallmark cards," Johnny said. Then, in 1998, Johnny starred as Hunter S. Thompson's alter ego Raoul Duke in Terry Gilliam's *Fear and Loathing in Las Vegas*, a role that would change him forever.

Bill Murray had also played Hunter in the 1980 film *Where the Buffalo Roam*. He offered Johnny some advice before he started filming: "Make your next role drastically different from Hunter. Otherwise you'll find yourself ten years from now still doing him." After he finished filming, Bill continued wearing dark sunglasses and smoking cigarettes with a holder. The same thing happened to Johnny. In a *Rolling Stone* interview four weeks after the *Fear and Loathing* shooting wrapped, Johnny was still acting like Hunter, with the same physical tics and chaotic speaking style. "Man, he's a sickness," he said. "I can't shake it."

Johnny did eventually shake it, and he let a few years—and a handful of Pirates films—pass before stepping back into Hunter's shoes to play the troubled, alcohol-soaked Paul Kemp in *The Rum Diary*. This time, he'd subsume himself further into the role, falling for the same woman Hunter fell for—Chenault, or Amber. Hunter had said the right Chenault was someone who could destroy Johnny; Johnny apparently wanted that too. By the time shooting wrapped, his placid lifestyle of doing safe blockbuster family films, watching his kids grow up, and savoring a single glass of wine wasn't enough anymore.

Hunter's earlier prediction seemed to ring true—Johnny wasn't cut out for the happy, settled family existence. Hunter recognized a twin spirit in his Kentucky brethren: someone who also lusted after chaos, oblivion, and self-destruction. Hunter said of his friend Johnny, "He's too prone to walking out to the edge of a limb."

CHAPTER 4

The En "GAG" ment

In the fall of 2013, after a rocky few months in their relationship since Hicksville, Johnny was in London with Amber, who was filming a starring role in a movie based on the Martin Amis novel *London Fields*. While in London, Johnny would also shoot a small part in the Disney musical fantasy *Into the Woods*. He booked a room at the Corinthia, a grand five-star Victorian hotel in central London overlooking the Thames, where the couple had first fallen in love during the press tour for *The Rum Diary*. Booking the same hotels around the world was the closest he could get to "home."

Even though Johnny was bringing in money—his latest film, *The Lone Ranger,* had hit theaters that summer, he'd booked *Pirates of the Caribbean 5*, and he was in talks for *Houdini* and *Alice in Wonderland 2*—his finances were in dire straits. His business manager, Joel Mandel, flew from LA to London to meet with him, and emails were pinging back and forth between his sister, Christi, and his agent, Tracey Jacobs. "We really must run like clockwork to make all these movies and the financials work," Tracey wrote. "I'm not willing to gamble on Johnny's financial future knowing what I currently know about April." April was the month when

Houdini, a project created by Jerry Bruckheimer and produced by Infinitum Nihil about the famous magician and escape artist, was supposed to film, but it never materialized. According to Tracey, even though he desperately needed the money, Johnny "hemmed and hawed" about doing it.

In *London Fields*, Amber was playing the female lead, Nicola Six, a psychic femme fatale who foretells her own murder on her thirtieth birthday at the hands of one of three men she meets at a bar. In the film, she begins romantic affairs with all three men, assuming a different personality in order to manipulate each one into revealing themselves as her future killer, alternating between a sexpot vixen, a sensuous dreamgirl, and a naive virgin. The film's producer, Chris Hanley, who also produced *American Psycho*, described Amber as a simulacrum of the character she played: "She destroys herself, but she also destroys the people that are drawn in."

Back in Los Angeles, Amber had still been living on her own in an apartment east of Beverly Hills but was spending more time at Sweetzer, Johnny's four-acre West Hollywood compound. The main house was a 1930s replica of a Bavarian castle, built on its own cul-de-sac. Johnny had spent a fortune fixing up the property, which had fallen into disrepair, and then he started buying up the neighboring houses. The historic mansion boasted an underground conveyor belt to the street for deliveries, 125 stained-glass windows, and hand-painted wallpaper. Even though Amber hadn't yet moved in with Johnny, his estate manager noticed Amber spent close to $80,000 changing paint colors around the house. One close friend of Amber's, who asked to remain anonymous, watched as she transformed from a self-possessed woman by day to an acquiescent nymph by night. She styled her hair, put on makeup, and donned a slinky nightgown for Johnny. She patiently crouched down to take off Johnny's boots before she poured him a glass of wine. She acted like "Betty Boop or Jessica Rabbit," the friend recalled. When Johnny was entertaining friends, Amber would keep up the role, sidling up to them to ask, "Boys, baby, do you need anything?" Though her display of old-fashioned domesticity seemed to confuse Johnny, he was attracted to her intellect, and perhaps she had the same feral spirit inside that he did.

Inside their suite at the Corinthia, in a move that even took Amber by surprise, Johnny got down on one knee. "I want you to be my girl, be my girl forever," he said. "I promise to make you smile at least once a day, every day." Amber beamed and said "Yes" to his proposal.

For the next few days, she said she felt like she had butterflies beneath her skin. She didn't know if it was real or not, because Johnny could be so impulsive.

But Johnny had flown Amber's dad, David, out to London. In David, Johnny saw his hero, Hunter Thompson, reincarnate. "He's about the closest thing to Hunter S. Thompson I've ever met," Johnny said. "We get along well."

David confirmed for Amber the seriousness of Johnny's intentions: "Johnny has asked me for permission for your hand in marriage."

"I felt like the luckiest woman in the world," Amber said.

When Johnny's assistant Nathan Holmes learned of the engagement the next day, he was in disbelief. Before working for Johnny, Nathan had been Heath Ledger's assistant until his death in 2008. Johnny had taken over Ledger's role in *The Imaginarium of Doctor Parnassus*, and also took on Nathan as an additional assistant. According to Nathan, Johnny and Amber had a huge argument on the night of the proposal. But Johnny followed through with his plan to propose anyway. "I thought, now why have you done that?" He compared Johnny and Amber to two like magnets that couldn't be pushed all the way together. They repelled each other. Nathan developed stress hives, and blamed the condition on having to be around their relationship. "I hated it. I hated their conflicts."

In December, Johnny gave Amber a $100,000 five-carat diamond ring.

The following spring, in March 2014, Johnny and Amber hosted an engagement party in Los Angeles. Amber took the helm in planning the celebration. The invitations were sent via post, printed on thick black cardstock decorated with a white starburst border, an outline of Amber's home state of Texas adorning the bottom of the page. There was no reference to Kentucky, or anywhere else Johnny had ever lived. "Amber & Johnny" was inked in thick letters up top, and in the middle of the page, in vintage tattoo-style lettering, it read, "In Celebration of Our Engagment."

Sam Sarkar read his invitation with disbelief. "Our EnGAGment?"

Despite being in the business since the late '80s, Sam didn't fit the Hollywood mold. He loathed what he considered the empty glitz of the industry and was more at home in greasy-spoon diners and art museums than movie premieres and galas. Sam and his longtime girlfriend Kris hadn't seen much of their friend Johnny since he started dating Amber. Before Johnny's breakup from Vanessa Paradis, Sam and Kris would see the couple often for birthday parties, family vacations, and sailing trips. After Johnny got with Amber, they rarely saw him. He was, according to Sam, "in her web of people."

Like Bruce Witkin, Sam never understood Johnny's infatuation with Amber. In his eyes, she represented everything about Hollywood that Johnny had tried to avoid. He saw her as a "stereotypical climber," young, ultra-ambitious, and eager to join the Hollywood fold. "Does she have a theater background? No. Was she a Broadway person? No. She's not honing her craft working on Cordelia from *King Lear*. No. That's not who we're talking about."

But how could he express such reservations to his good friend who was seemingly in love? Plus, he said, nobody could foresee how bad it would get. "It wasn't as if you got alarm bells like, she's gonna fucking cut your finger off with a bottle," Sam reflected. "Her character just seemed more benign. It just seemed like she was out to hitch a ride with a famous person."

The engagement party took place far from the manicured trees and marble fountains of Hollywood and Beverly Hills, tucked on a side street in Macarthur Park at the Carondelet House, a 1920s Italian-inspired brick villa. The attire was "vintage cocktail." Sam wore a red pinstripe suit topped off with a red velvet smoking jacket and black bow tie. Kris wore a black-and-white lace swing-skirt dress with sequin accents, her brown pixie cut accented by large diamond studs. They arrived hungry, eager for the "spirits and fare" promised on the invitation. As they queued to enter the party, the couple watched as a cluster of paparazzi clambered around a red velvet tent erected at the entrance to snap photos of the guests ahead of them. "Steven! Steven!" It was Steven Tyler. They screamed his name in desperation, trying to elicit something, anything.

Inside, the villa felt like old world Europe: medieval arches, stone floors, dark wood, velvet curtains, and dim light. Guests were required to stop at a desk near the front door to present their party invites and turn in their cell phones. It was a no-social-media party. After the checkpoint, guests were handed a glass of champagne and ushered in through a lush courtyard to a brick-walled central room with thick wood rafters and chandeliers.

A DJ played old classics like "Jailhouse Rock" and "Wild Thing." Sam and Kris joined the other guests milling about the darkened rooms of the house filled with leather couches, toile wallpaper, paintings, and old books, as waiters walked figure-eights holding trays of various amuse-bouches. In the back of the house was a softly lit courtyard where people smoked cigarettes and sipped champagne.

When Amber and Johnny arrived, they walked inside the villa with their arms around each other's waists. Neither acknowledged the screams and pleas of the paparazzi at their backs, entering into the house with their heads hung low, away from the eager lenses. Johnny wore a black suit and black brimmed hat, and Amber exuded old Hollywood glamour in a baby-pink silk camisole and a black satin high-waisted skirt. Her hair was worn long like Veronica Lake. Once inside, they posed for photos with friends and said a few hellos. Johnny's mom, Betty Sue Palmer, arrived wearing her signature circular glasses, cropped gray hair, and a burgundy velvet dress. Amber's friend Brittany "Bang Bang" Eustis was there partying with her fellow bridesmaid Whitney and her best man, iO Tillett Wright. "There was lots of booze. Everyone was drunk," Brittany recalled.

Sam and Kris watched as Amber laughed with her friends and displayed the enormous diamond on her finger. As they mingled, Sam and Kris couldn't help but wonder: *Where is Johnny?* They didn't see the old familiar faces they expected. Sam had known Johnny and his crew since the '80s, but aside from family, it was a roomful of strangers. And where was the food? A waiter approached with a tray of miniature tacos so small he needed tweezers to serve them. Kris tried to fill up on these "one-inch tacos" after she realized a proper dinner was not coming.

As the night wore on, Sam and Kris barely saw Johnny. At

one point, they spotted him standing by Amber's side, but just as soon as he appeared, he disappeared again. Later they learned he had spent most of the party in a "green room" upstairs. Sam had seen and heard a lot in his career in Hollywood and friendship with Johnny, but a green room at an engagement party was a first. Wasn't this just the type of occasion in which you're spending time with your fiancée and friends?

In the green room, Johnny received guests, including Banksy, Rick Rubin, Marilyn Manson, Ryan Adams, and Mandy Moore. Jerry Bruckheimer and Johnny's tattoo artist were there, and his business managers and lawyers were scattered about the party. Amber remained downstairs entertaining. She'd invited her childhood friends, family friends, even her therapist. According to partygoers, Amber didn't mingle much with Johnny's guests. Several people recall Amber asking after her fiancé throughout the night. Years later, at trial, she'd say that Johnny was doing drugs with her dad in the green room.

Kris recalled that Johnny looked different—that he seemed unwell. *He should look happy,* she thought, *newly engaged with a beautiful young fiancée.* But he looked like a shell of himself. Sam had a sinking feeling inside. "It started to become more sinister. She was pushing for the wedding to happen in a certain time-frame."

Sam and Kris bumped into Gibby Haynes of the Butthole Surfers. In the early '90s, Johnny and Gibby were in a band called P, and in 1993 they'd made *Stuff,* a documentary about their heroin-addicted friend, Red Hot Chili Peppers' guitarist John Frusciante, and his chaotically disheveled home. Sam and Kris talked with Gibby for a while before deciding it was time to go home and eat a real meal. There had been no dinner, no toasts, no speeches. Sam and Kris collected their things at the door. An attendant unlocked their cell phones from a lockbox and handed them the invitation they'd turned in upon arrival.

Sam and Kris arrived home from the party giggly and tipsy after drinking on nearly empty stomachs. Putting their stuff away, Kris glanced at the invitation returned to them and noticed something was different. Amber and Johnny had switched out the En"GAG"ment invitations, replacing the old ones with a new, copyedited version. There, in the middle of the card, it read perfectly, without typos, "In Celebration of Our Engagement."

CHAPTER 5

Neurontin and Seroquel

In the months following the engagement party, Johnny and Amber's relationship remained unsettled, and close friends and family weren't sure a wedding would even happen. That Johnny was also drinking and taking pills again only contributed to their troubles.

On May 24, 2014, Johnny and Amber flew to Los Angeles from Boston, where he'd been filming *Black Mass*, a movie in which he'd play the infamous American crime boss Whitey Bulger. On board his private jet, Johnny got so drunk he passed out in the bathroom. In a recording taken by Amber, he could be heard moaning through the door. A series of texts the following day between Amber, Johnny's assistant Stephen Deuters, Amber's own assistant Kate James, and Christi corroborate that *something* combative went down on that flight. Amber said that he was jealous of her working relationship with James Franco on the movie *The Adderall Diaries*, which they were in the midst of filming. Johnny thought she was having an affair and, according to Amber, he kicked her in the back and she fell over. Johnny would later testify that he'd been drinking on the flight, but the "kick" Amber spoke of was actually his attempt to tap her bottom with his foot, a playful gesture he made to say, "Hey, c'mon let's get past this," and defuse the situation. He said there'd been no physical violence, and that in fact he'd locked himself in the bathroom with a pillow and slept on the floor to avoid Amber.

After the plane arrived at LAX, Amber had a long text exchange with Stephen, who was looking after Johnny. "He's in some pain, as you might guess. He's been sick. We're gonna get him straight to bed," Stephen wrote to Amber. "When I told him he kicked you, he cried. It was disgusting. And he knows it . . . He's a little lost boy, he needs all the help he can get." Years later, Stephen would testify that he was doing what he often did as mediator and placater: trying to appease Amber.

But Amber was fed up. She told Stephen she was leaving Los Angeles and taking a red-eye back to the East Coast, where she was working on *The Adderall Diaries* in New York.

"It feels like we're at a critical juncture," Stephen texted her, referring to Johnny's substance use.

Stephen told Amber that Johnny had agreed to meet with Dr. David Kipper. He was a classic Beverly Hills concierge doctor, complete with coiffed hair, tanned skin, and a gleaming white smile. He carried a Screen Actors Guild card and had played bit parts in films like *Jackass: The Movie* and *Shallow Hal*. His celebrity client list was long. Danny DeVito and his wife, Rhea Perlman, described him as "the most honest, caring, selfless, responsible doctor" they'd ever had.

Dr. Kipper also specialized in addiction care for his celebrity clients. Christi and Tracey Jacobs had also noticed that Johnny's drinking and drug use were out of control again, so Tracey had suggested Dr. Kipper. "He has a lot of experience with high-profile people and really helping them seriously get and stay sober," Tracey said. For his agent, Johnny's substance use was becoming a problem for the bottom line. Johnny, who'd become a one-man industry on whom dozens of people were financially dependent, was frequently late to set and didn't learn his lines. He wasn't bringing in the same money as he used to.

Kipper may have been a questionable choice. In 2003, his medical license had been moved to revoke following accusations that he over prescribed medications to his client Ozzy Osbourne, as evidenced by his perpetual stupor and slurring on his family's reality TV series, *The Osbournes*. According to the Osbournes, Kipper had prescribed Ozzy with 13,000 doses of 32 different drugs in one year. The Medical Board of California charged Kipper with gross negligence for, among other things, overprescribing habit-forming drugs and running an unlicensed detox program. Despite all this, Kipper managed to keep his medical license and remained popular in Hollywood circles. He was also able to keep running his detox program, which seemed to consist of checking celebrities into swanky hotels and monitoring their prescribed drug use, promising a more comfortable and confidential alternative to in-patient drug rehab programs.

Dr. Kipper's medical notes from his first consultation revealed his initial impressions of Johnny's condition: primary dopamine imbalance, ADHD, bipolar one, depression secondary to above, insomnia, chronic substance abuse disorder, and chronic nicotine use. But Johnny had just started filming, and a total detox would have to wait. Under his supervision, Kipper planned to maintain Johnny on the drugs he was already habitually taking—Roxicodone, a highly addictive opioid painkiller, and Klonopin, a sedative—until his shoot was over.

Amber later drafted an email to herself that would become a contentious piece of evidence at trial, ultimately disallowed by the US court as hearsay. "I love you. You're my Steve," she wrote, referring to the nicknames they used for each other, "Slim" and "Steve." It was a reference to Humphrey Bogart and Lauren Bacall's characters in the movie *To Have and Have Not*, one of Johnny's favorite films. Bogart and Bacall were a rare example of high-profile actors who actually had a successful and lasting relationship. Amber continued in her email draft, "But there is this man, this other part of you, a shadow that exists in that hole in you . . . that's the part, the demon, that is killing us . . . I'm scared, Johnny. So scared." Hours later she texted Johnny some of the same language. She assured him that she knew he had a sickness and she wanted to help, but "Seeing such a beautiful thing as our love slaughtered right in front of my eyes, and not being able to do anything about it. That is what, who I am running from, that demon."

Johnny texted his friend, the actor Paul Bettany, confessing, "Drank all night before I picked Amber up to fly . . . no food for days, powder, half a bottle of whiskey, a thousand red bull and vodkas, pills, 2 bottles of Champers on plane and what do you get? An angry, aggro Injun in a fuckin' blackout, screaming obscenities and insulting any fuck who got near. I'm done. I am admittedly too fucked in the head to spray my rage at the one I love."

Within a week, it was business as usual. Amber and Johnny were a couple in love again.

On June 1, while back in Boston filming *Black Mass*, Johnny wrote his house manager, Kevin Murphy, that Amber's best friend from Texas, Raquel "Rocky" Pennington, was going through a breakup and would be moving into one of the Eastern Columbia Building penthouses in downtown LA. The Eastern Columbia Building, or ECB, is a Claud Beelman–designed Art Deco building clad in glossy turquoise terra-cotta tile with gold motifs and a four-sided clock tower on top. Johnny paid $7 million for all five penthouses from 2007 to 2008. Each was professionally decorated and had original steel paned windows, exposed brickwork, stunning city views, and a shared rooftop swimming pool. Johnny instructed Kevin to treat Rocky like a princess, saying, "She's a very kind, sweet, fragile girly."

After Rocky moved in, her new boyfriend, Josh Drew, a chef in LA, often stayed over. Amber's sister, Whitney, took up residence in another penthouse, and Johnny's longtime friend, the painter Isaac Baruch, moved into another. They all lived at the penthouses rent-free. When not occupied by other visiting friends, one penthouse was used as Amber's closet, filled with racks of clothing and boxes of shoes. Eventually, Johnny and Amber would move into Penthouse 3, where they lived together "sporadically," according to Josh Drew.

Over the next few months, Johnny continued to meet with Dr. Kipper and his nurse, Debbie Lloyd. On one visit, Debbie noted that "Fiance voiced concerns of patient's behavior while using drugs and alcohol. She is in agreement of treatment plan and supportive of patient's decision to detox after he finishes filming." When filming wrapped in early August 2014, Johnny headed to the Bahamas to begin a full detox.

Johnny was scared to go off drugs and alcohol, but Amber and his nurse would be there to coach him through it. According to Johnny's later court testimony, Christi was originally going to accompany him in the Bahamas, but Amber "insisted" on being with him, so she went instead of his sister. Johnny said that even though he was being treated by Nurse Debbie, Amber would intervene, claiming that she'd even withheld medicine when he was on the verge of having a seizure, one of the "cruelest things that she has ever done."

"It feels like the inside of you is trying to escape the body," he later explained to a jury, describing how painful withdrawal was. According to Amber, he'd wanted to quit the detox, but in the end he thanked Amber for getting him clean. "There is no luckier man on this earth to have the strength that Amber gives me," Johnny gushed in a text to Amber's mother, Paige, after the detox. "I don't need to explain the horrors to you . . . You know as well as I. What you do need to know is that your daughter has risen far above the nightmarish task of taking care of this poor old junkie. Never a second has gone by that she didn't look out for me or have her eyes on me to make sure that I was ok . . ." Johnny signed his text to Paige, "Your son out-law."

Johnny knew Paige would understand because she struggled with her own substance use. Amber's father, David, struggled with addiction too and was notorious among Johnny and Amber's friends for becoming belligerently drunk and abusing whatever drugs he could get his hands on. Later, a source who lived with Paige and David in their Texas home in 2017 and 2018 reported that David went into decline after Amber's divorce from Johnny because "all the fun money was gone." David would drink bourbon while popping muscle relaxants, "anything that was a drug, he would try it." The source described Paige as timid and afraid of her husband and said David would crack down on her any time she showed independence. "She had a lot of self-doubt and demons." Meanwhile, David "would fall down the stairs, crash into furniture, there were holes in the wall."

When Amber and Johnny returned to LA from the Bahamas so that Johnny could finish his detox at home, Johnny begged her to let him be alone for a few days. Go to the Beverly Hills Hotel with your friends, he told her. He'd pay to book them a luxury poolside bungalow. Amber agreed and threw a party with her friends but made sure to call and text Johnny frequently. Nurse Debbie Lloyd's notes near the conclusion of his detox in late August stated that Johnny had made great progress, but he wanted to give up because of tension with Amber. "Him and his fiancé are having a hard time communicating and understanding each other's point of view and feelings. A few times during the meeting the patient wanted to give up [the] process and talked about going out and relapsing." In September, less than a month after finishing the detox, while Johnny was filming *Alice Through the Looking Glass* in London, Nurse Debbie, who'd traveled with him, wrote in her notes that he and Amber had a "nasty freakout" and Johnny requested some "fuckin knock out yum yum" from her, in the form of prescription Neurontin and Seroquel. She described his knuckles as bloody and scraped, and Johnny told her he'd punched a white board in the kitchen after their fight. The next month, while still in London, he filmed additional scenes for *Mortdecai*, an upcoming comedy in which he played an eccentric art dealer. Nurse Debbie noted that one day after filming, Johnny was "extremely agitated" and kicked in the door of his trailer and refused to speak to the director. He was also "verbally aggressive" to someone on set "for no apparent reason."

Johnny's periods of true sobriety are difficult to track, and it's unclear what being sober meant to him. After Johnny returned to LA, Bruce Witkin recalled visiting Johnny at the ECB penthouses. He was there with a nurse who introduced herself as Johnny's "sober nurse."

"Johnny was smoking weed," Bruce recalled. "I'm like, 'Are you sober if you're smoking weed? Are you sober if you're drinking?' That's not sober."

In November, Nurse Debbie described Johnny as "hyper focused" on his relationship issues and seemed to be growing suspicious of Amber. "He feels she is not being truthful with him and he is not sure how to confront her about this when she arrives home." At the time, Amber was in Georgia filming *Magic Mike XXL*. Amber stayed out until 5 a.m. at the film's wrap party, which deeply rattled Johnny, according to texts with Nurse Debbie. "The lies are so clear now . . . They are making me NUTS, wondering WHAT WAS SO INTERESTING TO KEEP HER THERE THAT GODDAM LONG???" He concluded his text with, "Help. . . . .??? I don't know what's real and what is paranoiac jealousy!!!"

In mid-November, Johnny attended the Hollywood Film Awards to present the documentary award for Mike Myers's *Supermensch: The Legend of Shep Gordon*. Standing on stage, Johnny stumbled and struggled to stand up straight at the microphone. As he spoke of the legendary talent agent Shep Gordon, he slurred his words and had difficulty stringing sentences together. The media went wild with the story of Johnny's embarrassing performance. Some in the press joked that it seemed like he'd gotten into Captain Jack Sparrow's rum. He later explained that he'd been on "the medications, which were quite strong. There was Phenobarbital, there was Lithium, there was all kinds of things, and then I was also on Xanax, but I can tell you I was still in the throes of the kick, as it were." He described himself as a "drug addict who was coming off a very, very, unpleasant medication."

According to an email from Dr. Kipper to Dr. Connell Cowan, a psychiatrist he'd assigned to Amber to help her manage anxiety and stress, their recent fighting had been spurred by Johnny asking Amber to sign a prenuptial agreement. Kipper wrote Cowan, "She tried to push up the date of the wedding to avoid all this, but the reality is, he will need a pre-nup. If she fails to sign, they won't get married." In the email, Kipper described a chaotic flight to Japan in January 2015, in which the couple fought bitterly and openly, complete with "thrown coffee, attempts by him to storm the cockpit, attempts by her to leave the plane while they were over the fuckin ocean etc."

Members of Johnny's inner circle pleaded with Johnny to get a prenup. They said he initially agreed to do so, but then dropped it and announced he was getting married anyway.

CHAPTER 6

'Til Death

A mber and Johnny were engaged for just over a year before they finally tied the knot in February 2015. By the time they were saying their "I dos," their relationship was severely troubled. Years later, Amber would allege that by the time they got married, Johnny had already slapped her in the face on several occasions, once enough to spray blood from her mouth onto the wall; had shoved her several times, once onto a glass table; had kicked her in the back; had pulled her around by the hair; had given her a bloody nose; and had sexually assaulted her.

According to Amber, they were locked in a poisonous cycle. He was an out-of-control addict and rabidly jealous of other men and women, constantly accusing her of cheating. After turning violent toward her, he'd sober up and promise never to do it again, pouring on the love. Amber said she always stayed because she loved him and wanted to protect him, which is also why she hid the danger she was in from the people closest to her and the medical staff assigned to her. She said she was holding out hope that getting married would turn it all around.

For Johnny, who has maintained he never assaulted Amber, their nuptials were like a shotgun wedding without a baby. In the lead-up to the wedding, Bruce Witkin was spending time with Johnny in the recording studio. He remembered Johnny saying Amber wanted to get married quickly because they were both going away on film shoots. "She wanted to get it over with. Christi was there and we both told him, so what? You don't have to do it. Don't do it. We were trying to tell him—don't do this until you get a prenup. And Johnny kind of says to Christi, 'Well you tell her.' Christi cried and tried to convince Johnny not to go ahead with it. I tried to convince him too."

But Amber insisted. She wanted to get married before Johnny started filming the next Pirates of the Caribbean film, which required an intensive six-month shoot in Australia, where Johnny would have to live full-time. Amber said she was seeking stability by formalizing their union, but Johnny's camp saw the expeditious wedding plans differently. According to Johnny's assistant Nathan, "When they were married, Amber would get half of all he'd make on his films. So she wanted to be married before the next Pirates film."

"The next thing I know it's going along," Bruce recalled about the wedding plans. "And at first I'm like, is this really happening? It was rushed to me. I was freaked out, but what am I gonna do, not go? I gotta try to be there to support him, you know."

There would be two weddings in rapid succession: a small civil ceremony in Los Angeles, where they'd make it official, and a larger celebration on Johnny's private island in the Bahamas within the week.

The LA wedding was hastily arranged. On the day of the ceremony, Johnny's assistant Stephen Deuters and his wife, Gina, who'd traveled to LA from London to help Johnny prepare to film

Pirates 5, got a surprise phone call from musician Patti Smith. "Umm . . . I'm supposed to be at Betty Sue's house in thirty minutes," Patti told them, "but no one has been in touch with me." Amber and Johnny's civil ceremony was starting in the next hour at Johnny's mother's house, and Patti was expected to do a reading. Stephen had already spent the morning booking elaborate travel by airplane, seaplane, and boat for all the guests to attend the second ceremony. Like the civil ceremony, the Bahamas wedding had also been announced last minute. Not sure what else to do, Stephen and Gina grabbed their car keys and gunned it to Patti's hotel.

Stephen had started working as Johnny's assistant in the summer of 2004, joking that "he kidnapped me from a small town." They'd met when Stephen was twenty-six years old, while he was working as a producer's assistant on the *Charlie and the Chocolate Factory* remake. At the end of the shoot, Johnny approached Stephen and asked, "Do you like the Caribbean?" Stephen, confused, thought, "What kind of question is that?" before it dawned on him that Johnny was trying to hire him for the second Pirates of the Caribbean film. Before long, Johnny's agent, Tracey, was reaching out to Stephen for everything. "He's me, listen to Stephen," Johnny said in 2023. "He survived being my friend." After work, Stephen and Johnny would decompress by drinking red wine and watching Sherlock Holmes or Marx Brothers movies. Stephen would eventually rise in the ranks from Johnny's assistant to CEO of IN.2, the European arm of Infinitum Nihil.

Stephen had also met Gina on the set of *Charlie and the Chocolate Factory*, where she'd worked in the visual FX department. Even when Johnny kept Stephen away on months-long production shoots in faraway locations, Johnny swore to him that he wouldn't be the reason Stephen and Gina broke up. "In the brackets of time

I wasn't working, I was very welcome to fly out and spend time with Stephen while he was on location if I wanted to," Gina said. "Johnny would pay for my flights."

Amber was always nice and charming to Gina and Stephen, even if they felt she was a bit "off." It took awhile for Stephen to catch on to the problems in their relationship, but he eventually started to pick up on the signs of trouble: the little arguments, the snide remarks. Early on in their relationship, Johnny told Stephen he was worried he might wake up in the middle of the night and she'd be straddling him with a knife. "He'd make sort of offhand comments like that, you know?" Stephen said. "He doesn't like to moan, or whine or complain. He doesn't like to show fear. So he would say things like that to me, but kind of giggle."

During the lawsuits that would later come, Stephen tried to tell Johnny's lawyers about an even more alarming incident, but he could never nail down the precise date. He and Johnny were at the Infinitum Nihil office on Melrose going over work matters. "I could tell he wasn't really listening to me, which in and of itself, isn't that uncommon," Stephen said with a laugh. "He would often drift off when I was talking about work. But something was different this time, and he was looking down at his shoes. And I just said, 'Are you ok? What's up?' And he just sort of looked at me, touched his head, and he had a loose clump of hair on his head and there was a little bit of blood on it. And he went, 'That was 2 am.' This time he wasn't laughing."

When Stephen learned Johnny and Amber were engaged, he felt "inevitable dread."

Patti Smith was worried too, even as she was about to perform a reading at their wedding. On the car ride with Stephen and Gina to Betty Sue's house, Patti echoed their concerns. She told them she'd seen this situation before: a rushed wedding, a young woman, and an older, richer man. It didn't typically end well. But it was important to her to support her friend and his soon-to-be bride.

Most of the people in Johnny's life were aware of the red flags in the relationship. In the early days, Jerry Judge, Johnny's late chief of security, would tell Stephen and Gina about having to separate Johnny and Amber so they'd stop arguing. Whenever Amber traveled with Johnny, his team always rented out an extra hotel room in case a fight broke out and they needed to be sent to their own corners.

"It was hard to see, because we knew him in his prior relationships and it was never like that. Voices weren't raised. It was such a stark difference with Amber," Gina said. "But if that's what they want, then you're going to support them and you're going to hope that it works out, and hope they find peace and happiness."

It was nearing dusk when Gina, Stephen, and Patti pulled up to Betty Sue's house. Amber and Johnny hadn't yet arrived. Gina and Stephen spotted Lily-Rose, fifteen at the time, and Jack, twelve, standing outside. They'd just gotten out of school and were loitering by the door looking confused. Guests and workers trickled in and out.

Walking inside, Gina encountered Amber's bridesmaids, Rocky and Whitney, wearing designer gowns. They were cheerfully capturing the intimate occasion, each holding brand-new Leica cameras, which Johnny had paid for. Gina looked down at her own outfit: a hot-pink Moschino sweatshirt, ripped jeans, and matching hot-pink Adidas slide sandals. Stephen was wearing a green military jacket and faded gray denim. They entered the living room where the ceremony was to take place. It was a small room, filled with paintings and flower arrangements. Two cream couches faced each other in front of a travertine fireplace flanked by shelves filled with colorful Murano glass vases.

Gina looked over and asked Lily-Rose if she was going to the bigger wedding ceremony on the island the following week. "Oh . . . um, no? I can't. I have to do something for school. No one told me." *This is all so rushed,* Gina thought.

Johnny and Amber rumbled through the streets of Beverly Hills in Johnny's truck, making their way to Betty Sue's house as the sun was starting to set. Johnny's bodyguard of more than ten years, Malcolm Connolly, followed behind. Malcolm arrived in London from Glasgow in the '90s to lay brick and found himself working the nightclubs before a marine approached him about being a private bodyguard. In 2012, during the production of *Lone Ranger*, Malcolm was diagnosed with walking pneumonia. "I almost died, but Johnny paid close to a million dollars to save my life," he said. According to Malcolm, Johnny flew him to a good hospital and told the doctor, "It doesn't matter what this costs, fix it." Malcolm's mom called Johnny to thank him for saving her baby, but Johnny wouldn't hear it. "Don't worry about it," he told her. Malcolm vowed never to leave Johnny's side. "We will end like those two old guys in the Muppets," he said.

Malcolm ended up at Betty Sue's driveway first, watching as Johnny pulled up and parked behind him. Christi emerged from the house and began walking down the driveway toward them. Johnny got out on the same side as Malcolm. As Amber got out of the truck, Christi walked around the back and started chatting with her about the ceremony. "Fucking perfect," Malcolm thought to himself. Now was the moment he was looking for. He walked over to Johnny and pulled him aside.

"Do you really want to do this?" Malcolm asked him in his gravelly Scottish accent.

"No man, I don't," Johnny replied.

Malcolm remembered Johnny had a look on his face that said it all. "Get back in the truck," Malcolm said. "We'll fucking drive to Vegas and we'll talk about it in Vegas, and we'll fucking face the music after. Get in the truck." But Johnny wouldn't get in.

"No. No, I can't. I wouldn't do that." And with that, they turned and walked inside.

"I had him for two seconds, you know," Malcolm said. "He didn't have a best man except for [his son] Jack and he's just a kid. He didn't have someone to say let's fuck off. Let's get out of here. I tried."

As the ceremony started, Gina and Stephen stood in the back of the room, out of the way. There were maybe twenty people there in all. Amber and Johnny stood in front of the fireplace facing each other. Betty Sue was seated on one of the couches. All the other guests stood in the back. Johnny was wearing a short-sleeved black shirt, black vest, and black trousers. Amber wore a slinky white silk slip dress with a short lace veil over the back of her head. Jack stood to the couple's right in a gray T-shirt holding the large black ring box. Patti said a few simple words about love and the importance of communication. Then the hired officiant, a Russian woman named Maria Kharlash, owner of "Instant Marriage LA," a one-stop-shop for marriage licenses and officiating, positioned herself to the right of Betty Sue and began to read the wedding vows in her thick accent. She turned to Amber and asked her to repeat the vows.

As Amber solemnly repeated the vows, looking into Johnny's eyes, his mother muttered something unforgettable. "She don't love him," Betty Sue said venomously, loud enough for everyone in the small room, including Amber, to hear.

The officiant carried on. "Do you take Amber as your lawful wedded wife?"

"Yeah," Johnny drawled, casual as ever, as if she'd asked him to borrow a twenty.

The officiant, her voice lilting, said, "You do?"

"Yes, I do," he responded, smiling, and swinging his head back toward the officiant. She asked Amber the same question.

"I do," Amber said softly.

"She knows her lines," Johnny joked.

Jack handed his father the ring, which Johnny placed on Amber's finger. The room looked on as Johnny and Amber sealed their vows with a kiss.

Four days later, wedding guests arrived on Johnny's private island. The attendees flew first to Nassau, followed by a trip by tiny seaplane or boat to Little Halls Pond Cay. They were greeted with a black skull and crossbones flag mounted on a rocky jetty, whipping in the warm winds.

Johnny's forty-five-acre island looked like a Corona commercial, covered in brilliant green flora, with bleached white sand beaches and crystal-blue waters. Johnny bought the island in 2004 for $3.6 million with zero existing infrastructure. He'd named the various beaches on the island after those he loved: Lily-Rose Beach, Jack Beach, Gonzo Beach (for Hunter S. Thompson), Brando Beach (for Marlon), Heath's Place (for Heath Ledger), and Amber's Cove (formerly known as Vanessa's Beach). Johnny built a modest round bungalow with a thatched roof. The home was scattered with small trinkets and books and art, and the windows were covered in makeshift curtains made of scarves.

As the guests arrived, the island was aflutter with activity ahead of Johnny and Amber's second wedding ceremony. Chef Russell Borrill, Johnny's freelance personal chef, had arrived by seaplane two days before the wedding guests and knew he had to get to work right away if he was going to pull off this job. Only a few days earlier, he'd gotten a call from Stephen asking if he could do a rush job catering Johnny and Amber's wedding: breakfast, lunch, and dinner over several days for up to forty people on a remote private island. All the food would have to be flown in. It was a Herculean task, but Russell loved Johnny as a boss and as a friend, so he'd do whatever he needed to get the job done. He scrambled for a crew, but only his chef friend Robbie was around to help.

Russell, who was born in the UK and based in London, met Johnny in 2011 on the set of the Warner Bros. film *Dark Shadows*, a Tim Burton–directed remake of the 1960s gothic soap opera by the same name. Russell had previously been working for Martin Scorsese, and someone recommended him to Stephen Deuters and Nathan Holmes because Johnny needed to diet to become a "skinny vampire" for the film. "At first he was very quiet and timid around me. I remember one day I knew Lily-Rose [twelve at the time] was coming to set so I got this machine to make pizza dough because I knew she liked pizza. And he asked me, what's that for? And I said, 'I'm making pizza for Lily-Rose.' From then on he was just sweet to me, and once he got comfortable around me he was just a good friend."

In the beginning, Chef Russell liked Amber. When Johnny was away filming, he'd make Amber her favorite snack, fresh figs wrapped in prosciutto with basil and goat cheese. One night in London, Amber invited him and Malcolm, Johnny's bodyguard, to join her and Rocky for the premiere of *Anchorman 2*. Afterward, they all went to Nobu, Amber's treat. "We had a nice meal and she was lovely." But the next time they went out together was different. Johnny was out late filming *Alice Through the Looking Glass*, so Amber invited Russell and Malcolm to Nobu, her treat again. The English model and actress Cara Delevingne joined them. During dinner, Cara and Amber decided that Russell should cook them dessert back at the house. Russell prepared a chocolate fondant with ice cream, caramelized ginger, and honeycomb, but said he "suddenly felt like a third wheel. They were being flirty and I felt I wasn't welcome anymore. So I left. It was unusual, it went from a very friendly vibe to a 'why are you here' vibe." Josh Drew, the LA chef who'd begun dating Amber's friend Rocky, would later testify in a deposition that Amber had an affair with Cara while she was with Johnny.

According to Russell, at first Johnny and Amber behaved the way you would imagine a couple newly in love would. They'd leave "lovey-dovey" Post-it notes for each other around the London house, a rental they lived in while Johnny was in production on *Alice Through the Looking Glass* in 2014. Russell lived in the same house, his room separated from theirs by only a small corridor. The house was large, with a courtyard and a wooden gate out front, and a comfortable kitchen for Russell to work in. Amber's friends were often around, and Russell cooked for them, preparing large spreads of different themed foods: Portuguese, French, English, Thai. There was always a protein and a starch. When it was just Johnny and Amber, Russell would prepare buffet-style dinners for them that they'd enjoy together in front of the TV while watching documentaries.

But by the time of the wedding, Russell said he'd come to some realizations about Amber. "Anything with Amber, I mean—it's either an amazing kind of time, where everyone's really happy, or they're just at each other's throats. That's just how it was, whether it was with her parents, whether it was with friends, or whether it was with Johnny—that always seemed to be what it was. There never seemed to be any calm. When she was being nice to Johnny it was very intense. And when she was horrible to him it was very aggressive."

The prep days before the wedding were chaotic. Russell was emailing with Stephen and the staff on the island trying to gather intel on guests and timing of festivities, but everyone seemed to be as confused as he was. This wasn't how Johnny's close team of personal assistants normally operated. Russell messaged Nathan Holmes to find out what was going on. "Nathan had no idea that the wedding was even happening." At the time, Nathan was in Coomera, Australia, setting up the house where Johnny would stay during the filming of the next Pirates movie following the wedding.

When Russell landed on the island, Amber and some of her guests were already there. According to Stephen, 90 percent of the guests were Amber's friends and family. He'd asked Johnny if he wanted to invite Tim Burton and Helena Bonham Carter, or any other close friends aside from Bruce Witkin, but Johnny appeared embarrassed and told him he didn't want to invite anyone. "It was very clear whose party it was, it didn't feel like a mutual enterprise in any way," Stephen said.

The island staff was busy setting up lounging areas around the beaches, consisting of Moroccan rugs thrown on the sand with colorful oversized pillows and poufs, as well as white yurts farther inland for the wedding guests to sleep in. Chef Russell and his assistant were dismayed to realize there were more logistical challenges facing them. The kitchen was a fifteen-minute golf cart ride from the main dining area and bar, down by the beach. They'd have to transport all the food in chafing dishes, round after round.

"It was just absolute chaos, to be honest," Russell said. "I don't work that way. But they just wanted me to do my best, I suppose."

Russell had to work with the supplies that he could get to the island last minute. Tara Roberts, the island manager, ended up ordering double of everything because she said Amber wasn't communicating with her. "I tried to do the fig and prosciutto thing that Amber liked, but we couldn't get fresh figs on the island, so we used dried, and it ended up being a completely different thing. I did a miso cod dish Johnny likes, filet of beef for a fancy dinner. Each day had a theme; we did a BBQ day with pulled pork and ribs, a Spanish day, Caribbean." Russell recalled a particularly stressful moment one day in between the lunch and dinner service when Amber and her friends decided they wanted fish tacos. Robbie and Russell quickly defrosted fish, found some avocados in the fridge, and tried to turn out a platter of tacos all while prepping and cooking dinner for the dozens of guests.

Russell described the mood of the wedding as tense. And drug-fueled. "I was offered MDMA on the beach by one of Amber's bridesmaids," he recalled. Most of his observations were made transporting food from the kitchen to the dining area and overhearing the discussions among the island staff. On the first day after the guests arrived, Russell took a chafing dish from the golf cart over to the main bar area and saw Rocky Pennington, iO Tillett Wright, and Amber down on the beach angrily gesticulating and shouting at one another. According to a declaration later admitted to the circuit court of Fairfax County by Johnny's longtime friend Josh Richman, iO slapped Rocky and earned the nickname

"I Slap Rocky," a reference to the rapper A$AP Rocky. He said iO was proud of the nickname, especially after others picked up on it, wearing it like a "badge of honor." iO denied in sworn testimony that he had ever slapped Rocky.

That night, Johnny pulled Russell aside to give him a hug, thanking him. "He told Christi to look after me, and by that he meant give me the really nice wine. That was the Château Pichon, and I heard it was because Amber and her friends were going through it like nobody's business. There were people walking around with the bottle in their hands, drinking out of the bottle," Russell recalled. A single bottle costs nearly $500. "When you get a Pichon '88, you want to decant it and aerate it. Guzzling it down your throat doesn't really do it justice." Russell was dismayed by the wastefulness. "Food would be sitting in chafing dishes for hours. People were hungover, people were doing drugs. Some meals were a waste, because no one would actually turn up."

On Saturday, February 7, the ceremony was held on the shoreline under a large square-shaped arbor draped in gauzy white fabric, each post wrapped in greenery and white roses. Amber walked down the aisle as Van Morrison's "Sweet Thing" played over a PA speaker, arms linked with her dad, who was beaming. Whitney officiated, standing up front with a microphone, smiling ear to ear. Rocky stood to Amber's left in a mauve silk slip dress. Jack stood to Johnny's right, his best man. The majestic Atlantic Ocean coursed in the background. After the nuptials, Amber and Johnny posed for photos taken with a bright flash beneath the cinematically lit arbor, the sky a rich navy blue. Johnny wore a white suit with a black vest and pocket chain. Amber's dress was white patterned lace with long sleeves and a plunging back with a long sheer veil trailing behind her hair, which was swept in an elegant updo.

They embraced and smiled for the clicking cameras. "They looked high as kites," Bruce Witkin recalled. Of the thirty-odd guests, Bruce and his wife clocked several members of Johnny's concierge medical staff. Dr. Kipper and his wife were guests, as well as Nurse Debbie Lloyd and Amber's newly assigned personal nurse, Erin Falati. "Johnny looked sedated. Amber too," Bruce said. "They looked like fuckin' zombies. If you need that much medication to get along with the person you love, there's something fucking wrong."

Suddenly, everyone looked up. There was a helicopter pulsing above. Amber and Johnny stuck their middle fingers indignantly to the sky. The bridal party followed suit, giving the bird and laughing.

Later, the zoomed-out helicopter photos of the island ceremony appeared in several tabloids. Johnny's friends assumed they were tipped off by Amber and her friends. Their theory was that the ceremony, which Amber had inexplicably moved from the evening to earlier in the day, was intentionally rescheduled to get ahead of the designated no-fly-zone window in order to accommodate the cameras.

"They were bringing so much stuff from the mainland, someone could've figured out a wedding was happening," Bruce Witkin recalled. "But I wouldn't put it past her."

After the ceremony, people gathered up the shore for cocktails while DJ Kelly Cole spun music. Guests looked on as Amber threw her bouquet of white roses and eucalyptus into the evening air. It hit the sand without anyone catching it.

The wedding reception was held in Amber's very own Cafe

Cabrones, the wooden cantina Johnny had built for Amber as a gift, a replica of the bar from the set of *The Rum Diary*. It was dive-bar chic, filled with beachy knickknacks, lit by neon bar signs and a Schmidt Beer stained-glass lamp.

Amber and Johnny danced their first dance to "When I Get My Hands on You," a ballad written by Bob Dylan and performed by the New Basement Tapes. They held each other closely and looked into each other's eyes, lit by the videographer's bright white box light and the sporadic flashes of cameras, the slow song punctuated by animated and elongated "whoops" and "yeahs" from guests looking on. At the end of the dance, Amber held her fist up to Johnny's face and pretended to punch at him, smiling. Once seated, the toasts began. Bruce Witkin and his wife, Suzanne, remembered an emotional toast from Whitney, in which she was "basically just crying." Johnny's dad stood for a toast in a tan jacket and bolo tie; he looked down at Johnny and joked in a thick country accent, "Well, I've known this young fella for quite a few years." The most memorable toast of the night came from David Heard, who gestured to the island around him, proclaiming it was all Amber's now, before saying the same of Johnny's numerous properties in LA. They were all hers now too.

The toasts drew to a close and the music was turned up for dancing. Amber changed into a silver lamé slip dress and donned a crown made of flowers. She held hands and swung Jack around the dance floor. He smiled awkwardly while wearing a black Spitfire Wheels hoodie. Lily-Rose didn't make it to the wedding. Betty Sue, who was being treated for aggressive cancer in Los Angeles, couldn't come either. Johnny danced with Amber's mom, Paige, who looked frail but happy, to "I'm on Fire" by Bruce Springsteen. Amber appeared effusive and joyful; Johnny detached and withdrawn.

Later that night, sitting next to Gina Deuters at the reception inside the cantina, Amber leaned in and asked her, "Do you and Stephen ever fight?"

Slightly weirded out by the question being posed on Amber's wedding night, Gina replied, "I mean, no, not really."

Amber grabbed Gina's arm in emphasis. "No. No. Gina. I mean, like . . . *really* fight?"

PART II

CHAPTER 7

Trust and Discretion

While Amber and Johnny were still celebrating their nuptials, Johnny's freelance butler Ben King pulled into the palatial carport at Diamond Head, a colonial estate and riverfront mega mansion on the Gold Coast of Australia, just south of Brisbane. The carport was lined with tile, stone, and two massive planters brimming with flowers. Palm trees swayed in the breeze and cotton candy clouds floated overhead. It was forty-five acres of paradise. Ben opened the mansion's grandiose oak door and combed his way through the ten bedrooms and bathrooms.

Soon, the newlyweds—whose wedding photos were still splashed across the pages of *People*—would arrive at the estate. There was no time for a honeymoon; both Johnny and Amber were due back at work to start shooting their new films.

Diamond Head's owner, Mick Doohan, an Aussie motorcycling champion, was away on tour. Mick had previously rented his place to Brad Pitt, Angelina Jolie, and Pink. Now the mansion would be Johnny and Amber's home for several months while Johnny filmed the fifth installment of the Pirates of the Caribbean franchise, *Dead Men Tell No Tales*. The film would be shot exclusively in Australia after the Australian government offered Disney $20 million in tax incentives. It was the largest international feature film shoot in the country's history. The directors of the film, Joachim Rønning and Espen Sandberg, said the newest installment of the series was inspired by none other than the first Pirates film and would be an emotional exploration of Jack Sparrow's backstory. Young Jack would be portrayed by Anthony De La Torre, his face replaced by a CGI reanimation of Johnny's as he looked in 21 *Jump Street* and *What's Eating Gilbert Grape*. Johnny needed a win—his box office power had taken a dip after the spectacular failures of *The Lone Ranger* and *Mortdecai*. One review called *Mortdecai* "psychotically unfunny." A month earlier, the *New York Post* asked, "Has Johnny Depp become Hollywood's biggest joke?"

At Diamond Head, Ben took the elevator to the ground floor, dusted off the pool table, then scoped out the movie theater and gym. He rode the elevator back to the top floor and entered the primary suite. Inside the enormous walk-in closet, he sat down on the leather bench in the middle of the room. He was surrounded by stacks of suitcases containing everything Johnny and Amber would need for their home away from home. Inside one case, there was a box filled entirely with candles. Several more suitcases were filled with art supplies. Then he unpacked and hung up Johnny's clothes, mostly an assortment of tattered, patched, and stained bohemian garb—though they looked thrifted, some of the items were made by high-end designer Magnolia Pearl.

As far as British butlers went, Ben was crème de la crème. He began as a royal butler at the age of twenty to the Queen of England, living in Buckingham Palace. He then worked for Andrew Lloyd Webber, Nelson Mandela, and other aristocrats before going freelance and joining Johnny. Compact and slight with bright blue eyes, Ben presented as clean and elegant with impeccable manners. "Trust and discretion are the two things required for the job," he said.

Ben was in Australia with Johnny's assistant Nathan and the rest of Johnny's staff, including his chief of security, Jerry Judge, and bodyguard, Malcolm Connolly. The staff would live off-site in either an apartment block or neighboring hotel in the town of Broadbeach, a thirty-minute drive away. But at Diamond Head, Amber and Johnny would never be left entirely alone. There were two local security guards who never left the grounds, circling the property like clockwork, even after staff went home for the day.

After surveying the mansion's interior, Ben walked behind the house across the private landing strip to the oversized hangar where a helicopter and dozens of motorcycles and other vehicles were parked. He came back inside and sat down at the long wooden table and began to sketch out the table setting—his favorite thing to do. Nathan got the Apple TV set up with YouTube and Netflix, Johnny's favorites. After that, he checked a few more tasks off his list. He ordered good-quality towels for the house. He made some bedside flower arrangements. He went to the local department store to buy trays because, as Ben said, "Nobody ever has enough trays to carry stuff. Do it properly." And he met the pool guy, because the infinity pool overlooking the backyard, a giant marshland full of reeds, needed cleaning.

Nathan had arrived earlier in the week. Between him and Ben, most everything had been taken care of for Johnny and Amber's arrival. Nathan rented go-karts for the racetrack outside. He also found an art teacher for Amber because she wanted to take painting classes. The two men were soon joined by Chef Russell. With only Johnny and Amber to feed, this job was sure to be much easier.

Johnny arrived in Australia first and began filming in mid-February. Amber was in London filming *The Danish Girl* and was slated to join her husband in Australia after she wrapped in early March.

The day before her arrival, Johnny texted Nathan looking for drugs. He had said he'd been sober from booze for nine months to a year, but he was still taking ecstasy. Nathan replied that "the guy," a film crew member, could only carry two grams because if he's caught with more, it's twenty years in Australian prison.

Johnny exploded at Nathan. "Any ONE of ANY of you guys start to lecture me . . . I just do not want to hear it . . . No stupid bullshit about sappy bollocks."

Nathan apologized profusely, but Johnny was livid.

"I'm a grown fucking man and I will NOT BE JUDGED . . . AND I WILL NEVER . . . EVER . . . LIVE . . . IN THIS WORLD CAGE ANY LONGER."

"You are my legend!!" Nathan replied, doing damage control. "Fuck Disney . . . I know you will . . . And I will never stop you from doing whatever you please."

This seemed to pacify Johnny. "That's very sweet and you know I love you," he said.

Nathan stated that he "would die" for Johnny and for Johnny's kids. "I will do anything in my power ever to make you happy . . . ANYTHING!!!"

Johnny, fully quelled, told Nathan he didn't want to risk getting anyone in trouble and he'd get what he needed on his own. But a few days later he texted Nathan again, begging once more for drugs. "May I be ecstatic again?" he asked, referring to ecstasy. Later, he asked Nathan again, "NEED more whitey stuff ASAP brotherman . . . and the e-business!!! Please I'm in a bad bad shape. Say NOTHING to NOBODY!!!!"

Things were also off to a rocky start on the Pirates set. Ten days into filming, Sean Bailey, the president of Disney, called Tracey Jacobs and told her that on one day of filming, Johnny was four to six hours late to set and three hundred extras sat for hours waiting. The following day, Johnny was late again, this time by eight hours. A week later, Johnny sent an angry text message to Stephen Deuters about working on the film: "Honestly I will not again be doing anything that involves this discussion of furthering my embarrassment of having whored for all these fucking wasted piece of shit characters that I so ignorantly started to think of as my legacy . . ."

As soon as Amber arrived in Australia, on March 3, she and Johnny began to fight. According to Johnny, Amber was "irate" and "possessed" over discussions of a postnuptial agreement following their failure to execute a prenup before the weddings. He said Amber believed he was trying to "trick her" into receiving nothing from the postnup and complained that she wasn't even listed in his will. "All I could do was try to calm her down and say that I was not out to screw her over or put her in a position that was uncomfortable," Johnny said later, referring to the postnup-deal points his lawyer presented to Amber's attorney. Amber later said *she* was the one who spearheaded the postnuptial agreement conversation but that Johnny simply told her that the only way out of it was death. Amber said Johnny expressed that notion "probably 25 times." Without a pre- or postnup, per California law, Amber would automatically be entitled to 50 percent of everything Johnny made during their marriage if they split.

Johnny told Malcolm to look after Amber while he was away on set. Malcolm retrieved soy lattes for Amber and took her into town to go vintage shopping during the day. Amber was easy, according to Malcolm, because no one recognized her. Mornings in the house were reserved for Chef Russell. Since Johnny would eat his breakfast on set, Russell woke up early and went to the market to buy fresh food for the day.

On the evening of Friday, March 6, Russell texted his wife that he'd be working late. Johnny and Amber would have the weekend off together, so he wanted to make sure the house was stocked with groceries and prepared meals. He put the finishing touches on a selection of food that he placed on the coffee table in front of the TV for Johnny and Amber. The two of them snuggled under a blanket to watch TV as Russell said good-bye for the weekend. He reminded the pair that he'd prepared meals for the weekend that only needed to be reheated. That night, Diamond Head was eerily quiet as security did their hourly rounds.

On Sunday, Malcolm got a call from Jerry Judge, Johnny's head of security, who was out scouting locations. "Something's happened with the boss, man," Jerry said. "You need to extract him. Just extract him, take him out of there."

Malcolm raced with Johnny's driver to Diamond Head. That's when "the pantomime" started.

When Malcolm walked in the door, Amber was wearing a cardigan and a shiny slip, screaming at Johnny. Johnny was wearing his jacket, and a gray canvas bag filled with notebooks was slung across his shoulder. He screamed back at Amber, clutching one of his fingers.

"She cut my finger clean off . . ." Johnny said. "She slapped me with a vodka bottle." He leaned over to Malcolm showing him the injured appendage.

Malcolm looked at Johnny's finger and thought, "This looks like a captain cigar, like what you see in the cartoons." He said to Johnny, "Let's move, get in the car." He crossed over to Johnny and pushed him toward the door.

Johnny and Amber continued to argue as Malcolm tried to pull Johnny away and into the car outside.

"Johnny, that's all you do. You fuck off. You fuck off with your guys. You're a fucking coward, you big man," Amber screamed at him.

Johnny kept running back up the stairs to continue the fight, begging Malcolm, "Let me stay for a few more minutes."

Finally, Malcolm pulled him down the stairs and out of the house. He put him in the car and walked around to the other side to sit behind Johnny in the back seat.

"What's going on here? Want to chat? Want to talk?" Malcolm asked. But Johnny was already halfway out of the car again before Malcolm could finish asking questions. Johnny ran back up the stairs inside the house.

"Johnny, LET'S GO!" Malcolm demanded, this time with more force. He pulled him back outside, locked him into the back seat of the car, jumped in, and told the driver to speed away. Fast.

With Johnny in the back seat wailing, Malcolm and the driver raced back to Malcolm's apartment in Broadbeach. "It's going to be all right, boss," he reassured Johnny. The driver parked in the underground garage, and Malcolm snuck Johnny inside through a back passageway. As Malcolm washed Johnny's bloody hand, he could see the bone sticking out of his finger. There was dirt and paint in the wound too. He sat Johnny down on his bed and phoned Nurse Debbie. She and Dr. Kipper had also been flown out to Australia and installed in apartments near the mansion to be on call.

"Get here fast," he said. Johnny moaned behind him.

Kipper and Debbie arrived at Malcolm's apartment, took one look at Johnny's hand, and drove him to the hospital. Inside the ER, Johnny, still wearing his sunglasses, laid on a stretcher, his bloody finger wrapped in a green napkin laid on top of a large fabric pad. Malcolm stood next to Johnny, fuming. "I stood on top of a chair and I took pictures of him. I had enough. She could have killed him." Malcolm was convinced Amber was responsible and he wanted to document Johnny's injuries. "Every time I see him, he's got marks or scratches. She had a scary, scary temper. It really was dangerous, man, dangerous. I thought I could show up one morning and he'll be dead. She could kill him." Since he'd met her, Malcolm had observed Amber as upbeat and happy, while Johnny looked like he was dying inside. "She was la-la-ing around like Mary Poppins," he said.

Back at the Diamond Head mansion, Dr. Kipper and Nurse Debbie tried to locate Johnny's missing fingertip. There was still time to stitch it back on.

At some point that morning, Amber's cell phone had been positioned on the first floor near the front entrance. Still actively recording audio, it captured Dr. Kipper and Nurse Debbie's conversation. When questioned about it later, Amber explained that Johnny "took her phone and pressed record" before security got there.

The recording would eventually become a significant piece of evidence at trial. Amber would later assert that on that Sunday morning, she was fresh out of a "three-day hostage situation," in which Johnny inflicted grievous bodily harm on her, including rape with a glass liquor bottle. But on the recording, in the presence of her doctor and a nurse, Amber didn't mention any of the bloodied cuts and gashes covering her arms, her "shredded" feet caused by several broken glass bottles, a "busted" lip, cuts to her nose—injuries she would claim, in shockingly graphic detail, on the stand years later. Based on the audio, Kipper and Debbie also didn't appear to see any blood or physical injuries on Amber's body, even though several alleged criminal acts had occurred hours beforehand, assaults that could have sent Johnny to prison for decades if tried in court. Debbie later testified that she saw a bruise on Amber's arm, but didn't recall seeing cuts or injuries. Kipper said he didn't see any bruises, or cuts, or injuries.

As the medical team tried to find Johnny's finger, Amber became fixated on returning to Johnny and being by his side, but Dr. Kipper wouldn't hear it. Addressing Nurse Debbie, Kipper insisted that Amber fly back to LA with Jerry Judge. Debbie told him Amber would refuse. "She doesn't have a choice," Kipper said flatly. He explained to Debbie why Amber needed to fly with Jerry and no one else: "He's not gonna be manipulated, he's a strong guy." In the background of the recording, you can hear the sound of piles of broken glass being swept up. "You gotta love somebody to go through this," Kipper muttered.

Amber sobbed in the background—"He needs me right now! Me!"—while Kipper and Debbie discussed what meds to give her to calm her down.

"She only usually takes twenty-five. Do you want to go to fifty?" Kipper said.

"Of the Seroquel?" Nurse Debbie asked.

"Yeah," Kipper answered. "Take her upstairs."

Once Amber was out of earshot, Kipper said to Debbie, "I'll tell you what's suddenly happening with her. This is guilt. This is guilt."

"I feel like this is a nightmare!" Amber exclaimed. "I don't want to go if [Johnny] stays. I don't want people talking about this! I don't feel like it! I am losing him! I don't want him to run away! I might never see him again!" She stomped upstairs and closed herself in a bedroom. Jerry Judge tried to console Amber, who was still hysterical and sobbing, urging her to go back home to Los Angeles, but she remained reluctant. She believed the relationship would be over if she did. "I can't leave, I can't leave. It'll be the end if I leave," she said.

While Amber was sequestered upstairs, Jerry Judge called Christi, filling her in on what had happened that morning. The audio recording captured his end of the conversation. "There's been bottles thrown, and she—she admits to me she threw the first— she threw a bottle at him. She did it first." He continued, "She has scratches on her left arm, which Debbie told me about. Look, I've seen those scratches before on other people, and as far as I'm concerned, they're self-inflicted. I'm convinced of that. Self-inflicted." Jerry also mentioned seeing bruises on Amber. "She's got a bruise here, she's got a bruise underneath," he said.

He went on, "And she admitted, also, that she hit him first. She actually hit him in the face." He told Christi about another injury to Johnny's face. "She said on Friday he got a cigarette and put it out on his own face. With a cigarette, he was so out of it." Johnny would later claim that Amber was the one who put the cigarette out on his cheek after throwing the vodka bottle at him and slicing his finger; it was all part of the same rageful outburst. But Amber would claim Johnny was out of his mind on drugs, having taken ten ecstasy pills at once, as well as cocaine and liquor. She said she'd watched him smash a wall phone into pieces and lose his fingertip that way, though no evidence was found of a smashed phone.

Jerry talked to Amber several more times before she agreed to go back to Los Angeles. Plans were made for her to fly out early the next morning, March 9, 2015.

Hours later, while Dr. Kipper and Nurse Debbie continued looking for the piece of flesh from Johnny's finger, and with Amber still sequestered upstairs, Ben King returned to Diamond Head to find the rental home destroyed. Inside the art room, Johnny had drawn a penis on top of a picture of Amber in a bikini, and drips of black paint covered the cream carpets. Red wine was splashed across the fabric wallpaper and white shag rug. Expensive lampshades had been painted with globs of black paint. Inside the bedrooms, drops of blood dotted the white duvets. A flatscreen TV hanging on the wall had a hole in the middle where a coffee mug had been hurled at it. Written on the mirrors in the bathrooms were disjointed phrases scrawled in black paint and blood: "Starring Billy Bob Easy Amber," "She loves naked photos of herself, she's an artist," "So modern, So hot." Then, written in different handwriting with red lipstick *over* the bloody paint it read: "Call Carly Simon, She said it better, babe."

Ben said that when he walked through the aftermath, there was a clear trail of blood leading from one bedroom to the next, and in and out of several bathrooms. Inside one bedroom, the bed linens were covered in blood, and there was also a bloody iPad and a blood-smeared guitar. Both Johnny and Amber later claimed to have been hiding from each other in various rooms of the house.

As the manager of the house, Ben knew it would all fall on him to repair the damage to Diamond Head. Broken glass and crushed aluminum cans littered the polished marble floor, the Ping-Pong table was collapsed in half, a window had been smashed, more expensive textiles were splattered with blood and paint. "I think it's safe to say we lost our deposit," Ben said aloud, trying to make light of it.

Ben followed another trail of blood to the downstairs bar, which was set back from a pool table, lit with blue lighting. On the floor was a bloody paper towel sitting next to cans, bottles, and broken glass. Inside the towel was Johnny's fingertip.

Ben went upstairs and placed the flesh inside a ziplock bag and put the bag in a bowl of ice inside a plastic container. The fingertip was rushed to the hospital to give it to the doctors, but according to Ben, "The fingertip didn't find its way back to his finger, because it was too late."

That night, Ben pulled an all-nighter cleaning up blood, broken glass, paint stains, and booze. He did what he could on his own, but he'd have to hire out for the larger repairs: resanding the floors, cleaning the curtains, and repairing the plasterwork and a chipped staircase that was damaged by a hurled potted plant. After hours of working in the house, he drove back to his apartment in town to pack a bag, take a shower, and grab his passport, before returning to Diamond Head early Monday morning to pick up Amber. Instead of Jerry Judge, it had been decided that Ben would escort her back to LA.

On the ride to the airport with Ben, Amber talked on her phone to several people, one of them Johnny. She'd later testify that he called her from the hospital to ask if he had "killed it," meaning the relationship. At the airport, she stayed in the car, glued to her phone, while Ben went inside to check their bags. They'd barely made it on time for their flight.

Once on the plane, Amber sealed herself in the first-class bathroom, where she continued to talk on the phone. After some time, the cabin crew knocked on the door, telling her that the flight would be leaving and she needed to take her seat. She ignored their requests for another fifteen minutes before hanging up and returning to her seat next to Ben. As they taxied down the runway, Ben asked the question that had been burning into him. "What happened to the house?"

Amber turned to look at him. "Have you ever been so angry with someone, you just lost it with them?"

Ben hesitated. "No. I'm a pretty calm and even-tempered guy."

"You've never gotten so angry with someone, you just lost it?" she repeated, incredulous.

"With a person? No. Never."

Twelve hours later, Amber and Ben woke up as their plane descended into Los Angeles. Just before they landed, Ben spotted a row of scratches on Amber's left forearm, the same wounds Jerry had spotted on her and which he'd called "self-inflicted." They were long, thin, uniform vertical scratches, like hash marks. They stuck out to him because they were so consistent-looking.

Travis McGivern, Johnny and Amber's head of security in LA, picked up Ben and Amber from the airport. Back at the penthouses at the Eastern Columbia Building, Amber gave Ben a tour of the space before writing him a list of restaurants he should check out while in town. The next day, Amber went out to dinner with friends, including her personal nurse, Erin Falati, who had been contracted by Dr. Kipper's office. Erin's notes from the dinner read, "Ct [client] appears in good spirits; laughing, socialising. Appetite normal."

The next day, Amber requested to meet with Nurse Erin in private. Erin's notes from their private meeting stated, "Ct is well groomed, appetite appears normal, is hydrating adequately." Johnny would be back in LA soon for medical treatment, and

Kipper firmly requested that Nurse Erin keep Amber away from Johnny while he saw the hand surgeon and got "his meds balanced." Kipper's email to Erin told her to pin the blame on him, knowing that Amber would push back. He was frustrated by how willful Amber was being about seeing Johnny again. "Please use the excuse that Dr. Kipper insists that JD stay quiet without any distraction for the rest of the week while we get his medication organized and balanced," his email read. "None of this will be accepted by her, but I will be very upset. You can tell her this. If there is any stress created by a visit that's premature." In a separate message to Amber, Kipper stated, "If you are convinced that all problems between the two of you stem from his drug abuse, why would you have participated with mushrooms on the island during the wedding and Ecstasy in Australia? I want to help you both so please help me." Apparently, Amber had also consumed ecstasy during the three-day "hostage situation."

Six days later, Kipper emailed Johnny and told him that "with a very sad heart," he was withdrawing his care. It was not because of Amber's interference, but because he didn't feel assured that Johnny would stay sober ahead of the finger surgery, and he feared his substance use could jeopardize the procedure. "I refuse to put you in this dangerous position," Kipper ended the email. In his medical notes, Kipper wrote, "Johnny romanticizes the entire drug culture and has no accountability for his behavior."

Meanwhile, Jerry Bruckheimer's production company, JBF Inc., needed a story to give the public explaining why production on Pirates 5 had come to a halt. Three days after the finger incident, Chad Oman, an executive producer on the Pirates film and president of production at JBF, texted Stephen Deuters a press release with their "official" story: "Pirate steers off course! Johnny Depp injured his hand GO-KARTING with Mick Doohan at Australian motorbike champion's luxury estate—forcing the star to fly home."

An article in the *Daily Mail* on March 11 reported that the production would be "minimally affected" and filming would resume in two weeks. Photos showed Johnny boarding his private jet, flashing a gold-toothed grin for the paparazzi. He held his injured hand like a sock puppet against his chest, his forearm and hand sheathed in black skull-and-crossbones fabric that was sloppily wrapped up with silver duct tape. Soon he'd be on an operating table in Los Angeles for a skin grafting, in which skin from another part of his hand would be used to cover the portion of his finger that had been severed. A pin would also be placed in the broken bone. (Over the course of his healing, Johnny had three different hand surgeries and contracted MRSA three times. He'd later testify that special effects were required to hide the surgical bandage on his finger because it was so large, and that he had to continue wearing bandages for at least five months.) After the operation, Johnny posed for a picture wearing shades and a brimmed hat, flipping off the camera with a massive middle finger bandaged up in pink gauze patterned with little purple hearts. Reports stated that Disney lost $350,000 for every day that the production was shut down.

Ben flew back to Australia to help Nathan Holmes with continued damage control at Diamond Head. Together, they strategized how to restore the house without the owner, Mick Doohan, learning about the drama. The total amount of damages has been disputed, ranging anywhere from $50,000 to $150,000. But Nathan said the last-minute emergency job wasn't so bad. "I mean, to be honest, I had quite a lovely time. While they were all back in LA, me and Ben just fixed up the house for a couple of weeks. I won't lie. I felt a bit bad, but I got over that pretty quick."

Ben found a woman in the countryside who specialized in custom lampshades, and she made a perfect copy of an antique lampshade on which Johnny had painted "Good Luck and Be Careful at the Top" in dark, thick smears. He also found someone who could replace the big chunk of marble that had come off the bar in the downstairs game room. He replaced the broken Ping-Pong table and found carpet specialists who could handle the complicated replacement job. He did this work piece by piece, so it wouldn't raise any flags with contractors. Trust. And discretion.

Incredibly, four and a half weeks later, Johnny and Amber returned to the same house where the bloody nightmare had unfolded. "When they came back together in April, it was like a honeymoon. It was tickety-boo and lovey smiley," Ben said.

Amber's parents, Paige and David, joined the pair in Australia on the second trip. David was mad because Customs wouldn't let him into the country with a massive amount of frozen meat he'd brought from Texas. He asked airport officials to keep it in their freezer until his departure two weeks later. Many of Johnny's staff didn't care for David, deeming him crass and obnoxious, but Chef Russell tolerated him because he liked to connect about cooking. David always had menu suggestions for Russell too. "I tried to explain to [David], if I cooked mac and cheese for Johnny every day, he would be obese."

The second leg of Johnny and Amber's Australia stay mostly went off without a hitch—with the exception of a federal smuggling investigation.

On the private jet flight from LA back to Australia, Amber had illegally smuggled into the country not Texas BBQ, but her and Johnny's two teacup Yorkies, Pistol and Boo. She'd neglected to fill out the necessary paperwork and had falsified the Customs declaration, declaring that she was traveling without animals. She was found out when Ben King took the dogs to a grooming parlor, Happy Dogz, while the couple took a weekend trip away. He told the staff who the owners of the dogs were, and Happy Dogz's owner posted pictures on Facebook of the dogs being groomed, saying that it had been "an honor" to take care of the pets. The owner said that Amber wanted their hair trimmed back and their faces styled.

Australia's minister of agriculture, Barnaby Joyce, was livid. Animals without proper permits can bring rabies and other illnesses into the country. He gave Johnny and Amber fifty hours to get the dogs back to the United States or they'd be euthanized. "It's time that Pistol and Boo buggered off back to the United States," Joyce said. He knew that his stance wouldn't make him particularly popular. "I don't expect to be invited to the opening of *Pirates of the Caribbean*," he said.

Ben was frantic. He thought he'd lose his job when Amber complained about him to Johnny, but Johnny took him aside and told him he'd done nothing wrong and not to worry. Johnny's bodyguard Malcolm smuggled the Yorkies back to the States inside a hatbox that was placed onto his private jet.

While Amber was being investigated for perjury, she tried to convince Johnny's LA house manager, Kevin Murphy, to make a false statement to the Australian government.

"She wanted me to say essentially that it was my fault in one way or another that the paperwork wasn't completed, so that I could take the blame for her." Kevin said this made him feel "extremely uncomfortable."

"I want your help on this," she'd warned him. "I wouldn't want you to have a problem with your job."

The dog-smuggling story went viral, just the type of incon-sequential celebrity headline that people love to click and share. Amber eventually pleaded guilty to providing a false immigration document, and she and Johnny later recorded an awkward apol-ogy video that was submitted to the Australian court, seemingly in hopes that it would take their contrition into consideration when determining punishment.

"Australia is a wonderful island, with a treasure trove of unique plants, animals, and people," Amber began in the video.

"It has to be protected," Johnny continued.

"Australia is free of many pests and diseases that are com-monplace around the world," Amber said. "That is why Australia has to have such strong biosecurity laws."

"And Australians are just as unique, both warm, and direct," Johnny added. "When you disrespect Australian law, they will tell you firmly."

Amber and Johnny go on to say they're "truly sorry" that Pis-tol and Boo weren't declared, imploring viewers themselves to "declare everything when you enter Australia."

When the video appeared online, social media reacted swiftly, comparing their somber, stone-faced performance to hostage vid-eos and North Korean propaganda films. Johnny's insipid delivery was ridiculed by some but celebrated by others who called it his "finest performance in years." GQ called it "borderline perfor-mance art." Johnny joined in on the fun and told reporters af-terward, "I killed my dogs and ate them under direct orders from some kind of sweaty, big-gutted man from Australia." He said more apology videos were on the horizon, joking, "I'm going to do this everywhere I go."

For Amber, the incident wasn't so funny. She had recently au-ditioned for the part of Mera, an aquatic warrior-princess in the underwater superhero epic *Aquaman*, also set to film in Australia. With the movie's $160 million budget, it would be her biggest job to date and had the potential to propel her career to a new level of stardom. Amber was concerned about the investigation, and so was Warner Bros. What if she was banned from entering Australia? According to Johnny, Amber asked him to reach out to the executives at Warner Bros. on her behalf. Johnny obliged, calling up three of the top executives at the studio, and ultimately, Amber got the job.

CHAPTER 8

Poopgate

Despite the relative tranquility of the second trip to Australia, Amber and Johnny's relationship had been in a turbulent state since the weddings, oscillating between all-consuming love and explosive fighting. Just two weeks after the Diamond Head melee, they'd fought again in their downtown LA penthouse. Amber had discovered text messages that Johnny sent to Rochelle Hathaway, his private-jet flight attendant, with whom he'd previously been romantically involved. She later admitted that she did punch Johnny in the face, but only because her sister Whitney was close by, and she said she thought Johnny would push Whitney down the stairs. Johnny claimed that when he tried to escape the fight, Amber threw a can of Red Bull and her purse at him and then punched him in the face. His security guard Travis McGivern, who was standing in between them at that point, said, "I saw a fist and an arm come across my right shoulder and I heard and saw a closed fist contact Mr. Depp in the left side of his face." Travis said that when the punch happened, Johnny's reaction was a look of shock before Travis pulled him away and told him they were leaving. As they approached the front door, Johnny pointed to his face and told him, "That's your fault," to which Travis agreed. Travis said that Johnny had a "shiner" afterward.

By Whitney's account, Johnny punched Amber "really hard" in the head several times while holding her hair back with his other hand—all in front of Travis, who didn't immediately intervene. Whitney said Johnny used his left hand to hit Amber, as his dominant right hand was bandaged with the skin graft and a pin still in his finger. During the fight, Johnny allegedly trashed one of the other penthouses (the one that served as Amber's closet), and Whitney took several photos of tumbled-over clothing racks. Hours later, Whitney texted Amber's nurse, Erin Falati, and told her that Amber kept saying she wanted to kill herself.

A few months later, on May 22, 2015, Amber addressed Johnny as "My One and Only" in the couple's shared love journal, telling him that in him she found "the madness of passion" as well as "the safety of peace." Amber would later allege that five more incidents of violence occurred after writing those words. One of the alleged incidents occurred during their belated honeymoon trip in July 2015 on the luxury Eastern Oriental train. As evidence, Amber produced for the court a handwritten page from her diary in which she wrote that he choked and hit her on the trip. But at the end of the honeymoon, Amber also wrote in their love journal, "There is nothing on Earth I love more than waking up to your sweet soft beeps in my ear or the intoxicating warmth of your touch upon slowly climbing out of my dreams." Another entry wrote, "WHAT A BEAUTIFUL, EXTRAORDINARY, MAGICAL, MEMORABLE, WONDERFUL, stunning, SURPRISINGLY EVOLVING AND IMPULSIVE ADVENTURE. I COULDN'T HAVE IMAGINED A MORE GORGEOUS honeymoon."

There was an alleged incident on Thanksgiving that year, and another in mid-December, where both would accuse the other of violence and produce photos of injuries sustained. Johnny texted his friend Isaac Baruch on December 18, 2015, saying, "And then her fuckin' temper. Can't live like that man . . . She's gonna fuckin' kill me one day!!!" Amber, meanwhile, texted her friends that things were "really bad" between them, and by early 2016, it seemed like they'd soon be separating. Amber even asked her and Johnny's couples therapist, Laurel Anderson, who'd been recommended by their shared commercial agent, Christian Carino, if she'd have an advantage in her divorce if she filed domestic-violence charges with the police first, according to Laurel's session notes.

Yet by March 30, 2016, Amber wrote a letter to Johnny saying she was the luckiest woman on earth to be with him.

A few days later, Johnny texted his security team. "Please get her out of this room NOW!!!. She has struck me about ten times, can't take any more."

And then came the poop.

Penthouse 3 was quiet as Johnny's housekeeper Hilda Vargas cleaned up the morning after Amber's thirtieth birthday party. It was April 22, 2016. Amber and her best friend Rocky departed the penthouse in the late morning to drive to Coachella in Amber's 1968 red Mustang. There was a big celebration planned with dinners, and a party bus, plus Johnny had rented the Gene Autry suite at the glamorous Parker Hotel in Palm Springs. Many of Amber's friends, and Johnny, would be joining to continue the birthday festivities in the desert.

Hilda entered Johnny and Amber's unmade bedroom and prepared to strip the sheets. Upon lifting the top sheet, she discovered "a large pile of feces" in the bed. She was certain that it didn't belong to either of Johnny and Amber's two-pound Yorkshire terriers, Pistol and Boo. "I have cleaned up after those dogs many times," she said, "and their feces are much smaller." Shocked, Hilda took cell phone photos of the scene and informed Johnny's property manager Kevin Murphy, who forwarded the feces photos to Johnny.

The night before, Amber had celebrated her birthday by hosting a dinner party at the penthouse with her closest friends. Rocky's partner, Josh Drew, prepared a meal of carnitas with arroz verde. Outside on the penthouse patio, a long table was set, lights strung above it, candles offering a warm glow. Fresh bouquets of flowers covered the apartment inside and out. Amber charged thirteen bottles of wine to Johnny's wine account for her party, including five bottles of her favorite Spanish wine, Vega Sicilia, at approximately five hundred dollars a bottle. Johnny texted Amber before the party, "I am so sorry, but I am going to be late, I know I am going to be late and I will get out of here as quickly as possible." He went on to explain he had a 7 p.m. appointment with his business manager, Ed White, to discuss his still-dismal finances. Amber responded that it was okay.

"I just want to say I love you," she told Johnny.

"I love you too," he replied.

Johnny finally showed up around 11 p.m., several hours late, feeling "tired and subdued" after the long and discouraging meeting with his business manager. Moments before his arrival Amber texted him, "Hey, baby, bring up something to drink and or a joint? I'm in if you are."

According to Amber's later testimony, Johnny was drunk and high when he got home, joining her friends at the table as they took turns describing their favorite memories with Amber. "Johnny didn't want to participate," Amber recalled. "[Rocky] helped him out by offering a story that he has told before that is kind of sweet and endearing. And he couldn't really, he stumbled through it." A friend who was there, who didn't want to be named and described the evening as jovial and casually luxurious, recalled that when Johnny arrived his pupils were "well-dilated." As Amber's friends went around the table describing what they loved about her—her kindness, her generosity, how intelligent she is—"Johnny starts talking about when he met her and there was a beautiful white couch and when she gets up, she made a perfect impression of her ass on the couch." This friend didn't think Johnny's story was ill-intentioned, but coming from an older man describing meeting a beautiful younger woman, to the friend, it was patriarchy personified. They could tell there would be a fight later.

"His lack of awareness," they said, "it was unkind . . . He was older and richer, no matter what he always had the upper hand. She thought this would be a marriage of equals and he made sure over and over that that wasn't true." Amber's feminist friends at the table were shocked and offended. Amber was mortified.

The guests eventually left and, as predicted, a fight between Johnny and Amber ensued. Johnny claimed to have been reading in bed when the fight started. Amber said Johnny threw a magnum champagne bottle at the wall, and a wineglass at her, then grabbed her by the shoulders and pushed her onto the bed, before pulling her by the hair and shoving her to the floor. Johnny claimed Amber had been drinking heavily and punched him twice in the face as he lay in bed, and that he defended himself after the second punch by grabbing her arms and asking her to stop. Security guard Sean Bett was stationed at a penthouse next door, and Johnny called and texted him around 4 a.m.: "Got to go, time to get out of here." Then Amber threw Johnny's phone out of the thirteenth-floor window. Amber claimed Johnny threw *her* phone out of the window first, which she said was never recovered. Johnny's was later found in the possession of a homeless man living on Skid Row, who turned it over to Johnny's driver right away. He was rewarded with $420, chicken tacos, chips, apples, and Fiji water.

That night was the last time Johnny ever stayed at the penthouse at the Eastern Columbia Building in downtown Los Angeles. The couple wouldn't see each other in person again for a month.

The following day, Amber went to Coachella with her best friends. They were excited to see Guns N' Roses, who were headlining. Rami Sarabi, an architecture student at USC, was among the crew. Amber knew Rami through his parents, whom she'd met at a charity event during her early days in Hollywood. Rami, six years her junior, said he saw Amber as an older sister figure. He described Amber as a great friend, "nurturing and motherly," and that "she always knew the right thing to say." That morning, Rami met up with everyone at the ECB, but they were running late because they were looking for Johnny's phone. Amber was frantic but eventually got in her Mustang with Rocky, Whitney, and Rami. He spent the rest of the trip consoling Amber; Johnny had decided not to come and she was devastated. To calm her down, Rami took her on the Ferris wheel and played *Schitt's Creek* on his phone while some of their friends ate mushroom chocolate. Amber just wanted to go home.

At the festival, Whitney texted Johnny and said she was not "meaning to stick my nose where it shouldn't be," but Amber was "missing him like crazy" and really wanted to hear from him. According to Whitney's later testimony, when she sent this text, she already knew that Johnny had "hit" Amber the night before.

After the weekend, Amber returned to LA and went to work

on a movie called *I Do . . . Until I Don't*, about three couples on the verge of separating. Later in the week, she flew to New York for the Met Gala, where she was dressed by Ralph Lauren. Because Johnny had allegedly thrown her phone out of the window during their heated birthday argument a few days before, she had no idea if Johnny would join her there or not. "No one would talk to me on his team. No one would tell me. I didn't know," she said.

Waiting in line on the red carpet, Amber ran into Elon Musk, who was with his mother, Maye Musk. "I sat next to an empty place setting for Johnny that they cleared as soon as they realized that he'd effectively stood me up on the carpet," Amber later testified. "I was standing in line right in front of a gentleman. It was Elon. I didn't recognize him until we started talking and he had reminded me that we had met once before." They'd met in 2013 when Amber visited Elon at SpaceX. He'd given her a tour of the SpaceX campus and took her for a ride in a Tesla. It was on this trip that she decided he "looked attractive for a rocket engineer," Amber later told Elon's biographer, Walter Isaacson.

The night of the Met Gala, Amber and Elon stuck by each other's side, talking over dinner and at the gala afterparty. Over time, Amber divulged to Elon that her marriage to Johnny was on the rocks and she hadn't seen him in a while. When he heard the horror story of her marriage, Elon couldn't help but get involved.

After three weeks of estrangement from Amber, Johnny texted her dad, David. "We've not spoken to one another since I left [the penthouse] at 4:30am on the morning of the 22nd, her birthday, the argument, once again, brought her straight to that uncontrollable rage and she started throwing fuckin' haymakers around again, I cannot allow ANYONE to believe that it's okay to insult me, disrespect me and then feel as though she can apply violence to a situation that is already spinning out of control . . ."

The next day, May 12, 2016, Johnny texted Amber a picture of feces on their bed and said nothing else. To Amber, it was obvious. The dogs had shit in the bed. Accidents were a regular occurrence, she said, reminding him that one of the dogs had even shit on top of Johnny while he was in that bed. According to Amber's friend Brittany Eustis, there'd been discussions in the friend group about pooping in a bed and about placing "Saran wrap on the toilet." Before Coachella, Amber had been angry with Johnny and the friends had been talking about funny ways to get revenge. But Amber thought Johnny was bizarrely "obsessed" with the feces and that he was experiencing drug-related "delusions," blaming his wife for shitting the bed when everyone knew their dogs weren't housebroken.

A few days later, Johnny texted Amber to let her know that his mother's condition was not good. "I'm with Betty Sue, this will be it, the end is nigh. I've spoken your words of love and respect for her and then some. She's ready to split. Thank you for loving her."

Johnny had just returned from the UK for the London premiere of *Alice Through the Looking Glass*. "He looked terrible, physically drained," Gina Deuters recalled. Stephen and Johnny stayed up all night together. Johnny was sobbing about his mother and his failing relationship with Amber. After the premiere, Johnny flew back to the States to spend time with Betty Sue in her final days.

"It was a lot of shit Johnny was going through," said Bruce Witkin, who was at Johnny's side at the hospital.

At eighty-one, Betty Sue had lived longer with cancer than her family had expected. In mid-2013, Johnny wrote to Elton John soon after moving his mom out to LA, saying that the team at

Cedars-Sinai had given Betty Sue a year to a year and a half, versus the doctors in Kentucky who told him they'd be lucky to get three months.

Betty Sue's passing on May 20, 2016, sparked an epiphany for Johnny. He had to break it off with Amber. Johnny realized just how short life was. "Life is a birdsong, what feels like 100 years, is in fact, a second, millisecond . . . I understood that she had not had the proper training, or proper teaching, or proper background to be anything other than what she had been when we were younger. I forgave her for all that, as one would, should. It opened my eyes to the fact that, yes, try, in relationships . . . try your best, try. If it's not going to work, it's not going to work. And more importantly, if you're going to get out, if you're going to make an end, which I had decided that I . . . it was . . . somebody had to call it."

The evening after she died, on May 21, Johnny planned to go to the downtown penthouses and break up with Amber.

On Saturday, May 21, Bruce texted Johnny in the afternoon, checking in on his friend: "Hey brother. Just got to NY. How you doing? You no answer my text. Just thinking about you. Bwoosie."

Johnny replied to him on the drive over to the penthouses. "Still a big question mark, Am on my way to see her and breakup . . . I'm all butterflies . . . I hate myself!!! X."

Once Johnny was inside Penthouse 3, he told Amber he wanted a divorce. It was the first time they'd seen each other since her birthday. Johnny also confronted Amber again about the feces in the bed. Together, they called house manager Kevin Murphy and put him on speakerphone and asked him about the facts surrounding what would come to be known as "Poopgate." Amber screamed at Kevin, calling him a liar. Next they called

Amber's friend iO Tillett Wright in New York City. Johnny was mistakenly convinced that Amber had directed iO to commit the deed.

What happened next between Amber and Johnny in the few minutes that iO was on speakerphone is highly contested, not unlike the other private incidents of violence later alleged by both parties. Amber claimed that Johnny lobbed his phone at her eye and then assaulted her, pulling her hair and smashing objects with a magnum wine bottle. Rocky, still living in one of the other penthouses, heard yelling, so she entered Penthouse 3. Amber said Johnny then put his hands on Rocky, who was trying to intervene, and was screaming at her while continuing to destroy property. The security guards entered and eventually escorted him from the penthouse, but not before Amber screamed "Call 911!" loud enough for iO, who was still on the line, to hear. Johnny allegedly roughed up more of the penthouse and spilled wine in the hallway as he left.

Johnny's recollection of the event implies he was set up by Amber and her friends that night. He said he told iO on the phone that he could "have" Amber now, tossed the phone onto the couch beside her, and then walked toward the kitchen while Amber screamed, pretending that she was being hit. Hearing the commotion, Johnny's security team entered and observed Amber yelling, "Stop hitting me Johnny!" while he stood twenty feet from her. Johnny claimed Amber switched to "Call 911" because she knew iO was still on the line.

Minutes before the first LAPD officers arrived, Amber texted iO, "Please."

"I did already, are the cops not there??" iO replied.

"No."

"Fuck man, they said they were on their way."

It remains unclear why Rocky didn't dial 911 as a witness on the scene, whereas iO was across the country in New York.

According to Amber, after Johnny left, and before the police had arrived, Rocky and Josh Drew brought Amber into their apartment next door, where they comforted her and took a photo of her face. The photo showed redness around her right cheekbone. Then Amber said she called Samantha Spector, a divorce lawyer, for advice.

As the police pulled up to the downtown building, Johnny texted Bruce Witkin from the car. "It's done!!!"

LAPD Officers Melissa Saenz and Tyler Hadden arrived on the scene and were inside Johnny and Amber's penthouse for approximately fifteen minutes. But Amber declined to speak to the officers. "I was afraid to speak to police at this point," she'd later explain. "I knew it would cause an international media incident for us both and I wasn't ready to be in the middle of a media storm, on top of everything else."

Saenz and Hadden left a business card with Amber. Their report on the incident read, "Radio call of dispute. Refused report. Adv'd [advised] can call at later time if changes mind." After they left, another series of photos were taken by Amber, Rocky, and Josh documenting Amber's face, red and swollen around her eye, and the damage around the apartment. Photos were also taken of the LAPD business card lying flat on a table. While they were snapping photos, at 9:30 p.m., Johnny sent a farewell text to Amber, Rocky, and Josh in a group chat. He didn't yet know that the cops had been called.

"That was it. The last encounter forever. You were already ready to strike!!! Why did I even come in there in the 1st place?? To be yelled at by you!!!" He signed off, "I will miss the moments of beauty and truth . . . goodbye, Amber . . . What the fuck was I thinking?? I wish you all merit, The Former Him."

Responding to a second 911 call, another pair of officers arrived at the penthouse around 10:28 p.m. After dialing 911 from New York City, iO had called his friend Lauren in Los Angeles, explained the situation, and asked her to call 911 too, even though she was miles away from the scene and barely knew Amber. Approximately six minutes after those officers arrived on the scene, they exited.

Three of the four LAPD officers that visited the penthouse that night would go on to testify about what they witnessed. Speaking years later, Amber stated, "I didn't call 911. I didn't call the police. I refused to cooperate with them to protect Johnny . . . Every bit of this was to protect Johnny and protect the secret that I fought really hard to keep for nearly five years, which was behind closed doors." This episode would be repeatedly referred to by Amber and her lawyers as forensic proof that the relationship had gone off the rails—the turning point seen in so many relationships rife with domestic violence.

The next day, Amber went to Rocky's jewelry and bead show and took several photos standing in the booth wearing sunglasses and laughing.

"Can I post the pic of us?" Rocky texted her afterward.

Amber appeared happy in the photos, wearing sunglasses concealing the location of her injuries. After the bead show, Amber attended the birthday party of her friend Amanda de Cadenet, a British socialite turned feminist media maven. An Instagram photo showed Amanda at the party posing with supermodel Amber Valletta and Amber, who was smiling, leaning her head to her left, a thick lock of hair cascading over the right side of her face. Amber later said she had to ask her friends to help her place the hair specifically over her right cheek to cover "a bruise, swelling and scratches." The image was deleted soon after it was posted.

Whitney later testified that when she saw Amber that day, "her eye was bruised and swollen, her lip was busted open and there was a chunk of her hair missing." But no one else who testified claimed to have seen injuries to her lip or missing hair from her scalp, and Amber didn't mention suffering those injuries. Amber did text her mother the photos she'd taken with Rocky and Josh, telling Paige that the night before Johnny had been "hitting" her in the face with the phone, and that he'd thrown her down and hit her on the head. Later that day, iO emailed Amber his full account of the phone call for use in a future witness statement, subject line: *What Happened*. In iO's email, he wrote that he'd heard the phone being thrown, and afterward that Amber had picked it up and told iO that Johnny had thrown the phone at her face, saying, "Oh you think I hit you? What if I pull your hair back?" One hour after receiving iO's statement, Amber texted her mom again, clarifying that Johnny had hurled the iPhone at her face like a baseball.

The night of May 22, around 11 p.m., Amber rode the penthouse elevator down to the lobby wearing a bulky jacket with her hair down. Forty seconds later, she returned to the elevator with James Franco, who was wearing a black baseball hat and a large black backpack. They'd seen each other earlier that month at James's brother's art show during her estranged period with Johnny. Inside the elevator, they stood close to each other in the corner, faced away from the security camera. As they ascended, they nestled their heads together. James would later be subpoenaed in Virginia, but he'd never testify, even though he would've heard and seen the fight's aftermath up close.

Six days after the penthouse brawl, the photos of Amber's injuries and the officer's business card would appear in an exclusive story on TMZ. For almost two years, Johnny and Amber had managed to keep the volatility of their relationship hidden from the press, though Amber acknowledged rumors in an interview with *Marie Claire* months earlier. "I try not to react to the horrible misrepresentation of our lives," she said. "But it is strange and hard."

Now, the feeding frenzy would begin.

CHAPTER 9

Media Antics

Four days before TMZ published the photos, on Monday, May 23, 2016, a clear spring day in Los Angeles, Amber quietly filed for divorce from Johnny at the Superior Courthouse in downtown Los Angeles, citing irreconcilable differences. After just fifteen months, their turbulent marriage was finally coming to an end. Another short-lived celebrity romance for the books.

The next day, Amber's divorce attorney, Samantha Spector, sent a letter via postal mail and email to Johnny's entertainment lawyer, Jake Bloom, in Los Angeles. Johnny was in New York City at the time to play a show with his band, the Hollywood Vampires, after which he'd head to Europe to go on tour. The band was named after a nocturnal celebrity drinking club formed by the Godfather of Shock Rock, Alice Cooper. The original club members, made up of rock stars like Ringo Starr, Harry Nilsson, and Keith Moon, gathered to outdrink each other at the Rainbow Bar and Grill in West Hollywood in the early 1970s. In 2015, Alice Cooper formed a band named after the club with Johnny and Joe Perry.

Samantha's letter, which would come to be known as "the extortion letter" among Johnny's supporters, informed Jake that

Amber had officially filed for divorce and stated that Johnny had committed domestic violence (DV) against Amber on May 21, claiming he "violently attacked and threatened" Amber that night at the penthouse and they had witnesses and evidence to back up her claims. Two other instances of DV from the past six months were also cited in the letter. These were the first allegations formally made by Amber to Johnny.

"Although Amber is afraid of Johnny, she strongly insists that we do everything possible to keep this matter out of the media spotlight, which is why she has not yet sought a CLETS DV TRO [California Law Enforcement Telecommunications System Domestic Violence Temporary Restraining Order] and why we did not arrange for Johnny to have been personally served at last night's movie premiere. Amber wishes to work quickly toward a private and amicable resolution of all matters, but she will need Johnny's immediate cooperation to do so."

Samantha instructed Jake Bloom to have Johnny sign and return the notice of divorce within three days of the letter, by Friday, May 27, or "we will have no alternative but to arrange for Johnny to be personally served." The letter listed out a series of Amber's immediate requests: appropriate temporary alimony (eventually requested at $50,000 a month), exclusive use and possession of a black Range Rover owned by Johnny, exclusive use and possession of three of the downtown penthouses where she and several of her friends were still living, and a contribution to Amber's attorney's fees in the amount of $100,000 and $25,000 for "forensic accounting costs," also to be paid by Friday.

The same day Amber filed for divorce, and throughout the following day that Samantha Spector sent the letter to Johnny's lawyer, Amber was frantically trying to reach Johnny in New York City. The story hadn't yet broken in the media, and she was begging him to call her, texting him "please" over and over again, and "Emergency," and "I'm dying."

On Tuesday, Amber and Rocky also paid a visit to Johnny's house on Sweetzer Avenue in West Hollywood. It was in the afternoon, and housekeeper Hilda Vargas was there. She was surprised because she hadn't seen Amber for weeks. Amber pulled her aside and confronted her about the photos of the feces in the bed from April 21. According to Hilda, Amber told her the photos "destroyed her marriage." Hilda said she talked to Amber at length in the bright daylight, and that she didn't notice any injuries to her face.

That night, having not yet made contact with Johnny, Amber sent him a text explaining aspects of Spector's letter. Her text downplayed the domestic-violence allegations and threats of a restraining order. Johnny had two days left to comply with her stated demands.

"Just confirmed that the cover letter is completely private and has nothing to do with any public record. (And only included the domestic violence/restraining order stuff because I called the lawyer when the cops were here and I didn't know what to do or why that happened and was scared) But that letter is private." She continued, "We can take as long or quick as we want. And do this or undo this as we see fit. You and I have the control. And love each other." She ended with, "I'm sorry if I've hurt you. I have nothing but love for you."

According to this text, Amber was still willing to "undo" the wheels she'd set in motion with her lawyer. She told Johnny the situation was being steered by her attorneys, and that when the cops had arrived at the penthouse on May 21, she "didn't know what to do or why that happened." Amber shifted the blame to her lawyers and away from Johnny, suggesting that they were still on the same team.

Amber's apologetic and loving text to Johnny that day sharply contrasted her communications with friends and family in the fallout of the penthouse fight. In the immediate aftermath, Amber texted several people that she was planning to get a restraining order against Johnny right away, saying he was "crazy" and that "shit got bad." Within twenty-four hours of the LAPD visits, Amber texted iO, makeup artist Mélanie Inglessis, Nurse Erin, both of her parents, assistant Savannah McMillan, Josh Drew, her ex-girlfriend Tasya van Ree, and Elon Musk to inform each that she'd called the cops on Johnny and would pursue a restraining order against him that Monday. The next day she'd had the locks changed on three of the penthouse doors. As Amber was texting Johnny that she loved him and that they both had "the control," she was also gathering evidence, asking for photos and witness declarations from her friends iO, Raquel, and Josh Drew.

Behavior like this isn't abnormal for victims of domestic violence, who often oscillate between extremes: making plans to leave and telling others of their plans, while at the same time maintaining the status quo with their loved one who is abusing them. Amber loved Johnny and it *was* difficult for her to walk away. According to some experts, it often takes survivors seven attempts to leave before they're able to end it for good. But another, vexing way to look at Amber's behavior, if you believe Johnny's version of the story, is that of someone trying to leverage power in the divorce and wrest control of the narrative.

Ignoring Amber's pleas, on Wednesday, Johnny filed his response to Amber in court through his divorce lawyer, Laura Wasser, rejecting all of Amber's requests for spousal support. Within hours, countless media outlets, from Page Six to *Vanity Fair* to the BBC to the *Los Angeles Times*, rushed to publish stories breaking the divorce news, commenting primarily on the marriage's brevity, and citing their "irreconcilable differences." "Johnny Depp's wife, Amber Depp, throwing in the towel," CBS News wrote. Many of the articles breathlessly reporting on their divorce mentioned the awkward Australia apology video, seeming to link the split with the couple's public embarrassment. Several mentioned the callous timing, noting that Johnny's mother, Betty Sue, had passed away three days before Amber filed.

Johnny then released a public statement, which, in hindsight, can only be viewed as brutally ironic: "Given the brevity of this marriage and the most recent and tragic loss of his mother, Johnny will not respond to any of the salacious false stories, gossip, misinformation and lies about his personal life. Hopefully the dissolution of this short marriage will be resolved quickly."

That hope would be quickly dashed.

On Friday, May 27, 2016, KCAL news anchor Pat Harvey swiveled her chair to face the camera and announced the top news headline of the day. "Actor Johnny Depp was slapped with a restraining order today after his estranged wife Amber Heard shows up in court with bruises on her face," Harvey stated before they cut to footage of Amber leaving Los Angeles Superior Court. "Flanked by security, Amber Heard doesn't try to hide the bruise on her cheek, and neither does her lawyer." The footage showed Amber swinging her head and turning her face to the left, displaying a purple bruise on her right cheek as she solemnly walked from the courthouse doors to the black car waiting for her on the street.

Amber was crowded by bodies, cameras, and microphones as reporters asked if she was okay, begging for some kind of comment. A security guard in a black suit stayed close by her side while Samantha Spector led the charge, bulldozing through the crowd, trying to keep the reporters at bay. "You guys, she showed a lot of courage today," she announced to the group. Amber wore a high-necked plain black dress with a thin belt at the waist and kept her hands modestly clasped in front of her. She looked wan and mournful. Once inside the SUV, the cameras kept rolling, zooming their lenses into the car to capture Amber crying in the back seat, holding her face in her hands.

Inside the courthouse, Amber had presented multiple photos documenting injuries to her cheek and eye area from the night the cops were called, along with a sworn written declaration in which she requested legal protection and restated the requests detailed in Spector's earlier letters for alimony payments in the amount of $50,000 a month. "During the entirety of our relationship," Amber wrote, "Johnny has been verbally and physically abusive to me. I endured excessive emotional, verbal and physical abuse from Johnny, which has included angry, hostile, humiliating and threatening assaults to me whenever I questioned his authority or disagreed with him." She went on to discuss her fear of her husband. "As Johnny's paranoia, delusions and aggression increased throughout our relationship so has my awareness of his continued substance abuse. Because of this, I am extremely afraid of Johnny and for my safety. I am petrified he will return at any moment to the Broadway residence, to which he has full access to despite my repeated pleas to his security team to prevent otherwise and to protect me, if restraining orders are not immediately issued. I strongly believe that in addition to DVROs [domestic-violence restraining orders], Johnny also requires enrollment in anger management courses and a Batterer's intervention program." Her DVRO request cited three separate incidents over the prior six months—including the May 21 fight, when the LAPD was called, and her thirtieth birthday party in April, when Johnny had allegedly thrown a magnum champagne bottle at the wall, hurled a wineglass at Amber, pushed her onto the bed, and grabbed her by the hair and violently shoved her to the floor. It also cited a "severe incident" in December 2015 in which she "truly feared that her life was in danger." "I live in fear that Johnny will return to the Broadway residence unannounced to terrorize me, physically and emotionally. I require the protection of this Court via the issuance of Domestic Violence restraining orders."

Later that day, TMZ, who'd been on the scene at the courthouse, published the photos of Amber's injured face and the LAPD business card, splashed with the headline: "Amber Heard Claims Domestic Violence, Gets Restraining Order Against Johnny Depp."

It was done. Her domestic-violence allegations were now out in the world.

Years later, former TMZ employee Morgan Tremaine would testify about the tabloid's movements that day. Morgan was a field assignment manager at the time and his job was to dispatch camera people to the downtown courthouse. On the stand, Johnny's lawyer asked him if TMZ normally sent paparazzi to the courthouse. "Only if we had been informed prior. It's not by any means a celebrity hotspot. We would only ever send people there if we had been tipped off that something was occurring and there was somebody present there." According to the courthouse records, TMZ, *Entertainment Tonight*, and KCAL were the only news organizations that filed media requests with the court on the 27th. Morgan explained what his team of paparazzi were supposed to do that day. "Their objective was to capture her leaving the courthouse and then she was going to sort of stop and turn toward the camera to display the bruise on the right side of her face, the alleged bruise."

Since that fateful day at the courthouse, much has been made about the visible or nonvisible mark on Amber's face: whether it was there or not there; apparent to see or covered with makeup. Rocky, who'd been at the penthouse that night the injuries were allegedly inflicted, said she saw "just a swollen, like, red swollen cheek." Josh Drew, who was also on the scene that night, said he saw injuries and swelling. Her makeup artist and close friend Mélanie Inglessis, who saw Amber three days after the incident, said she didn't recall seeing any injuries. Some online commentators observed that the mark resembled the aftereffects of cosmetic filler injections. Later witnesses at trial, including ECB concierge Alejandro Romero, Johnny's friend and neighbor Isaac Baruch, house cleaner Hilda Vargas, two building employees, and three police officers who saw Amber between May 21 and May 27 and *did not* see a bruise on her face, were interrogated about the makeup she was possibly wearing, the Arnica cream she may have used, the icing she may have done to reduce swelling, the quality of the light in the locations where they saw her.

Whatever the truth, the pictures of Amber's injured face were now immortalized on TMZ and in the pages of *People* magazine.

Photos uncovered the day after the TRO (temporary restraining order) hearing caused even more speculation. A series of paparazzi shots showed Amber walking down the street with Rocky and Josh Drew looking joyous, throwing her head back in laughter. Though she appeared not to be wearing makeup, with her hair pulled back, the purplish-brown mark that was prominent in photos twenty-four hours prior wasn't easily discernible in the photo.

Immediately after Amber filed her request for a temporary restraining order, Johnny's divorce lawyer, Laura Wasser, submitted her opposition memo to the court, which was clipped and quoted in the media as many times as Amber's statement.

"Amber is attempting to secure a premature financial resolution by alleging abuse," the memo read. "Her current application for a temporary restraining order along with her financial requests appears to be in response to the negative media attention she received earlier this week after filing for divorce." That Amber had received sexist backlash after her divorce filing was undeniable. Many tabloids questioned the young starlet's financial motives; others painted her the evil stepmother. One TMZ article from May 26 quoted anonymous sources close to Johnny who told the tabloid that Lily-Rose and Jack "hated" Amber because they thought she treated Johnny "like crap," and that Betty Sue thought Amber was "a terrible person" who was using Johnny for his money and fame. The TMZ article ended on a note that seemed to ask, *How could she?* "Amber filed for divorce Monday . . . three days after Betty Sue died. There was no prenup, and Amber wants spousal support."

"Due process requires reasonable notice and an opportunity to be heard," Wasser's memo continued. She argued that ex parte or one-sided applications for TROs are reserved for emergency scenarios where substantial harm could result if a protective order isn't put in place immediately. Even though Johnny was out of the country, Amber had applied ex parte, which didn't require a response from Johnny before a TRO was granted. "Amber is nonetheless seeking ex parte relief for several matters which do not constitute an emergency, including the payment of spousal support and attorney's fees. Not only are such matters devoid of any exigency, but they are also wildly premature."

Where there are claims of domestic violence, family law courts are often afraid to not issue ex parte TROs. They'd rather issue an emergency temporary order than not and have someone turn up seriously injured or dead. Erring on the side of caution, the court granted Amber the temporary protective orders. After May 27, 2016, Johnny was prohibited by law from contacting Amber or getting closer than a hundred feet to her. The court also set a hearing date for June 17, when a judge would determine if Amber's temporary restraining order should be made permanent.

But Amber didn't just want a restraining order; she wanted Johnny to be criminally charged. TMZ and the tabloid paper the *Daily Mail*, which had been covering the TRO story around the clock, were starting to raise questions around Amber's story, citing the lack of a police report from the night of the penthouse fight. On Tuesday, May 31, her lawyers released a statement, via Amber's publicist, explaining that Amber had made a visit to the LAPD. "Johnny's team has forced Amber to give a statement to the LAPD to set the record straight as to the true facts, as she cannot continue to leave herself open to the vicious false and malicious allegations that have infected the media," the statement read.

In California, the most serious charge possible was a felony intimate partner violence charge pursuant to California Penal Code §273.5, which carried up to four years in prison.

Five days later, on June 1, 2016, *People* magazine hit newsstands featuring an explosive cover story with exclusive new photos of Amber's injuries. "Inside Their Toxic Marriage," the headline read. The cover photo showed a pale and forlorn Amber with discoloration under her eyes and a lesion on her lower lip. The words "Exclusive Photo" were splashed next to the image, which was credited to a friend of Amber's and dated from December 2015.

Bruce Witkin, who was on tour in Denmark with Johnny and the Hollywood Vampires at the time, remembered the moment they saw the *People* cover story. "We're on the road. You know, he was freaked out. And I'm like, 'What is this?'" Bruce thought it looked suspicious. "Do I think they both hit each other? Yeah. But do I think it was to the extent that she said? Absolutely not. I never witnessed anything physical, but it was that kind of volatile relationship."

Gina and Stephen Deuters had also traveled from London to Copenhagen to see their friends on tour. Gina said she and Stephen were speechless when they saw the story. "We were meant to be having a nice day, a nice dinner, the Hollywood Vampires were coming into town . . . and then, this."

"When we saw him that night, we didn't even know what to say," Gina continued. "Like, 'Sorry your mom died. Sorry your wife sold a bullshit story to the papers.'" Gina described it as "a really devastating day" for Johnny's children. May 27, the day Amber had been photographed with the mark on her face at the courthouse, was also Lily-Rose's birthday. "The kids had to protect themselves by kind of dissociating, putting a boundary up."

Johnny later said he "felt ill" when the *People* story dropped. "I felt sick in the sense there was no truth in it. There was no truth in it whatsoever . . . Then you notice people looking at you differently. And then you notice calls stop coming from agents and producers." He'd finish a show and then go to the back of the tour bus so he could "get it out." "I just sat in the back of the bus and cried and hid it from people." The weekend after the piece ran, Johnny took a break from tour and spent a few days visiting castles in Romania with Tim Burton, who'd flown out to support Johnny through the difficult time.

The following week, on June 7, 2016, TMZ published another shocking story—this time about Amber and her ex-girlfriend, Tasya van Ree, that had never been made public. "Amber Heard Arrested for Domestic Violence Against Girlfriend," the headline read. In 2009, the same year she met Johnny, Amber had been arrested at the Seattle-Tacoma airport for misdemeanor domestic violence against Tasya. The judge told her they weren't filing charges, but that they could reopen the case within two years. Two years later, Washington police received a request to delete the arrest information on the case. They granted the request, but the records weren't fully deleted from the system. Seven years after that, they got into the hands of TMZ reporters.

Immediately, Tasya disseminated a strongly worded statement in Amber's defense, calling her "wrongly accused," and said the incident was "misinterpreted and over sensationalized" by the two involved cops. "I recount hints of misogynistic attitudes toward us which later appeared to be homophobic when they found out we were domestic partners and not just 'friends.'"

Beverly Leonard, one of the two female arresting officers, was "incensed" that Tasya suggested homophobia was a motive behind Amber's arrest. Now retired, she lives outside of Yuma, Arizona, near rolling hills of agriculture and livestock. "I've been an out lesbian since I was eighteen years old. I've marched on Washington, I have been in multiple Pride parades and I'm an advocate for the LGBTQ community." For Beverly, it had been a normal day on duty as a uniformed police officer on patrol at the Seattle-Tacoma airport. She'd been inside the police substation on the ground level when she noticed two attractive women descending the escalator from the arrivals level down to the baggage claim area. She didn't know at the time that one of the women was the actress Amber Heard.

Both tall, stylish, and beautiful, the women were hard not to notice, but they also stood out because they were arguing intensely. As they approached the plexiglass window of the substation, they stopped walking, and Beverly said she watched as

Amber turned toward Tasya and lunged at her with her hands, reaching toward Tasya's neck as if she was going to choke her. Tasya leaned back, away from Amber, but Amber was able to get her fingers under Tasya's metal chain necklace and rip it off her neck. "She ended up having marks on her neck from the grasping and pulling toward her . . . That's what I saw—the overt movement of Amber's reach and Ms. Van Ree pulling back." Beverly said that as an airport police officer, she'd seen a lot of fights go down. "You see things you don't normally ever see because of the stress of traveling. So I recognized what was happening and I wanted to stop it before it got to blows."

The minute Beverly saw Amber's hands lunge for Tasya's neck, red flags went off. She stood up, clicked on her mic and called for backup, communicating that a potential assault in progress was taking place. Beverly stepped out of the structure and stood in between Amber and Tasya, who were less than ten feet from the plexiglass window of the substation. Beverly's backup arrived, another female officer, and they separated the two women to calm them down. Amber was holding Tasya's broken necklace in her hand. She noticed that they appeared to have been drinking; both of their eyes were watery and they smelled of alcohol. Beverly talked with Amber while her backup talked to Tasya.

"We're fine," Amber told her. "That's my girlfriend, we just got into an argument. We're fine."

The minute Amber said "girlfriend," everything changed. Despite their insistence everything was fine, Beverly had to treat the incident like a domestic-violence assault according to state laws. "We had no discretion at that point in the state of Washington . . . Because I saw what I saw. We had to arrest Amber."

When prosecutors weigh the risk of homicide in domestic abuse cases, the biggest indicator, more than gun ownership, stalking, and forced sex, is any prior attempt at choking or obstructing an airway, because statistically, choking behaviors are the most common correlative to homicide. Beverly's no-nonsense approach to domestic violence was a direct result of the O. J. Simpson case and the Violence Against Women Act—the federal law that Amber would go on to advocate for years later.

"Regarding domestic violence, when things get to the point of choking, that's an indicator that there's been other things," Beverly continued. "Most of the time, I'm referring to a heterosexual couple. So if we arrest a man for choking you, that's bumped up almost to the level of attempted murder. Once you reach for the airway, it's not like you're just grabbing the person's arm. It's a whole other level of violence. That alone made it more urgent to break them up because of where she was grabbing and reaching. It wasn't like she punched her, that would have been completely different. This was leveled up by the virtue of her going for the throat, for the airway."

The timing of the TMZ story couldn't have been worse for Amber. Just as she was mounting her own domestic-violence case against Johnny, her history of violent behavior toward an intimate partner had surfaced. But this was the trouble with the tabloid media. Try to control your story, and it can turn on you all too quickly.

Two days later, on June 9, Trinity Esparza, the front desk supervisor at the ECB building, received a call from Amber, who was upstairs in her penthouse. Amber wanted to discuss the media reports coming out about her and Johnny; it seemed the building staff had been talking to the press. After Trinity told her she'd need to speak to the general manager, Brandon Patterson, Amber came downstairs to meet with both of them. Amber was upset that certain building employees had told reporters she was visibly uninjured following the May 21 fight. "I'm sure the front desk would never compromise the privacy of residents," she told them. Then Amber asked Trinity and Brandon to speak to her "friends" at *People* and deny that building staff had made statements disputing her injury allegations. They declined, explaining that they weren't authorized to speak to the press (though some on staff purportedly had) and that Amber should call the building's lawyers. Later, Brandon stood next to Trinity as she showed him security footage from three days after the alleged phone-throwing incident, which captured Whitney and Rocky Pennington in the ECB lobby with Amber. In the footage, Whitney throws a pretend punch at Amber's face and they all laugh.

On June 13, *People* published a follow-up story: "Amber Heard's Neighbor Speaks Out About Seeing Bruises on Her Face." In the story, the unnamed source tells the magazine that they saw "definite bruising" and that Amber "winced" when he went in for a hug on May 31, ten days after Johnny allegedly threw the phone at her. The source for the story was architecture student Rami Sarabi, who'd moved into the ECB building a month before the abuse allegations went public to be closer to Amber, because he knew things were "dark" for her. Rami said when she announced the abuse allegations, he told her he was willing to back her up publicly. "At first I had my lawyer write a statement for me, an affidavit. Then Amber told me that *People* might reach out." Soon after, Mia McNiece, an editor at *People*, contacted Rami and the follow-up piece was underway.

In June, Amber saw her therapist Dr. Connell Cowan for the first time since February 2016. His progress notes from their session described her affect as "Anxious/sad—in crisis mode." She told him she felt "demoralized by the story spun by the media," which was that Johnny had been victimized by a "cold gold-digger." In perhaps one of the earliest signs of the online bullying that would soon descend on her, someone had briefly altered Amber's Wikipedia page to read, "Amber Laura Heard is an American gold-digger. She married the super talented and respected actor Johnny Depp to take advantage of his kind nature. She feels she no longer needed him therefore began blackmailing him with abuse allegations." To dispel the accusations, Amber withdrew her request for $20,000 a month in spousal support (reduced from $50,000, which already had been denied by a judge) "in light of the coordinated false and negative media campaign falsely depicting my attempts to attain a CLETS Domestic Violence Restraining Order as being financially motivated."

In the same therapy session, Amber also expressed to Dr. Cowan that it was still hard for her to fully and finally let go of Johnny. Her feelings were complicated. She really missed him. He *was* the love of her life.

She found another way to distract herself, with a high-profile billionaire who'd been waiting in the wings.

CHAPTER 10

The Rocketman and the Pirate

S oon after the restraining order against Johnny was granted, Trinity Esparza said a large plant was delivered to Amber at the front desk of the ECB. She called Amber's interior decorator, Laura Divenere, who also acted as Amber's assistant, to tell her it had arrived. Laura took the plant up to the penthouse, but she didn't realize a card had fallen out and onto the floor of the elevator. A resident later picked it up and brought the note to Trinity, who gave it to Laura after she checked security camera footage to be certain it had fallen from the plant.

"I had a wonderful weekend with you, —E," the note read.

According to a source that worked closely with Elon Musk at the time, Amber had confided in him about her harrowing marriage to Johnny. On May 22, the day after the blowout at the penthouse, Elon texted Amber, "Well, I'm just glad you're ok. You talked about J being violent in the past and still having keys to the apartment, so I thought something might have happened."

"It did," Amber shot back. "But that's irrelevant. I had the locks changed." She continued, "Legal divorce filing tomorrow. Restraining order—all that."

"Wtf!? But you're ok, right? Is there anything I can do?"

"To Elon, it sounded like this woman had been abused," the source close to him said. Listening to her stories of being brutally attacked by one of the world's most powerful movie stars, and seeing photos, "Elon's sense of justice led him to want to help her."

"I'm happy to engage 24/7 security for you, if you'd like," he texted Amber. "It would be utterly confidential."

According to the sworn testimony of Eastern Columbia Building concierge and trial witness Alejandro Romero, Elon already had his own key fob for the penthouse garage, and had been visiting Amber regularly there for over a year, late at night, when Johnny was away. Trinity reported seeing Elon with "messy hair" around 9 a.m. at the ECB one morning in late June or early July. Trinity didn't know who he was, but one of the building residents told her he was his hero. That same day, Amber asked Trinity for help retrieving her keys, which had fallen down the trash chute. In a later witness statement, Trinity said she noticed three round bruises on Amber's neck and two Band-Aids on her arm. She also recalled that Amber had a mark on her left cheek, below her eye, about half an inch in length.

In late June, Amber surprised Elon for his birthday. She flew to the Tesla factory in Fremont, California. On the way she picked wildflowers, and when she arrived, his security team helped her hide in the back of a Tesla. As Elon approached the car, Amber popped out of the back clutching a bouquet. Two weeks later, in mid-July, Elon and Amber were spotted together in Miami, Florida. Amber was there with Whitney. The trio stayed in poolside villas at the Delano Hotel in South Beach, and Elon flew Amber and Whitney up to Cape Canaveral, where a SpaceX launch of Falcon 9 was scheduled to take place. Amber told Elon's biographer Walter Isaacson that it was "the most interesting date" she'd ever been on.

These were the first buds of a relationship that would evolve and grow into something serious for the both of them. What no one knew until much later was that Amber and Elon's relationship was also turbulent and toxic, plagued by fighting, jealousy, and dramatic accusations. Witnesses in Elon's inner circle would go on to state strikingly similar things about Amber's character as Johnny's people did.

While she was in Miami, Amber communicated with Christian Carino, her agent at CAA, and asked him in a text to please tell Johnny that she loved him. Christian understood at the time that Amber wanted to talk with Johnny, to find a resolution to their legal battle, and agreed to help try to set up an in-person meeting between them. Christian asked Amber about the restraining order in place. He then texted Johnny, who was reluctant to meet but eventually agreed and offered his travel schedule after Amber promised she'd never accuse him of violating the court order. Johnny hoped that by meeting "she would retract her lies that the world had been fed."

Unlike Amber, Johnny didn't express lingering feelings for his estranged wife. He did, however, seem a bit pissed at Elon Musk. In a text to Christian, Johnny talked like a pirate: "I'll show him things he's never seen before like the other side of his dick when I slice it off." In the month after the allegations of domestic violence went public, he'd altered all three tattoos he'd gotten for Amber, most notably the tattoo on his knuckles, which was changed from her pet name "SLIM" to "SCUM" (and years later, to "SCAM"). He wrote to Paige, Amber's mom, in late May: "a restraining order . . . and a doctored photo??? that is not love, darlin' . . . i hope she is happy now, finally . . ." and told Paige that he was "shocked, disappointed and hurt" and that "she killed us." Paige, like Amber, pitted the blame on Amber's lawyers. "It's the lawyers on both sides doing this not Amber," she wrote back.

Paige said Amber's "dumb lawyer" had told her she'd be evicted from the penthouses in thirty days if she didn't go through with the restraining order. Johnny replied he'd "never do that" and insisted he told Amber she could stay as long as she needed. Paige said Amber still loved Johnny "madly" and wrote, "She DID NOT want to do this I swear to you. The lawyers are frigging things up." Despite the emergency restraining order, the photos of Amber's injuries, and her daughter's own descriptions of violence at his hands, Paige's love for Johnny was steadfast. She ended their exchange with "I love you son" and asked if she could be his adopted mom. Johnny told her he was taking his wedding ring off for good and that he and Amber would never see each other again.

Johnny would see Amber again. That July, Christian set up the mediation between the fractured pair at a friend's house in the Bay Area. Johnny was still on tour with the Hollywood Vampires and doing a show in San Francisco, so Christian and Amber flew up together and drove out to the house. Johnny met them a few hours later.

Amber would later say she wanted this mediation because "more and more attacks were coming out against me and accusing me of being a liar and was forcing me in a position where . . . I would have to at some point speak to prove it." She said she asked Christian to arrange the mediation because she didn't want the world or Johnny's kids to know what he was capable of. She also stated that she just wanted Johnny to leave her alone, even though it was Amber trying to get in contact with Johnny.

Amber and Johnny sat outside while Christian watched inside through a window. Johnny's security guard, Malcolm Connolly, sat in another room inside the house and vowed to intervene if things got too heated. Malcolm had begged Johnny not to come to this meeting. "She's setting you up," he said. He had reason to be concerned: in early June, the LAPD was called, citing a violation of the temporary restraining order, when members of Johnny's team came to the penthouses to collect some of his personal belongings. But Johnny wouldn't listen to Malcolm.

Johnny and Amber talked for hours. When Christian's friend eventually needed his house back, they relocated to a hotel suite at the historic Omni Hotel in San Francisco. Bruce Witkin, who was on tour with Johnny, also thought the meet-up was a bad idea—and soon his fears were confirmed.

Bruce was hanging out in the hotel lobby when he saw several of Johnny's security guys leaving in a hurry.

"What the fuck is going on?" he emailed an assistant of Johnny's.

"She's here," the assistant replied.

Bruce found out what room they were in and walked straight there to stop the meeting. "Are you sure you want to do this?" he asked Johnny, reminding him that he could get arrested for violating the TRO. As he sat next to Johnny in the hotel room, Amber walked in crying. Johnny's security guards threw their hands up.

"He's yours," they said to Bruce.

"All right . . . you guys talk," Bruce said to Amber and Johnny as he left the room, leaving the door cracked open. "If I heard any noise, I was going in."

Inside the suite, sitting beneath crystal chandeliers, Amber and Johnny continued their self-guided mediation, but their attempt at reconciliation soon devolved into another bitter fight—all secretly recorded by Amber on her phone.

At one point, Amber told him she just wanted to touch him.

"After all the shit you fucking accused me of? You wanna touch me? You're fucking nuts," he said.

Amber cried and told Johnny she didn't want things to end badly. She tried to take his sunglasses off to see his eyes. "Don't take my fucking glasses off," he spat. "You will not see my eyes again."

There were revealing moments in the recording that demonstrated a more honest side to their relationship: that they both emotionally tortured each other, and that Amber hit Johnny more than once. Johnny reminded her why he left her on her thirtieth birthday, because she "haymakered him" and "came around the bed and was punching" on him. Later, Amber would explain that she didn't deny this in the moment because she was "not having that conversation with Johnny," and she just wanted to get out of the hotel room. "Booze does not make me crazy. Drugs do not make me crazy," Johnny told her. "Here's the deal. YOU make me crazy."

"Stop it!" she said. "Stop the blame. Stop the nitpicking. Stop the fighting. I don't want to fight with you. All I can say is I love you."

At one point in the night, Johnny pulled a knife out and threatened to cut himself. It was the same foot-long turquoise-handled knife that Amber had given to Johnny as a birthday gift, the blade inscribed with "hasta la muerte" and his nickname for her, "Slim."

"Want to cut me somewhere?" Johnny asked Amber.

"Please do not cut yourself," she pleaded, begging him to "put the knife down." When housekeeping knocked on the hotel room door, Johnny sent them away with a crude joke. "No thank you, no thank you, there's sperm on the pillows." Johnny then continued to ask Amber to cut him, because she hates him, he said. Amber said she'd never do that to him.

"I know you're in pain, but stop. Please don't . . ."

"There's a way for the pain to go away," Johnny replied.

"It doesn't make it go away, trust me."

"How do you know?"

"I know, trust me. It doesn't make it go away."

Years later, when the recording was played in the courtroom, both Amber and Johnny appeared to be crying.

Bruce sat outside of the hotel room until sunrise. Eventually, Amber left the suite, and Malcolm volunteered to walk her down to the street to catch a cab. She looked Malcolm in the eyes as they took the elevator down. "I really love him, Mal. I really do," she said through tears.

"The shit has already hit the fan," Malcolm said as he escorted her through the opulent lobby. "It's too late."

A few weeks later, she was seen in London with Elon at a cabaret nightclub called The Box. Just a mile down the road, Amber and Johnny would meet again, years later, inside London's Royal Courts of Justice.

CHAPTER 11

The Cabinet Video

Johnny and Amber's ad hoc mediation attempt to prevent going to court had failed and the permanent restraining order trial was imminent. But after Amber missed a few scheduled depositions in LA, the trial was pushed from June to August. Johnny's lawyer Laura Wasser chafed at the delays. "Amber has provided innumerable excuses: I am in London. I am at a wedding. I have a costume fitting. My lawyer is unavailable. Amber is truly not interested in having the veracity of her claims examined." Amber's team claimed all of these statements were categorically false—she was simply busy and needed time to prepare.

The type of permanent restraining order that Amber was seeking against Johnny was called a Domestic Violence Restraining Order, or DVRO. DVROs have a lower burden of proof and broader outlines than a civil harassment restraining order, or CHRO, which is used to protect yourself against a stalker or someone harassing you that isn't family or an intimate partner. DVROs are issued on a "preponderance of evidence," whereas CHROs are issued at a much higher standard: "clear and convincing evidence." With a DVRO, the definitions of harm become more amorphous and broad—for example, an individual can introduce evidence of patterns of coercive control, or evidence of "disturbing the peace" by an intimate partner. DVROs have no requirement for any likelihood of future harm. What a spouse can demand from the other after a DVRO is issued is also much broader in terms of financial spousal support and custody of property.

The collateral consequences of having a DVRO issued against you are significant. After being entered into a state and national database, the restrained party may have to surrender their passport and any firearms in their possession until the end of the order. Many countries accept and recognize the authority of court orders issued in the US and bar entry for the restrained. Typically, a permanent DVRO will last between one to five years.

Amber eventually sat for her deposition on August 13, 2016, four days before a judge would hear the case. Leading up to the hearing, Amber repeatedly contacted Johnny, continuing to violate her own emergency protective order. In the few days before she was deposed, Amber called Johnny fourteen times.

Johnny had retained criminal defense attorney Blair Berk to cross-examine Amber on her claims in a taped deposition. Blair was known for her successful representation of preschool teachers in a case spawned during the time of moral hand-wringing known as the "Satanic Panic" before going on to represent A-list clients such as Kanye West, Lindsay Lohan, and Leonardo DiCaprio (and later, more famously, in the era of #MeToo, Harvey Weinstein, Marilyn Manson, and Armie Hammer). Over several tense hours, Blair questioned Amber on camera about the events surrounding her thirtieth birthday party and the May 21 penthouse fight, the incidents of domestic violence listed in her application for a TRO. During the deposition, Amber walked back several previous statements and made a revealing slip-up. Referring to Johnny learning about her divorce filing, she stated to Blair, "I'm specifically saying I would like him to know information coming from me, so that he finds out about the divorce filing [from me] other than TMZ, which was alerted—" letting slip that TMZ had been fed the scoop on their divorce. As soon as she realized what she said, she stopped short and held her hands up to her face, mouth agape, as she looked over at her lawyer. A pregnant pause filled the room as she wiped her palms across her cheeks, smoothed her hair, and then clasped her hands. She never picked the sentence back up.

On the eve of Amber's deposition there had been another big leak. A secretly filmed video of Johnny was published on TMZ's website. The footage, which would come to be known as "The Cabinet Video," showed Johnny in a fit of rage at home slamming his kitchen cabinets and kicking cabinet doors, the sound of glass shattering in the background while he repeatedly shouted "Motherfucker" in anger. It was daytime but Johnny was wearing sunglasses and a fedora inside. Amber stood in the corner in a T-shirt and jeans surreptitiously filming him before placing her phone behind an object on the kitchen table, still rolling.

It was February 2016, and Johnny had just had another grim talk with his business managers about the state of his financial affairs. Johnny was deep in loans he couldn't pay back, no matter how many big roles he took with Disney. For months, The Management Group had been urging him to sell off assets, such as his French villa near St. Tropez. Real estate appraisers had valued it at $13.5 million, but Johnny had spent $10 million to restore it and insisted on listing the property at double the appraised value.

Amber shifted and angled her body to conceal the camera as Johnny stormed around the kitchen.

"I woke up and you were so sweet and nice, we weren't even fighting this morning, all I did was say sorry," she said, trailing off softly.

"Did something happen to YOU this morning?" he yelled back at her, punching the table, breaking something fragile on top of it.

As he emptied most of a bottle of red wine into a large stemmed mason jar, later nicknamed his "megapint" of wine, Johnny noticed Amber's hidden camera. He walked over, picked up the phone, and shouted at her, "Oh, you got this going?" before throwing it down the hallway. The TMZ video ended there.

The footage was jarring. Johnny had almost always been captured on film as genial and lighthearted. The public had never seen him act belligerent and hostile like this. For the first time, the world could observe him candidly as emotionally volatile and prone to rage and violence. It was something Amber's camp could point to as proof that Johnny did spin out of control and had a scary temper. The media pounced on the story. Some righteously condemned Johnny's "rage." Some condemned Amber for having leaked the video, which she denied doing. Others condemned the media itself for condemning Amber. "Amber Heard Is Not Just Another 'Crazy Woman,'" one headline read.

But the video given to TMZ was not the full video. Both the beginning of the video, in which Amber sets up the camera, and the end, showing Amber picking her phone back up and laughing after Johnny yelled "Ass" at her as she walked away with a blank look on her face, were edited out. The video was published within fifteen minutes of landing at TMZ. Later, an employee of the tabloid would testify that they only publish material that quickly when it's sent directly from the copyright source.

Throughout her deposition, Amber's demeanor wavered between a kind of unworldly naivete to defensive, hostile, and self-assured. While listening to an audio recording in which Johnny described his head being slammed by Amber into a door, she munched on snacks. After it was over, she smiled, shaking her head no. In other moments, she smiled sarcastically and rolled her eyes.

Three days after her deposition, Amber asked that the proceeding for her restraining order request not move forward. The case was dismissed with prejudice, meaning it was permanently dissolved and could never be retried. In a matter of days, Amber went from a "petrified" wife requiring legal protection from Johnny to dropping the entire case against him, forever.

On the same day, August 16, 2016, Johnny and Amber settled their divorce. The dissolution of their fifteen-month marriage would result in three phonebook-sized volumes of family law records. Amber was awarded $7 million in the settlement. Two days later, she released a public statement saying she'd donate the entire settlement to the ACLU and the Children's Hospital Los Angeles, perhaps eager to disprove the "gold-digger" accusations.

Johnny retained all of his real estate properties and more than forty vehicles and vessels. Amber would keep the dogs and the horse, Arrow, he had gifted her. Neither would receive spousal support. The former couple, along with their suite of lawyers, signed a confidentiality agreement that barred them from ever discussing the details of the divorce publicly. They both agreed to release a joint statement to the press.

"Our relationship was intensely passionate and at times volatile, but always bound by love. Neither party has made false accusations for financial gain. There was never any intent of physical or emotional harm," the statement read. The statement contradicted and sanitized the previous accusatory statements they'd made about each other and ended with an attempt at reconciliation. After their DIY mediation attempt, the divorce agreement, and now their joint statement, it seemed like Johnny and Amber had finally reached some kind of accord. But the posture of peacetime wouldn't last long.

PART III

CHAPTER 12

Primal Screams

The red carpet was buzzing in front of the NeueHouse in Hollywood, a private members-only club and co-working space with locations in LA and NYC, on November 14, 2016. As Zendaya and Gwen Stefani lined up, Bono breezed past, one of the few men in sight. That night, he'd be awarded Man of the Year, a first ever, at the 27th annual *Glamour*'s Women of the Year Awards.

Amber strolled down the red carpet wearing a beige dress made of lace and tulle frills, posing for flashing cameras, her hair pulled back and lips painted dark red. Only a few months had passed since Amber and Johnny settled their divorce, and only a week since Donald Trump was elected 45th president of the United States, defeating Hillary Clinton. As Amber shifted angles for the camera, she subtly tilted her head. Behind her was a white wall emblazoned with logos for *Glamour* magazine, Condé Nast, and L'Oréal. Since the divorce was finalized, both Amber and Johnny had receded from the public eye, letting the media cycle move on to other scandals, like Trump's own leaked *Access Hollywood* tape. But tonight she was back in the spotlight as a presenter and would be announcing one of the evening's Women of the Year.

Glamour's Women of the Year Awards were established to honor "extraordinary and inspirational" women from a variety of fields, from entertainment to science, medicine, and politics. Madonna was one of the first to receive the award in 1990, but others have included Britney Spears, Serena Williams, and J. K. Rowling. Though this was an established celebrity award show, this year the event took on a particularly political note in the wake of Donald Trump's win. With a man who'd been caught on tape bragging about grabbing women by the pussy now the elected president, contemporary feminism was at an inflection point. That night, they'd dedicate a segment of the show to Hillary Clinton, honoring and thanking her for her career in public service, in a tribute that felt almost funereal.

At the beginning of the awards show, host Tracee Ellis Ross took to the stage and invited the audience to join her in a communal primal scream. As the night proceeded, honors were given to the gymnast Simone Biles, plus-size model Ashley Graham, and Iraqi-born Yazidi activist Nadia Murad, who was raped and beaten for three months when she was kidnapped by ISIS at age nineteen before escaping. During the raid and kidnapping, ISIS killed seven of her family members. Standing under the bright lights onstage, Nadia's demeanor remained markedly somber, a stark contrast to the telegenic presenters and honorees who'd come before her. As her translator interpreted her brief words condemning genocide and war crimes, she kept her eyes fixed on the audience.

An hour into the event, Lena Dunham walked onstage in a burgundy dress, tilting her head with a smile directed to a friend in the audience. Arriving at the podium, she looked solemnly toward the crowd. "When I was a junior in college I was sexually assaulted," Lena said. Two years before she'd published her bestselling memoir, *Not That Kind of Girl*, which included an essay about her sexual assault. Lena then began to tell the story of Chanel Miller (then still "Emily Doe") and the high-profile Stanford rape case that was, at the time, still dominating headlines. Chanel's victim impact statement, which she'd read aloud in court, had gone viral when it was published on BuzzFeed several months earlier.

After Lena shared Chanel's story, Amber walked onto the stage with actresses Freida Pinto and Gabourey Sidibe. They each read parts of the victim impact statement. Freida Pinto read the well-known first line, "You don't know me, but you've been inside of me," looking up at the audience. They ended the performance speaking in unison: "Victims are survivors. And survivors are going to be doing a hell of a lot more than surviving. To girls everywhere, I am with you." Emily Doe was then announced as the next recipient of the Woman of the Year award.

Amber was starting to shift her activism in a new direction. Previously she fit hearing aids for the hard of hearing, advocated for LGBTQ rights, and brought art to young girls at the Children's Hospital Los Angeles. Now, her work had a distinctly feminist edge. A few weeks after the awards show, Amber recorded an emotional video PSA about domestic violence for British socialite Amanda de Cadenet's newest project, Girlgaze, described as an "online multi-sided platform company" aimed at connecting businesses with "womxn & non-binary creatives." Leaning into the camera, Amber spoke with passion. "It happens to so many women, when it happens in your home behind closed doors with someone you love, it's not as straightforward." She ended with a forceful call to action. "Speak up. Speak up," she said, staring into the camera with defiant eyes. "Raise your voice. Your voice is the most powerful thing and we, together, as women standing shoulder to shoulder cannot and will not any longer accept silence." A card at the end of the PSA read, "Share this video if you think it's time to eliminate violence against women." The video's release coincided with the United Nations International Day for the Elimination of Violence Against Women. It was republished online by *People*, *Variety*, *Time*, and the *Daily Mail*.

As Amber was rebuilding her life and leaning into activism after her hostile divorce, things were heating up with Elon Musk. By April 2017, their relationship, which had been "on" for nearly a year, intensified. Soon she'd be returning to Australia's Gold Coast to film *Aquaman*, only this time she'd be traveling with Elon instead of Johnny.

In Australia, Elon rented Amber a beautiful home. It was here, away from the office, that his infatuation with Amber became more problematic for the executives at SpaceX and Tesla. For the first time, Elon became distracted from his life's work. "It would be a Tuesday night and she would keep him up all night. There was a blatant disregard for the fact that he had tens of thousands of employees and he had responsibilities," said a source close to Elon. "She did more to slow the advancement of electric cars than the CEO of Exxon Mobil."

Elon himself later described the relationship with Amber to his biographer, Walter Isaacson, as the most agonizing of all his romantic relationships, admitting that he carries a deep-seated pain about it to this day. "It was brutal," he said. For a man that has trouble accessing his humanity, Amber brought forth the most human of emotions: he was lovesick.

A few months after the Australia trip, during an interview at the SpaceX office for *Rolling Stone*, Elon, flustered, excused himself and had a pep talk with his chief of staff, Sam Teller. A few minutes later, he fessed up to the reporter: he and Amber had just broken up and he "was really in love and it hurt bad." In fact, he'd barely been able to function at the launch event of his Tesla Model 3 the night before. "I've been in severe emotional pain for the last few weeks. Severe. It took every ounce of will to be able to do the Model 3 event and not look like the most depressed guy around. For most of that day, I was morbid. And then I had to psych myself up: drink a couple of Red Bulls, hang out with positive people and then, like, tell myself: 'I have all these people depending on me. All right, do it!'"

This breakup wouldn't be their last—Amber and Elon continued to see each other, on and off, throughout the rest of 2017. A friend of Amber's, who chose to stay anonymous when interviewed for this book, hung out with Amber and Elon on at least three different occasions. She remembered a conversation she had with Amber after Amber moved out of the ECB penthouses and into a house of her own in the Hollywood Hills. Amber told her friend that Elon was crazy, possessive, and jealous, and that he'd placed cameras in her house, bugged her car, and was following her. But Amber's friend was skeptical. "Y'all, this is exactly the same shit we just did with this other guy, Johnny. How is no one seeing this?" All of Amber's friends had joined the ranks and turned against Elon, and yet, as they had with Johnny, they'd adored him initially and welcomed him into their friend-family. She tried to understand it from Amber's perspective, but she couldn't rationalize it based on what she already knew about Amber. "*She* was a chaotic, unstable character."

Elon's close family and friends didn't approve of Amber either. Kimbal Musk, Elon's younger brother, told Walter Isaacson that Amber was "a nightmare," stating "she was just so toxic." On a trip to Rio de Janeiro in December 2017, they had a fight that ended their relationship for good. Amber locked herself in their hotel room and started screaming that Elon had taken her passport and that she was scared she'd be attacked. The security guards and Kimbal's wife assured her that no one was trying to hurt her, she was safe, her passport was securely in her bag. They told her she should and could leave whenever she wanted. But, Kimbal said, her ability to shift her own reality was shocking. "She really is a very good actress, so she will say things that you're like 'Wow, maybe she's telling you the truth,' but she isn't. The way she can create her own reality reminds me of my dad." Elon had told the *Rolling Stone* reporter that his dad, Errol Musk, who infamously fathered two children with his stepdaughter, whom he first met when she was four, was evil. "You have no idea about how bad. Almost every crime you can possibly think of, he has done," Elon said. Johnny's legal team would later desperately try to subpoena Elon Musk, but he was too buffered by security.

After the breakup, Amber texted her agent, Christian Carino, the same person who arranged the mediation between her and Johnny the year before. "Dealing with breakup. I hate when things go public. See I'm so sad."

"You weren't in love with [Elon]," Christian replied. "You told me 1,000 times you were just filling space. Why would you be sad if you weren't in love with him to begin with?"

Amber asked Christian to give Johnny a letter she wrote expressing her love for him, and apologizing for what happened. "God I miss him," she said.

As an actress in Hollywood speaking out about gender inequality and power imbalances, Amber was ahead of the curve—but soon she'd have a global movement on her side, empowering her to go deeper into advocacy work on behalf of survivors of sexual harassment and domestic violence.

In October 2017, bombshell reporting from the *New York Times* and *The New Yorker* revealed that dozens of women, including high-profile actresses, had accused top film producer Harvey Weinstein of rape, sexual assault, and sexual harassment. The number of Weinstein accusers would eventually total more than eighty, with accusations that stretched back thirty years. Ten days after the story broke, actress Alyssa Milano tweeted, "If you've been sexually harassed or assaulted write 'me too' as a reply to this tweet." Within twenty-four hours, more than 12 million social-media posts referenced #MeToo, and the viral social feminism campaign soon spread across eighty-five countries. Alyssa Milano quickly credited the phrase "#MeToo" to its originator, the activist Tarana Burke, who coined the phrase in 2006 as a way to raise awareness and promote solidarity among women of color who'd suffered sexual assault.

And just like that, the #MeToo movement was born.

Even before the Weinstein exposé, a new women's movement was gaining steam. The day after Trump's inauguration in January 2017, millions of women across the US and the globe joined the National Women's March. Energy around expanded Title IX regulations and stopping campus sexual assault had been building since 2011. But with Alyssa's tweet, Hollywood swiftly jumped on the bandwagon. It was Hollywood's movement now—and the victims shown in the media were nearly always white, connected, and rich. As a succession of beautiful, famous actresses came forward with their stories of abuse and harassment, the #MeToo movement catapulted into a viral social campaign that, to many, was a righteous and overdue reckoning for an industry that, since its inception, had operated with few moral bounds.

To others, it was a dangerous moral panic. Accusers were taking down previously celebrated cultural figures from Louis C.K. to Charlie Rose to Matt Lauer, as well as politicians like Al Franken and Andrew Cuomo. New allegations seemed to emerge on a weekly basis. Some called it "the Weinstein Ripple Effect." Less than a month after the Weinstein articles dropped, NBC News published a list of more than forty high-profile men accused of sexual harassment or assault, or both. *Glamour* later published its own list of high-profile men who stood accused of #MeToo violations that included a hundred names. Many of the men listed were power players in Hollywood. At that time, an accusation was enough to prompt exile.

The nation was outraged at the picture emerging from Hollywood: an ethically bankrupt enterprise driven by sex and greed, lorded over by sleazy, misogynistic men who acted with impunity. Actresses in the industry, bearing witness to this predatory system, demanded change. It was time for every aspect of Hollywood, from directors to studios to agencies, to adopt the tenets of #MeToo: accountability and systemic change. It was time for Hollywood to listen to and amplify women's stories, especially women who were victims or survivors. By 2018, #MeToo had become the dominant discourse among a film world eager to wash its hands of Weinstein's lecherous legacy. Packaged by celebrities and then corporations, the reckoning was long overdue—but to some critics, its execution seemed to amount to a one-size-fits-all feminism.

Whether you believed #MeToo was revolution or histrionics, a new dawn for feminism or Satanic Panic Part II, Amber was poised for the moment. Since splitting from Johnny, her public persona had transformed from a silenced, persecuted victim to an outspoken survivor and advocate—an evolution that neatly coincided with the trending social causes of the moment: women's and LGBTQ rights and then, suddenly, #MeToo.

Through her role as a Hollywood activist, Amber's celebrity grew to new heights. In May 2018, she was selected to be a global celebrity ambassador at L'Oréal, a role that A-list actresses Dame Helen Mirren, Julianne Moore, and Eva Longoria also held, and which involved, in Amber's words, being "a spokesperson for this dynamic, world-loved beauty brand that's been telling women 'we're worth it' since before I was born . . . I feel like these women—my fellow ambassadors—represent a voice, a power, a movement, an opinion." As a global spokesperson for women's issues, she shot branded content and splashy commercials for blond hair dye, celebrating women who "own it" as part of L'Oréal's #OwningIt campaign, and walked in a Paris runway show during Fashion Week to raise awareness about the brand's training program, "Stand Up Against Street Harassment."

As more brands and corporations hurried to hop on the #MeToo train, they changed their messaging to raise awareness about issues concerning women. Nike launched the "Until We All Win" campaign to promote gender equality and empowerment. The condom brands Durex and Trojan focused their ad campaigns on sexual consent and sexual assault. Twitter bought its first-ever television ad during the 2018 Oscars, a sixty-second black-and-white spot focused on female empowerment and promoting a newly minted hashtag: #HereWeAre. Now these corporate brands could be concerned and "active," without directly and materially addressing the systemic issues plaguing women, like poverty and healthcare.

After Amber was made L'Oréal Global Ambassador of Women, which also involved starring in the "Worth It" talk show "honoring women in cinema, beauty, and beyond" at the 2018 Cannes Film

Festival, Amber received more prestigious appointments. The ACLU, slated to receive $3.5 million of her divorce settlement, selected Amber to be an ambassador of women's rights with a focus on gender-based violence. During the Brett Kavanaugh hearings in the fall of 2018, Amber aligned herself with Christine Blasey Ford and flew to DC to protest the Supreme Court nominee on the courthouse steps alongside other celebrities. Amber started working with "Mr. Charity," or Todd Krim, a self-described "charity matchmaker" who ran an advisory firm specializing in "leveraging the power of celebrity engagement to help nonprofits and brands make a lasting impact through special events, personal appearances, and social impact campaigns." In October 2018, he and Amber traveled to Geneva, after Amber was appointed a Human Rights Ambassador for the Office of the United Nations High Commissioner for Human Rights. Amber gave a talk about her role in "amplifying the voices of sexual-assault survivors and demanding justice, dignity and representation in the highest level of government." After returning to the States, she posted on Instagram from Dallas, Texas, where she campaigned for Beto O'Rourke, who was running for Senate. She hobnobbed with feminists and celebrities like Amy Schumer at a dinner for Time's Up, a nonprofit founded by Hollywood celebrities in the wake of the Weinstein scandal that raised money to support victims of sexual harassment. She made a video urging women not to suffer in silence for the UN's sixteen days of activism against gender-based violence.

Amber was also a featured guest at the 2018 "Incredible Women" gala in Hollywood. The event, themed "One Year Stronger," was co-hosted by Donna Langley, the Chairwoman of Universal Pictures, and celebrated the one year anniversary of #MeToo and Time's Up. Amber took to the stage in a red velvet tuxedo jacket and black cigarette pants to read aloud an open letter she wrote entitled "To My Silent Sisters," which she'd published two years earlier in *Porter* magazine, an editorial vertical of the luxury fashion ecommerce site Net-a-Porter. The letter didn't name Johnny, but it discussed the stigma of coming forward as a victim of domestic violence in Hollywood.

"No matter how terrible or terrifying surviving trauma may be," she read out to the star-studded audience, "the truth is, it can pale in comparison to what happens after." Amber hadn't been silent in private conversations about the fact that she believed her career and reputation had suffered because she went public as the abuse victim of an ultra-famous and beloved star. Now, she wanted the industry's support. "The fear of being ostracized by your community is just about the most terrifying prospect there is," she said. Amber concluded with a motivational message to women. "You may have suffered alone behind closed doors, but you are not alone."

CHAPTER 13

The Monster

While Amber was traveling the world telling her story and advocating on behalf of women everywhere, Johnny, with the help of a new lawyer named Adam Waldman, was working hard to do damage control to repair his tarnished public image and shore up his ruinous finances.

Johnny first met Adam at his new accountant Ed White's house in Bel Air around October 2016, a few months after his divorce from Amber. His life was in shambles. Aside from the ugly situation with Amber, The Management Group had just put nonjudicial foreclosure notices on certain properties he owned. In March, Johnny had fired TMG after seventeen years, and TMG claimed Johnny wasn't paying back a $5 million loan *they* had lent him in 2012. During the meeting at Ed White's house, the men conversed in White's garden overlooking the Bel-Air Golf Course. Ed told Adam that he believed TMG had taken "a cavalier approach to Depp's accounts." According to the *Hollywood Reporter*, after several hours of talking, Adam was convinced Johnny had grounds for a lawsuit.

Adam was a high-powered lawyer and lobbyist in Washington, DC, whose clients included Julian Assange and Russian oligarch

Oleg Deripaska. "I did not want a Hollywood attorney," Johnny said. Adam was in his early fifties and had a taut, lineless face thanks to his wife, Dr. Barbara Sturm, a celebrity cosmetologist who created the "vampire facial," a skin treatment utilizing her signature product, the MC1 moisturizer, a $1,400 cream infused with the buyer's own blood. Sources in Johnny's inner circle described Adam as a Svengali character who quickly became Johnny's chief confidant. Adam founded the Endeavor Group in 2001, a discreet financial management company for the ultra-wealthy. Their website, now shuttered, described their operation as representing "the business, philanthropic and special interests of a select group of high net worth individuals." Adam had cultivated links to Hollywood through his work at the intersection of entertainment, politics, and capital. In 2002, he helped create Debt, AIDS, Trade, Africa (DATA), a multinational NGO founded by Bono. Wyclef Jean, Angelina Jolie, and Brad Pitt were also his clients. Endeavor's website listed just two board members, one of whom was Jack Valenti, former special assistant to President Lyndon B. Johnson and president of the Motion Picture Association of America from 1966 to 2004. Valenti was massively influential in Hollywood, but his was a Hollywood of a bygone era, when the profits still came from box office sales and broadcast television.

Contemporary Hollywood was a shadow of its former self—defined by tested intellectual properties, Marvel franchises, large corporate streamers, and predatory agencies. Mega media corporations and investment firms dominated the space, reducing risk and maximizing efficiency—all before AI came into the picture. According to Johnny, he'd been pushed for years by his agent, Tracey Jacobs (and, according to some sources, by his sister, Christi), to do more commercial roles in big-budget films, playing fantastical and farcical characters like the Mad Hatter and Charlie

Mortdecai. When the script for the movie *Transcendence* came in, Stephen Deuters took one pass and told Johnny, "Well . . . that script is a piece of shit," but eventually he learned to keep his mouth shut. "I felt he was pushed to do things he wouldn't otherwise have done by the powers that be and he always insisted in himself that he would deliver artistically." Still, whether Johnny liked it or not, it was his commercial roles that enabled his lavish lifestyle, and it gave him leverage in the industry. He was one of the Hollywood elite.

Tracey Jacobs would later say in a deposition that Johnny blamed her and her talent agency, UTA, because they weren't setting up financing for his esoteric projects. One of the more niche projects he wanted to make was an adaptation of J. P. Donleavy's 1955 book, *The Ginger Man*, initially banned in Ireland and the United States for obscenity but later hailed as a classic. It was one of Johnny's favorite books—a comical picaresque following the adventures of a roguish but charming folk-hero, Sebastian Dangerfield, who chases booze and women and avoids hard work and polite society like the plague—which had been introduced to him by none other than Hunter S. Thompson. "Every man should read this, and spend at least one evening in his life impersonating this unapologetic horror of an individual!" Johnny said.

When his reps told him these projects weren't marketable, Johnny didn't want to hear it. According to Johnny, Tracey feigned interest, saying, "I think we can get funding," and then nothing would happen. "She didn't want me to do any films where the commission was $500,000," he said. She didn't always have the right instincts either. In an interview for this book, Johnny told the story of the time he was in former Disney studio chief Dick Cook's office, when he threw out an idea that Johnny loved—a movie called *Pirates of the Caribbean* based on the famous Disneyland theme park ride. Johnny agreed to do the movie, even though there wasn't a script yet. "I'm out of my fucking gourd. I'll do it," he said, emphatically. Tracey, who was sitting next to him, looked like Johnny attacked her with a thousand bees. She didn't want him to take the part. "Tracey got very famous because I was making a lot of money," Johnny said. Tracey remembered it differently, saying it was her idea to take Johnny to Dick Cook's office and that this meeting led to a relationship with Disney and the first Pirates movie. "He said, word for word, 'I'd love to do a movie that my kiddies can see.'"

Thirteen years had passed since he made the first Pirates film, and now, new marketable projects were what he needed most. Johnny had to be making $60 million a year to keep up with his bills. He loved to shop for his many collections of Hollywood memorabilia, occult ephemera, horses, and real estate properties. It cost him $500,000 a month in storage-facility rental fees alone to hold his inventory, which included personal belongings of Marilyn Monroe and Marlon Brando; Jack Kerouac's raincoat ($15,000); dozens of rare vintage guitars; a 1959 Corvette and a 1960 Rolls-Royce Silver Ghost; hundreds of blue-chip artworks, including pieces by Warhol, Modigliani, Basquiat; and a $245,000 Leonor Fini painting he bought Amber as a gift. Johnny spent $10,000 a day on security and $300,000 a month on full-time staff, many of whom managed the fourteen different properties he owned around the world, which had cost him nearly $75 million. To his critics, Johnny was quintessentially Hollywood, an out of touch A-list actor who indulged in excess, then found himself in crisis because of it. His addictive personality spiraled as the fat paychecks rolled in. Success became his biggest enabler.

Still, Johnny and his coterie stressed his immense star power—his films had brought in billions for Warner Bros. and

Disney. Aside from Tom Cruise and Robert Downey Jr., no actor was as profitable. More than a decade after he told a reporter that he rejected "the idea of being a product," his fate as a product had been irrevocably sealed. He felt disenfranchised from the Hollywood system, he hated being a commodity, a piece of "IP." Johnny escaped the synthetic world of fame by regularly obliterating his mind and body, entering an anarchic void of alcohol and drugs, a form of "freedom" he learned from Hunter S. Thompson. Perhaps he understood that his personal risk-taking assigned him an even higher cultural value. After all, his own Hollywood idols, the superstars turned tortured addicts Marilyn Monroe and Marlon Brando, were all the more legendary for their self-destructive ways and tragic declines.

Eventually Johnny and his team at Infinitum Nihil moved their offices—and productions—overseas, where there was less red tape and independent movies still had a life-form. Johnny's longtime friend and IN's head of development, Sam Sarkar, explained that in Europe there was much more freedom in moviemaking. "It's like, yeah, you've got a mansion. But, baby, I'm over there (in Europe). I do whatever the fuck I want and I answer to no one." Sam recalled doing a Q&A with Al Pacino when Pacino told the story of working with Francis Ford Coppola on *The Godfather* and he found Coppola hunched over crying at the end of a long day of filming. "They wouldn't let me do one more shot," Francis said.

"What director on a Marvel movie is sobbing at the end of the day because they didn't get the shot they wanted?" Sam asked.

In January 2017, a few months after their first meeting, represented by Adam Waldman alongside his attorneys Benjamin Chew and Camille Vasquez of the law firm Brown Rudnick, Johnny sued the Mandel brothers and The Management Group (TMG) for fraud, theft, and malfeasance in its mismanagement of his business and financial interests. He also sued Bloom Hergott, the firm of his longtime entertainment lawyer, Jake Bloom, for mishandling his divorce from Amber and allegedly charging millions of dollars in improper fees. That same month, TMG hit back with a cross-complaint of fraud, claiming Johnny's financial woes were the direct result of his reckless spending. They asserted that Johnny lied to the public and public authorities as a habit and required his employees, family, and friends to lie on his behalf as well. TMG called this Johnny's "modus operandi" to avoid personal responsibility for his "sad conduct."

Bruce Witkin, who was the head of a start-up record label called Unison that he and Johnny had formed in 2007, soon found himself roped into the Mandel lawsuit. The label had lost $4 million in its first four years. When Bruce apologized to Johnny and suggested they call it quits, Johnny told him it would take the world twenty years to catch up to Bruce's genius. "Keep going," he said. By 2015, Joel Mandel had finally convinced Johnny to stop funding the operation.

Adam had a nickname for Johnny's friends who he decided were more loyal to the Mandels than to Johnny: "Tessio," after the character played by Abe Vigoda who betrayed the Corleone family in *The Godfather*. Bruce said he was wrongly deemed a Tessio. "They just lumped me and a few of Johnny's friends into this lawsuit and I never heard from anyone in Johnny's camp again." Johnny's close friends Sal Jenco, James Russo, and his longtime assistant Nathan Holmes were folded into the lawsuit as well and had to be deposed. In TMG court filings, Johnny insisted he never authorized the funding for the record label. Soon after, Johnny stopped answering Bruce's calls. Bruce was left in the dark as to what he'd done wrong. "Someone once said to me, 'You're Johnny's mirror, and he doesn't want to look in the mirror.'"

Longtime agent Tracey Jacobs had also been given the boot. In October 2016, Johnny called Tracey, who was in London, and said, "I'm going to CAA." He told her he was unhappy at UTA and that he felt CAA would do a better job keeping him and his team at Infinitum Nihil happy. Tracey was livid. It was 2 a.m. in London, and she was returning to LA the next day—yet he'd knowingly woken her up in the middle of the night to tell her "almost gleefully" over the phone that, after thirty years, she was fired. Johnny ended the call by slamming down the phone.

Tracey's axing might have been a blessing in disguise. After the first Pirates of the Caribbean film in 2003, Johnny had been a prized client—one of the biggest stars in the world with earnings to match. But by 2016, according to Tracey, his star power had "dimmed." Johnny's baby, *The Rum Diary*, had lost $50 million, and producer Graham King let his three-year deal with Johnny's company Infinitum Nihil lapse. Warner Bros. stepped in to fund Infinitum Nihil for another three or four years, but it was becoming harder for Tracey to get Johnny high-paying jobs. His reputation for chronic lateness and unpredictability due to his substance-use issues made him a liability. Tracey said she'd get calls on "every movie" Johnny worked on.

While Johnny was filming *Mortdecai* in 2014, "I would get calls from Lionsgate, I would get calls from Gwyneth Paltrow because he just wouldn't show up," Tracey recalled. "And that was a movie he was not only starring in, he was producing it, then he didn't show up to his press conference in Japan because he was sleeping." Tracey denied Johnny's claims that UTA wasn't facilitating his artistic and indie film endeavors. She said starting in 2005, Johnny and Christi would put pressure on her to find him the highest-paying jobs. "I need to make some money," Johnny would tell her. Tracey discussed with Johnny that the high-paying jobs might compromise his artistic choices. "As I recall, he didn't seem very concerned about that."

Now Johnny was trying to claw back credibility from an industry he'd always derided, but his timing couldn't have been worse. A bomb was about to go off in Hollywood. And as the industry threw its arms around a new social movement called #MeToo, Johnny would soon find himself ranked among the disgraced—not just inside whisper networks, but by some of the most widely read media outlets in the world.

In the aftermath of the October 2017 Weinstein exposés, a string of actors embroiled in #MeToo scandals were pulled off or edited out of well-established movies and franchises. In November, Kevin Spacey was fired from the final season of *House of Cards,* in which he'd played the lead for five seasons. Scenes he'd just filmed in Ridley Scott's *All the Money in the World* were reshot with actor Christopher Plummer. Days later, Louis C.K.'s content was pulled from HBO and his film *I Love You, Daddy* was scrapped by its distributor. A comedy special that was planned with Netflix was also canceled. In February, beloved Emmy-winning actor Jeffrey Tambor was fired from the television series *Transparent* after he was accused of sexual harassment by two women on set.

Even before the #MeToo movement took off, some of J. K. Rowling's fans had been pissed that Johnny was still set up to repeat his role as dark wizard Gellert Grindelwald in the second of the Fantastic Beasts movies, a wildly successful Harry Potter spin-off, after Amber's initial abuse allegations went public. He was guilty as charged—by Amber, not a court of law—no ifs, ands, or buts. One Twitter user named Claudia posted in 2016, "a wild idea: what if we didn't put a domestic abuser in one of the most culturally significant and morally formative franchises of our time." But J. K. Rowling—not yet the polarizing figure she's become today for her controversial gender politics—was an outlier among other famously outspoken feminists in Hollywood. Rather than toeing the party line, she worried about what she perceived as #MeToo excesses. Though the press had dogged Johnny following Amber's TRO, their bitter divorce, and the *People* magazine stories, J.K. remained committed to moving forward with Johnny as a lead in the second installment of Fantastic Beasts, which was slated for release in fall 2018. On December 7, 2017, J. K. Rowling posted on her website, assuring fans that she heard their concerns—but it didn't matter. "Based on our understanding of the circumstances, the filmmakers and I are not only comfortable sticking with our original casting, but genuinely happy to have Johnny playing a major character in the movies." The first film brought in $814 million at the global box office, and though Johnny's reputation in Hollywood circles had faltered, he was still a draw for audiences.

A few weeks later, a hundred prominent French female intellectuals and artists issued an open letter in *Le Monde* criticizing the #MeToo movement for going too far, too fast. "The Harvey Weinstein scandal sparked a legitimate awakening about the sexual violence that women are subjected to," they wrote, "particularly in their professional lives, where some men abuse their power. This was necessary. But what was supposed to liberate voices has now been turned on its head: We are being told what is proper to say and what we must stay silent about—and the women who refuse to fall into line are considered traitors, accomplices!

"Just like in the good old witch-hunt days," their statement went on, "what we are once again witnessing here is puritanism in the name of a so-called greater good, claiming to promote the liberation and protection of women, only to enslave them to a status of eternal victim and reduce them to defenseless preys of male chauvinist demons."

Feminists like Catherine Deneuve offered a view in stark contrast to Amber's and other #MeToo champions. "This frenzy for sending the 'pigs' to the slaughterhouse, far from helping women empower themselves, actually serves the interests of the enemies of sexual freedom, the religious extremists, the reactionaries and those who believe—in their righteousness and the Victorian moral outlook that goes with it—that women are a species 'apart,' children with adult faces who demand to be protected.

"Men, for their part, are called on to embrace their guilt and rack their brains for 'inappropriate behavior' that they engaged in 10, 20, or 30 years earlier, and for which they must now repent. These public confessions, and the foray into the private sphere or self-proclaimed prosecutors, have led to a climate of totalitarian society."

Despite such emerging voices of dissent against "cancel culture" and J. K. Rowling's assurances to her fans that Johnny should remain cast in *Fantastic Beasts: The Crimes of Grindelwald*, by the spring of 2018, pressure was mounting to fire him from the franchise. Only now, it was not just fans calling for Johnny's removal, but also members of the mainstream media.

On April 27, 2018, the British tabloid newspaper *The Sun* printed a story with the headline "GONE POTTY: How can JK Rowling be 'genuinely happy' casting wife beater Johnny Depp in the new Fantastic Beasts Film?" Written by *The Sun*'s editor Dan Wootton, the article challenged J. K. Rowling on her decision to keep Johnny in the cast. With his article, Wootton hoped to "reveal a significant backlash from within the #MeToo and Time's Up movement because the Scot [J. K. Rowling] is hellbent on backing her famous pal [Johnny Depp]—despite his clearly inexcusable behaviour towards ex-wife Amber Heard."

The Sun, which reaches more than 30 million monthly readers, included in the article the same photo of Amber's bruised face that had appeared on TMZ and in *People* and detailed Amber's claims of abuse. For emphasis, Dan Wootton included a quote from actress, activist, and alleged Weinstein victim Katherine Kendall, who was described as one of two brave members of #MeToo/Time's Up who "went public" for *The Sun* to question J. K. Rowling's casting decision. "I don't stand behind hitting people or abusing people," she told the tabloid. "It seems that Amber got hurt. As someone who has been the victim of sexual abuse and a supporter of MeToo and telling my story to help others, I cannot advocate violence. I think it is a confusing message to put people in roles that are aimed at children and young people if there is a suggestion they have done something of that nature." Dan Wootton also challenged J. K. Rowling with five questions she "MUST answer," such as, *Do you take domestic violence accusations as seriously as sexual harassment given your support of the Me Too movement? If so, do you believe Amber Heard's detailed 2016 court filing detailing abuse allegations by Johnny Depp, which included pictures showing her injuries and on the record accounts by other witnesses?*

Something shifted for Johnny with this article. Seeing his name in print, attached to the word "wife beater," in a major (if unabashedly sensationalist) news publication was a bridge too far—he had to act.

One month later, on June 1, 2018, Johnny quietly sued *The Sun* and editor Dan Wootton for libel. In his filing, he asserted that the purpose of the article was to convince readers, falsely, that he was a domestic abuser and to persuade J. K. Rowling to drop him from the Fantastic Beasts franchise. He also claimed in court documents that *Amber* had been violent with *him*, punching him twice in the face the night of her thirtieth birthday.

A day after his fifty-fifth birthday, and a week after Johnny sued *The Sun* for defamation, Amber texted Johnny, "Happy Birthday."

In the months that followed, Johnny was photographed looking unrecognizable. Headlines described him as "gaunt" and "pale" and "shockingly thin." He took to wearing a black fitted cap that said FUGLY in large block letters across the front. He'd gone on tour with the Hollywood Vampires and several fan photos emerged in which he looked like a different person, the skin on his face sagged.

Even though work was slower for him now, Johnny had a new movie to shoot. After the tour, he'd play Colonel Joll in the adaptation of J. M. Coetzee's *Waiting for the Barbarians*. Before casting Johnny, producer Michael Fitzgerald had gone to lunch with him, and Johnny took out a sketchpad that he carried everywhere. He scrawled something on one of the pages, then tore it out and placed it next to Michael's plate. After lunch, Michael picked up the note. "Pain is true, all else is subject to doubt," Johnny had written. Though they'd later become close friends, theater star Mark Rylance, the film's lead, didn't want Johnny in the movie based on what he'd heard about him, which Johnny didn't know at the time.

Meanwhile, still in the midst of the lawsuits with the Mandel brothers and Johnny's former attorney Jake Bloom, Adam Waldman reached out to *Rolling Stone* pitching a story about the injustice being done to his client's reputation and his bank account. According to *Rolling Stone*, Adam cited as proof of the injustice an "anti-Depp" story in the *Hollywood Reporter* from 2017 titled "A Star in Crisis and the Insane Story of His 'Missing' Millions," which cast the Mandel brothers as reasonable professionals who'd tried to warn an ungovernable Johnny about the state of his finances. Adam believed the story had been orchestrated by the Mandels themselves, though they were never quoted in the piece.

Adam thought *Rolling Stone* would take Johnny's side. Johnny had a long history of good press with the magazine. Over two and a half decades, Johnny had been on the cover of the magazine seven times, with headlines ranging from "Sweet Sensation" to "Johnny Depp: The Last Buccaneer." *Rolling Stone* was also known for being transgressive and edgy. For decades, it had crusaded and embodied New Journalism, publishing writers like Tom Wolfe and Johnny's hero Hunter S. Thompson—authors with strong journalistic voices who didn't obey traditional notions of objectivity. In fact, *Fear and Loathing in Las Vegas* was first serialized in the magazine. If anyone could put a positive spin on Johnny's plight, it was *Rolling Stone*.

But in recent years, the counterculture magazine had moved away from its subversive, hippie roots, pivoting toward ambitious works of investigative journalism. Graham Ruddick of *The Guardian*, writing in 2017, described *Rolling Stone* as a "rock'n'roll magazine turned liberal cheerleader." The shift didn't come without missteps. In 2016, the magazine was sued for defamation for its infamous article "A Rape on Campus," originally published on November 19, 2014. The article described an alleged gang rape and initiation ritual at the Phi Kappa Psi frat house at the University of Virginia. After serious factual discrepancies and failures in the journalistic process were exposed by media watchdogs and legal investigators, the magazine's founder and publisher, Jann Wenner, commissioned the Columbia University Graduate School of Journalism to investigate the processes that led to the article's publication. When the 12,000-word report came out in 2015, *Rolling Stone* finally retracted the article. The fraternity, several of its members, and the associate dean of the university named in the article then sued its author and the magazine and won more than $4 million in collective damages. By September 2017, the storied magazine was so financially distressed it had to put itself up for sale, and by December, a majority of the shares had been acquired by Penske Media Corporation.

It was the Penske-controlled *Rolling Stone* that would profile Johnny the following year. According to the journalist assigned to the story, Stephen Rodrick, Adam Waldman reached out to *Rolling Stone* without the involvement of Johnny's longtime publicist, Robin Baum. Later, Adam would testify that it was Johnny who reached out to *Rolling Stone* first. Adam invited Stephen to Johnny's rented mansion in London to hang out for the story, which Adam envisaged as a redemptive puff piece that would win fans back over to Johnny's side.

It didn't go quite as planned.

"The Trouble with Johnny Depp" was published in *Rolling Stone*'s June 2018 issue. In it, Stephen Rodrick wrote, "Waldman seems to have convinced Depp that they are freedom fighters taking on the Hollywood machine rather than scavengers squabbling over the scraps of a fortune squandered." He detailed Johnny's elaborate, over-the-top spending, and seemingly pointed the blame at Johnny rather than the Mandels. "Maybe being a permanent Peter Pan is the key to Depp's onscreen charm. But time has passed. Boyish insouciance has slowly morphed into an aging man-child, still charismatic but only in glimpses. If his current life isn't a perfect copy of Elvis Presley's last days, it is a decent facsimile."

Johnny didn't help himself with sardonic comments about how The Management Group got a few things wrong about his spending—his monthly wine bill was far more than $30,000, he clarified, and it cost closer to $5 million to shoot Hunter S. Thompson's ashes out of a cannon, not $3 million as the Mandels stated. Johnny was painted as a pitiful star in decline, a delusional victim of his own lawless self-indulgence.

The following month, *Variety* reported that Johnny and Amber appeared "moments apart" on different panels for Warner Bros. at San Diego's annual Comic-Con. Toward the end of the Fantastic Beasts panel, Johnny showed up dressed as the evil wizard Grindel-wald with one blue eye and blinding white hair, after his other cast members had been musing about what they'd do if they had magical powers. Zoë Kravitz said she'd impeach Trump, while Ezra Miller said he'd destroy the patriarchy. Johnny chose to talk about "muggles" (translated from Harry Potter–speak to mean non-wizard humans), but his statements seemed almost confessional. "We who live for freedom, for truth, the moment has come to rise up and take our rightful place in the world," Johnny said. Amber took the stage an hour later with her *Aquaman* cast members, including Jason Momoa and Nicole Kidman, and director James Wan.

By the fall, still reeling from the bad press, Johnny did an interview with *British GQ*, in which he said he'd been "shafted" by *Rolling Stone*. In one of his first public statements about his ex-wife since the divorce, he also emphatically denied Amber's abuse allegations, saying "I will never stop fighting. I'll never stop," and contradicted her account of events around the May 2016 penthouse fight. "Why didn't [she] speak to the police?" he asked, in response to delicate questioning by the interviewer. "I mean, they spoke to the police, but the police saw nothing and they offered her an emergency medical technician. She said no. Police see nothing on her. Police see nothing broken in the place, no marks, and then they offer her an EMT to have a look at her and she says no and I don't know if it was the next day or a couple of days later, but then there was a bruise . . .

"She was at a party the next day," Johnny went on. "Her eye wasn't closed. She had her hair over her eye, but you could see the eye wasn't shut. Twenty-five feet away from her, how the fuck am I going to hit her? Which, by the way, is the last thing I would've done. I might look stupid, but I ain't fucking stupid."

The interview was published on October 2, 2018. Within days, Amber served Johnny papers for violating the NDA from their divorce settlement, including an arbitration demand. The suit would ultimately fizzle, but it sent a loud message—this would be a battle for control over the public narrative.

In November, *Aquaman* had its world premiere in London's Leicester Square. In the weeks leading up to the premiere, Amber had been gathering momentum from the film's upcoming release to talk about issues that mattered to her. "She's recast herself as a women's rights warrior following her split from Johnny Depp," the *Daily Mail* observed. "And Amber Heard is taking her new role seriously." In press junkets for the film, Amber pinned an orange ribbon to her shirt for the hashtag #HearMeToo, which commemorated the UN's International Day for the Elimination of violence against women.

As the new year approached, Johnny began preparing for his next film, *Minamata*, an indie set to begin filming in Serbia in January, in which he'd play famed photojournalist W. Eugene Smith, who in the 1970s documented government-sponsored environmental injustice in Japan. It had been a tumultuous and at times agonizing year, but Johnny had weathered the lawsuits against his former lawyer and business managers—he settled with the Mandel brothers in July, and with Jake Bloom in October—and up next was his libel case against *The Sun*, which would take place before a judge of the High Court of London (a trial date was set for March of the following year). Though the headwinds of #MeToo were against him, Johnny wasn't exiled *yet*—not like Kevin Spacey or Louis C.K. His reputation had taken several hits, but J. K. Rowling was still in his corner, he was still working on new films, and his nearly $23 million paycheck for Pirates 6 was on the horizon.

It wasn't until Amber published her own explosive #MeToo story in the *Washington Post* that his life would come crashing down.

CHAPTER 14

The Moment

The law firm of Ellis George Cipollone sits in a gleaming red-granite-and-glass high-rise overlooking Beverly Hills, Bel Air, and Westwood, on the Avenue of the Stars. The high-rise forms part of Century City's skyline, a district that was born out of the backlot of 20th Century Fox Studios. Eric George, a partner at the firm, occupied a two-room corner office on the thirtieth floor with views that stretched to the Pacific. Born and raised in Beverly Hills, and the son of the former chief justice of the Supreme Court of California, Eric was the consummate Hollywood lawyer: he was tall, gregarious, owned a steel-gray Range Rover, and worked on several high-profile cases, representing everyone from Michael Jackson's ex-wife Debbie Rowe in their child custody battle to the Kennedy family fighting the release of RFK's assassin. He has also repped the Kardashians and the City of Los Angeles.

On December 6, 2018, Amber wrote to Eric asking for his help. "Please see the proposed op-ed that would run in conjunction with my official announcement as the new Women's Rights Ambassador for the ACLU." He'd worked with Amber before, successfully getting dismissed a $10 million suit brought against her in

November 2016 by producers of the doomed film *London Fields* for breach of her performance and promotional obligations. But now Amber was going on the offensive—and she needed Eric's help.

A month before Amber reached back out to Eric, the nonpartisan nonprofit American Civil Liberties Union (ACLU) had approached Amber about authoring an op-ed discussing how survivors of GBV (gender-based violence) had been made less safe under the Trump administration. The op-ed would be run just after the November midterm elections, to "remind the newly elected Congress of their priorities." It would debut Amber's new title with the ACLU and, conveniently, would also coincide with the US release of Warner Bros.' *Aquaman* later that month. The film, which had already been released in the UK, was shaping up to be the biggest paycheck ever for the DC universe.

It's not unusual for nonprofits to court celebrities to raise the profile of the issues they champion—and, of course, to bring in large donations. Amber first got connected to the ACLU through Elon Musk in August 2016, the same month she settled her divorce with Johnny. Elon, who had an existing relationship with ACLU director Anthony Romero, served as intermediary, telling Anthony that Amber supported their work and wanted to make a financial contribution. Amber then pledged half of her divorce settlement, $3.5 million, to the organization. Elon donated too, boasting on Twitter that he was one of ACLU's top donors. Anthony was smitten with his new high-profile contacts. "Had a great meeting with Elon. Love that guy. Love you too," he wrote Amber in an email in June 2017.

When the ACLU reached out to Amber in November 2018 to propose the idea of writing an op-ed, they laid out the specific causes they wanted her to address—including the #MeToo movement and gender-based violence—and suggested that she "interweave her own personal story, saying how painful it is as a GBV survivor to witness these setbacks."

At the time, America was still searching for a new definition of feminism. Just two years had passed since the Trump election, and one since the Weinstein revelations and the explosion of #MeToo. Women were calling for the reauthorization of Joe Biden's Violence Against Women Act (VAWA), and to block proposed changes to Title IX. The #MeToo movement had ushered in a new paradigm of feminism that was battled online, in the media, and in the courts, lifting the curtain on the often dehumanizing lived experiences of women and enacting new federal and state laws to level gender inequalities. Women demanded anti-catcalling laws and strict definitions of consent. #MeToo activists framed men's indiscretions—not only sexual harassment and assault, but also the leveraging of power and position to control women—as a systemic, historical, and pervasive injustice long tacitly accepted by society. In order to enact true change, it seemed nothing less than a scorched-earth revolution was enough. Exiling offending men was one tool, but increasingly it became clear that the real work for #MeToo activists was to change structures in law and government that had allowed these imbalances and abuses to go unchecked for so long.

Many of the changes ushered in by #MeToo were necessary and long overdue, but frequently lost in the uproar were the time-honored principles of due process. When Amber and the ACLU conceived of the op-ed, no court of law, civil or criminal, had yet found Johnny guilty of domestic violence. The criminal restraining order Amber brought against Johnny had been dropped by her own lawyers. He was innocent in the eyes of the judicial system and owed due process, a principle of the law that the ACLU has, since its founding in 1920, always purported to hold sacred.

When asked later what kind of investigation and corroboration their organization did with respect to Johnny's alleged abuse of Amber, the ACLU's answer was that three of their employees had conversations with Amber and that they reviewed various news reports on the issue. During those conversations with Amber, they found her to be credible with "significant expertise" on gender-based violence. The ACLU didn't investigate her 2009 misdemeanor domestic-violence arrest at the Seattle-Tacoma airport as part of their ambassador vetting process. They also didn't attempt to contact Johnny or his reps about criminal allegations. "We did not believe there was any reason to reach out to Mr. Depp."

Amber asked ACLU communications director Gerry Johnson to place the op-ed where it would have "the biggest impact possible" because Amber's publicist Jodi Gottlieb was "tied up with all things *Aquaman*."

"Since the draft turned out pretty strong and *Aquaman* is slated to do huge numbers," Gerry Johnson replied, "I'm wondering what you think about pitching in this order: NYT, WaPo, Teen Vogue, USA Today."

At the time, the *New York Times* was the place to go for #MeToo opinion pieces, having published #MeToo-related op-eds from Lena Dunham, Salma Hayek, Lupita Nyong'o, and more. But Amber's ended up with the next one down the list, the *Washington Post*. "Wondering if we might interest you in a piece by Amber Heard (who, as you may recall, was beaten up during her brief marriage to Johnny Depp), on what the incoming Congress can do to help protect women in similar situations," a member of the ACLU Communications team wrote in its pitch.

The first draft of the op-ed was generated by ACLU Communications Strategist Robin Shulman, who sent it to Amber and her team for review. Robin wrote Amber in an email, "I tried to gather your fire and rage and interesting analysis and shape that into op-ed form—with mentions of a few policies and a growing movement. I hope it sounds true to you." She continued, "Your lawyer should review this for the way I skirted around talking about your marriage." Earlier drafts included the words "restraining order," "marriage," and "divorce," which were later scrapped. Eventually, the team settled on these eleven fateful words: "Two years ago I became a public figure representing domestic abuse."

Jen Robinson, a UK-based attorney at Doughty Street Chambers, whom Amber had hired to represent her in Johnny's upcoming libel case against *The Sun*, in which Amber would testify as a star witness, also weighed in on the op-ed. "This is an important story which is not about [Depp]; it's about societal and industry responses . . . It is so important that we ensure that you are protected and survive this, as an example of what's possible, even in such a powerful industry. That's why the Weinstein story was so big globally—for what it said to women everywhere." Jen, who was thirty-seven at the time, hailed from Australia and practiced as a high-profile human rights barrister in London. She was a minor celebrity herself, having represented clients like Julian Assange and Richard Dawkins and done work with the United Nations. She was also Amal Clooney's bridesmaid. Jen fit into the A-list celebrity scene seamlessly, donning stiletto heels, tailored-skirt suits, red lipstick, and shoulder-length blond hair kept in a neat side part. She told a reporter she kept nothing in her fridge except champagne. Jen had strong connections to several major papers and tabloids in the UK and would run point on the media messaging for Amber during her time as chief witness for *The Sun*.

Six days before Amber's *Washington Post* op-ed appeared online, Sean T. Walsh, a strategist who worked with Eric George, wrote to Amber, Jen, and Eric. "I think Eric's edits still get us 95% of what you want . . . I say send it off and dam [sic] the torpedoes ahead!" Like Jen Robinson, Sean Walsh—who was tall and wide as a linebacker, wore Drake's brand OVO over his buttonups, and lived in Oakland on a small ranch—had an impressive résumé. He'd worked as press spokesman under two presidents, Reagan and Bush Sr. He consulted for a major pharmaceutical company, helping the brand navigate the hit it took after the opioid epidemic. "Some jobs are boring and some are interesting," he quipped. Sean once said that if he was ever reincarnated he'd want to come back as his buddy and colleague Eric George. They loved their late nights over martinis at the legendary Los Angeles restaurant Dan Tana's, where they blended right in with the Hollywood elite amid the red lights and spaghetti-stained carpets.

Sean first met Amber after getting a call from Eric, who said his client needed help crafting an op-ed. He flew down from San Francisco to meet Amber in a Hollywood vegan joint, which, for Sean, lumbering man that he is, was "like holding a cross to a vampire." He listened as she told him stories from her marriage to Johnny. "She was telling me her history and I believed her. No one is that good of an actor." Sean agreed to help her out.

Though the ACLU had ghostwritten Amber's op-ed, the organization was primarily concerned with its brand and the issues that mattered most to them. It's inferred from several emails—now in the public record—that the ACLU had its own agenda and was pushing Amber to speak more directly to the marriage. But like Johnny, Amber was bound by a broad confidentiality agreement in their divorce judgment; writing directly about her relationship with her ex-husband would have put her in legal hot water. Amber had already tried to take Johnny to court for the same violation after his interview with *British GQ*.

As Eric would later testify in court proceedings, he urged Amber against publishing the op-ed to begin with, advising that Johnny was "litigious" and likely to sue if given any excuse to do so.

Amber's op-ed was published by the *Washington Post* on December 18, 2018. It first appeared on the *Post*'s website with the headline: "Amber Heard: I spoke up against sexual violence and faced our culture's wrath. That has to change." It appeared the next day in print with a different headline: "A Transformative Moment for Women."

"I knew certain things early on, without ever having to be told," Amber wrote. "I knew that men have the power—physically, socially and financially—and that a lot of institutions support that arrangement." She said that she'd been "harassed and sexually assaulted by the time I was of college age." Amber added that she "kept quiet" about these incidents. "I did not expect filing complaints to bring justice," she wrote. "And I didn't see myself as a victim." Her friends told her that coming out in public would mean she could be blacklisted. "I had the rare vantage point of seeing, in real time, how institutions protect men accused of abuse." After coming out with allegations (she left unsaid against whom), she said she had to change her phone number weekly because of death threats she was receiving. On top of that, she was dealing with societal and industry backlash for simply making a #MeToo accusation.

Though Amber never mentioned Johnny by name, the media response to her op-ed was quick to fill in the blanks, blasting his name across their headlines. *Refinery 29*: "This is what speaking out about Johnny Depp cost Amber Heard." *Elle*: "Amber Heard claims accusing Johnny Depp of domestic abuse lost her jobs." *People*: "Amber Heard says she was dropped from jobs after making Johnny Depp allegations."

The blowback came swiftly for Johnny. Two days after the op-ed was published, Disney executive Sean Bailey was interviewed in the *Hollywood Reporter* about the studio's upcoming movie plans. When the interviewer mentioned a possible reboot of the Pirates of the Caribbean franchise, she asked, "Can *Pirates* survive without Johnny Depp?" Bailey responded, "We want to bring in a new energy and vitality." Though Johnny had been verbally promised $22.5 million for the next installment, it seemed no one had bothered to call him or his agents and tell them that he'd been fired. They were dumbstruck when they received an email from Johnny's publicist, Robin Baum, who'd attached a MovieWeb article with the headline, "Johnny Depp's Jack Sparrow Won't Return in New Pirates of the Caribbean Movie." Johnny's agent, Christian Carino, who'd taken over from Tracey Jacobs, asked, "Were we told this officially from Disney?" and Jack Whigham, Johnny's manager, replied, "No."

"What do we do?" Christian said.

The next month, in January 2019, Amber graced the cover of *Glamour*'s final print issue, wearing a low-cut baby-blue satin suit, and leaning against a shiny red convertible. The headline: "Amber Heard: Silence Is Complacency." Two months later, in March, she was served with papers. Johnny was suing her for $50 million for defaming him in the *Washington Post*.

According to Jack Whigham, "After the op-ed, it was impossible to get him a studio film." Johnny's assistant Jason Forman also said the calls stopped coming in. Entertainment lawyer Richard Marks, who later testified as a witness for Johnny in his lawsuit against Amber, said that because the *Washington Post* wasn't a trade paper or an industry rag, but a flagship newspaper, its publication of Amber's op-ed had catastrophic effects on Johnny's career. It was the proverbial nail in the coffin. He also claimed there was a new unwritten policy in Hollywood: "They'll put up with divas and drugs to make money, but now we've drawn a line at domestic and sexual abuse."

Johnny's lawsuit categorically denied that he ever abused Amber, claiming that her allegations were part of an "elaborate hoax to generate positive publicity." He stated that her story had been "refuted" by two police officers, multiple third-party witnesses, and eighty-seven surveillance camera tapes. But the lawsuit was also a plot twist in the context of the wider #MeToo movement: Johnny was turning the tables on his accuser. "Ms. Heard is not a victim of domestic abuse; she is a perpetrator," Johnny claimed. "She hit, punched and kicked me. She also repeatedly and frequently threw objects into my body and head, including heavy bottles, soda cans, burning candles, television remote controls and paint thinner cans, which severely injured me." He added that she committed these acts "while mixing prescription amphetamines and non-prescription drugs with alcohol."

Here was a powerful male celebrity who'd been publicly accused of domestic violence not only asserting that her allegations were false, but claiming that *he* was the true victim in their relationship, and that his much younger wife, a devoted #MeToo advocate, was a systematic abuser. This was virtually unheard of—a high-profile man publicly accusing a woman of domestic violence—and it complicated the #MeToo narratives the world had heard up to that point. If we're to take women's accusations at face value, as the #MeToo movement had been endorsing, should we do the same for male victims?

"I have denied Ms. Heard's allegations vehemently since she first made them in May 2016 when she walked into court to obtain a temporary restraining order with painted-on bruises that witnesses and surveillance footage show she did not possess each day of the preceding week," his filing continued. "I will continue to deny them for the rest of my life. I never abused Ms. Heard or any other woman."

The following month, Amber hit back: she was now claiming thirteen incidents of domestic violence, stretching back to the start of their relationship; the three incidents she'd cited in the TRO were only the tip of the iceberg. The allegations were described in painstaking detail over fourteen pages. Her version of what happened behind closed doors was distressing and graphic: Amber described bloody gashes, being dragged through broken glass, bruised and swollen noses, black eyes, hair pulled from her scalp, being held against the wall by her neck, being suffocated on their marital bed, clothes torn clean off her body, repeated punches to her head, being dragged up sets of stairs by her hair.

After listing all the incidents of violence, Amber wrote, "I have never physically abused anyone. I know what that does to people." The motion insisted that Amber was resolved to fight for the victims of domestic violence and against the silencing of abuse victims. It also legitimized her as an expert on the issue, saying she speaks at "conferences worldwide about how to combat this pernicious and insidious issue affecting millions, if not billions of women and men worldwide." Her credibility was bolstered by her alliance with respected entities like the ACLU and the United Nations. With the detailed list of violent incidents, the public and official legal filing was also a sort of press release, letting the world know there were larger societal issues at stake. Johnny's attorney Adam Waldman had been asserting her claims were a hoax, but now with more violence on the table, how could they keep perpetrating this narrative?

Johnny's attorney Samuel Moniz of Brown Rudnick called the detailed motion listing these thirteen incidents a "public firebomb," as story after story republished the lurid claims of violence in the media. "Amber Heard describes the violent fight which prompted her to leave Johnny Depp in harrowing video where she recalls him 'yanking her by the head' and 'smashing his phone in her face'" (*Daily Mail*). "Amber Heard Says She Feared Johnny Depp Might Kill Her" (*The Cut*). "Amber Heard recounts horrific abuse at hands of 'Monster' Johnny Depp" (Page Six). Her motion was filed one day before the theatrical release of a film in which Amber had a supporting role, *Her Smell*. It also came just days after Johnny's security guard since the '90s, Jerry Judge, who was like a second father to him and had been a key witness to the relationship drama, passed away of cancer. Ten days later, Amber celebrated her thirty-third birthday in Mexico with a group of her friends, partying on a yacht, getting tattooed, and going horseback riding.

At the end of April, she traveled to DC to attend the 2019 Vital Voices Global Leadership Awards where her friend and fellow activist Amanda Nguyen, the founder of Rise, a sexual-assault advocacy group, won the "Light of Freedom" award. Amanda had publicly shared her story of being allegedly raped in 2013 while a student at Harvard. At the time, she chose not to press criminal charges, worried that the arduous process would have disrupted her burgeoning career—she'd just graduated and started a coveted job at the White House. In order to extend the shelf-life of her rape kit, and thus her window to press charges at the time she wished, she'd have to go through a lengthy and confusing legal process every six months, and so she decided to change the law.

She wrote the Sexual Assault Survivors' Bill of Rights, which included the right for survivors to have a rape kit procedure at no cost and for the kits to be preserved for the maximum applicable statute of limitations or twenty years—whichever is shorter. The bill was passed unanimously into federal law in 2016. It also mandated the right to equality under the law, the right to terminate all legal ties with the assailant, the right to survivors' advocacy, and the right to retention of all rights regardless of whether the assault is reported to law enforcement.

Amanda, a nominee for the Nobel Peace Prize, stated of her friend, "I've never seen someone as fired up as Amber." She reflected on their first dinner, which lasted six hours. "We discussed at length the process of how bills become law, how a coalition builds, how to shape your narrative to persuade people from different aisles. It really does go beyond showing up at events. Amber has a true desire to learn how to change the laws and change the world."

In DC, Amber rubbed shoulders with special guests like Nancy Pelosi and Hillary Clinton (a Vital Voices founder), along with corporate Hollywood leaders like Donna Langley, the chairman of Universal Pictures, and Bozoma Saint John, chief marketing officer at Endeavor, the billion-dollar holding company/talent agency in Beverly Hills. "Today, in the midst of some of the most challenging times the United States have ever seen, it's women who are doing the hard, essential work of reinvigorating our democracy," said Secretary Clinton during her closing address at the event. "Today more than ever before, women in the United States and around the world are raising their own vital voices, coming forward to tell their stories and demand equality."

Amber was doing just that. At the United Nations General Assembly in New York City in September, she spoke during a first-ever "Survivor's Town Hall," organized by Amanda Nguyen's group, Rise. Standing onstage at the UN Headquarters before numerous ambassadors and world leaders, Amber was defiant. "The MeToo movement has done a great deal," she told the crowd. "We need to take our outrage and determination to end sexual violence and we need to codify it. My story matters. My assault matters."

Amber was also leveraging her platform to push for new federal laws. As a victim of the celebrity iCloud hack in September 2014, in which Amber had more than fifty personal photos of herself, some nude, plastered all over the internet, she advocated on the Hill for a federal bill that would make "revenge porn" a crime. In a November 2019 opinion piece for the *New York Times* titled "Are We All Celebrities Now?" Amber wrote about the necessity of this federal law. In it she said something prophetic about the nature of social media: "The power of social media makes it possible for any person to be dragged before the eyes of the world."

The NDAs Amber and Johnny had signed after the divorce now seemed beside the point. Johnny had now made his own shocking accusations of domestic violence, and Amber had officially gone public with the full, ugly story of her life with Johnny. With two high-profile trials on the horizon, more lurid details would soon come to light.

CHAPTER 15

Hollywood Dicks

For decades, Johnny had strived to live in relative privacy for a global superstar. Now, as he was preparing for trial in his lawsuit against the Rupert Murdoch–owned British tabloid *The Sun*, that era was over. At fifty-six years old, and with zero American film projects lined up, he would soon be exposing the worst sides of himself to the world because, he maintained, even at his worst, he wasn't a "wife beater."

Amber, meanwhile, had re-engaged Eric George, the lawyer who'd reviewed her op-ed, to push back against the defamation claims made against her by her ex-husband. To build their case, Eric would have a hard look into Johnny's past violent behavior. For that nitty-gritty work, the legal team brought in Hollywood fixer and private investigator Paul Barresi.

Paul, who drove a shiny black Alfa Romeo and wore dark wraparound shades with tight sweaters unzipped at the top, called the job a "limited task," meaning the focus of his investigation was to find a pattern of violence: perhaps another woman Johnny had abused, or a guy he'd physically assaulted. "It's time for someone to speak up and call BS on his phony claim to be as nonviolent as Gandhi," Eric wrote to Paul in his first week on the job.

Paul, whose location on Twitter lists "The Underbelly of Hollywood," previously worked with Anthony Pellicano, the most notorious Hollywood fixer of the past several decades. Following an illustrious career as an unscrupulous "problem solver" for A-listers like Michael Jackson, Tom Cruise, and Chris Rock, Pellicano went to federal prison for a criminal enterprise he created around his business. He was ultimately charged with owning illegal firearms and explosives, racketeering, and wiretapping. In 2006, Eric George represented former Disney President and CAA superagent Michael Ovitz after he was sued by *Los Angeles Times* reporter Anita Busch. Anita claimed Michael Ovitz hired Pellicano to intimidate her and scare her away from writing negative articles about him as he was trying to sell one of his companies. In 2002 she'd found a dead fish with a rose in its mouth lying on the broken windshield of her car alongside a note reading "STOP." The dead fish incident triggered an FBI investigation and a flurry of other lawsuits against Pellicano.

Born in 1949, Paul Barresi grew up with his Italian American family in Lynn, Massachusetts, a town outside of Boston nicknamed "The City of Sin." He started his career as a fitness trainer which led him to nude modeling opportunities. In 1975 he posed with Cassandra Peterson, aka Elvira, in *Playgirl*, and in 1978 he was the first male to grace the cover of *Hustler* magazine. Eventually he got into directing, producing, and starring in adult films, where he had a thriving career as "undisputedly the king of military-themed videos" under his moniker "Joe Hammer." He said the adult films he directed were known for their good storylines, even more than the sex scenes.

In an interview for this book, Paul said his pivot from adult film star to Hollywood private eye didn't come easy, as "sordid revelations overshadow everything." Now, he's the one uncovering sordid revelations. "My turf is the gutter and the streets," he said. "The smoldering secrets beneath the red carpet are what I sift through."

Paul said that Amber's lawyers were certain Johnny was a violent person. "They were thoroughly convinced Depp was abusive just based on what Amber told them. They just believed that he was a woman beater and her entire defense rode on that . . . I entered into it thinking it was a slam dunk," he said.

In the first two or three days of Paul's investigation, Amber's lawyers asked him to watch several videos of Johnny. "They told me, there's a lot of stuff in these videos where Johnny's being abusive, you know, where he's throwing things and pushing people around. I looked at them extensively, and I didn't see anything there beyond a pathetic little man who couldn't hold his beer, couldn't hold his wine, who was stumbling, fumbling, could barely put a sentence together and could barely stand on his own two feet."

For someone with Johnny's fame, money, and stature, there were bound to be lawsuits. Paul investigated assault claims on the *City of Lies* shoot in Los Angeles in 2017. Gregg "Rocky" Brooks, a location manager on set, had accused Johnny of taunting him and punching him twice in the ribcage. He sued Johnny for creating a hostile workplace and inflicting emotional distress. A photo after the alleged incident shows Johnny and Rocky standing side by side, smiling. They eventually settled the matter in 2022; the terms weren't disclosed.

Another lawsuit was brought against Johnny by his ex-bodyguards Eugene Arreola and Miguel Sanchez, who complained about long hours with no overtime or meal breaks starting around April 2016, when they said Johnny's world was thrown into financial turmoil. They claimed their job turned into watching after Johnny's son, Jack, who lived in a separate home alone on the

Sweetzer compound. Sanchez worried he'd be fired if he didn't give in to Johnny's two children's every whim. They also cited an incident at a local nightclub in which they alerted Johnny of illegal substances on his face and had to conceal his condition from onlookers. (The parties eventually settled.)

Paul says he interviewed and "door stepped" countless people from Johnny's past over the course of three months. But he never found the dirt Amber and her lawyers were looking for.

Paul was fired and Amber eventually parted ways with Eric George. It was time to change her legal team.

In September 2019, Amber joined forces with powerhouse attorney and #MeToo ally Roberta Kaplan. In Roberta, who rose to prominence when she successfully argued *US vs Windsor*, a 2013 landmark Supreme Court decision that paved the way for the federal government to recognize same-sex marriages, Amber seemed to have found the perfect advocate and public face for her legal battles. In 2018, Kaplan had cofounded the Time's Up Legal Defense Fund, an arm of the newly formed Time's Up nonprofit created to help pay "the legal fees and costs for select cases of workplace or career-related sexual harassment and related retaliation." Led by a group of Hollywood celebrities in response to the Weinstein scandal and the burgeoning #MeToo movement, Time's Up quickly raised $22 million through the crowdfunding site GoFundMe.

A day after Roberta Kaplan, who was based in New York, was admitted pro hac vice as Amber's counsel, she released a strongly worded statement regarding the *Washington Post* op-ed to the press. "It cannot be true that every time Ms. Heard speaks about her experiences and beliefs regarding the #MeToo movement, or society's response to it, her statements will be interpreted as implying that Mr. Depp abused her. While Mr. Depp may believe that everything Ms. Heard says is actually about him, readers blessed with a grasp of English usage and context can readily discern otherwise, especially in a political opinion piece like this one."

First on the agenda for Kaplan was getting the $50 million defamation lawsuit moved from Virginia, where Johnny had filed it, to California, the logic being that Amber and Johnny both lived in California as individuals and as a couple, and it was the state where most of the abuse occurred and where all of the witnesses were located. But there was another reason. California had powerful anti-SLAPP (Strategic Lawsuit Against Public Participation) statutes designed to prevent defamation cases from moving forward. SLAPP suits are "lawsuits brought by individuals and entities to dissuade their critics from continuing to produce negative publicity." According to the ACLU, "SLAPPs are designed to discourage public discussion by using our legal system to choke the exercise of free speech"—a classic example being a real estate developer suing local residents who publicly criticize a proposed construction project for defamation. Amber was perhaps counting on California's anti-SLAPP statutes as a first line of defense. Virginia's anti-SLAPP laws are weaker, and defamation lawsuits aren't as easily thrown out.

How could Johnny bring a case in Virginia, a state he'd never lived in and had no association with? Because that's where the *Washington Post*'s printing presses and the servers that publish its stories online are located. Virginia is one of ten states that is a lex loci delicti jurisdiction, translated as "the law of the place of the wrong," meaning the laws of the state where the action took place determine the legal consequences. In a ten-page opinion letter, a Virginia judge affirmed that the publication of Amber's op-ed technically occurred in Fairfax County, denying Amber's motion to dismiss.

Unless a settlement could be reached, Amber and Johnny would be headed to court in Virginia. But first, they would square off at the Royal Courts of Justice for Johnny's defamation case against *The Sun*. Even though Paul wasn't able to dig up any damning new evidence for Amber, she had a trove of pictures, videos, audio recordings, and witnesses to support her claims of abuse before the British judge. Little did she know that Johnny's lawyers had unearthed new evidence of their own.

In January 2020, two months before the trial was due to begin in London, Stephen Deuters was doing picture approvals on his work computer for the *Minamata* film when a file popped up labeled "AVM" (for "Amber voice messages"). He opened the folder and scrolled through the audio recordings, all more than five years old, and totaling more than six hours. "Holy shit!" he said. He didn't need to listen anymore, he knew he'd found gold. Hours of recordings capturing their bitter fights were now in Team Depp's possession. He transferred the recordings to Adam Waldman, whom Stephen said did cartwheels. Then, just like that, a *Daily Mail* headline dropped like a bomb: "EXCLUSIVE: 'I can't promise I won't get physical again, I get so mad I lose it.' LISTEN as Amber Heard admits to 'hitting' ex-husband Johnny Depp and pelting him with pots, pans and vases in explosive audio confession."

"When you're in the middle of a storm, and you're getting pummeled and finally, you have something that's authentic and real and reflective of the situation, and even though the situation's gross; it was great," Stephen said.

The recording obtained by the *Daily Mail*, leaked by a "well-placed source," was a two-hour-long audio file that had been recorded consensually on Amber's phone in 2015. Within the leaked recordings were several instances of Amber admitting to being physically violent with Johnny, and mocking him whenever he claimed to be a victim. At the time, the newly married couple had just returned from a well-documented month of travel together. They'd been snapped on the red carpet in Venice and Toronto, appearing very much in love, inspiring headlines like, "Johnny Depp and Amber Heard's Chemistry Is Officially Out of Control," and then in Brazil, where they did charity work together, fitting hundreds of hearing-impaired people with hearing aids. Poignant publicity photos showed Amber fighting back tears as Johnny fit a young girl with hearing aids and she heard for the very first time.

The recordings Stephen unearthed presented a much more fractured and bleak picture of the couple's world. The first recording began with Amber describing Johnny as a "vacation husband," who "splits" every time tension or conflict arises. Johnny explained that he "splits" in order to avoid a violent situation with Amber. "I'm not going to be in a physical fucking altercation with you . . . you fucking hit me last night."

"What about all the other times you split?" Amber responded, obliquely.

"I'm not the one who throws pots and whatever the fuck else at me."

"That's different," Amber hit back. "One does not negate the other. That's irrelevant, that's a complete non sequitur. Just because I've thrown pots and pans does not mean you cannot come and knock on my door."

They discussed an altercation from the previous night in which Johnny claimed Amber punched him in the jaw with a closed fist and then lied about it to his security guard. Amber replied in a refrain that later echoed across social media: "You didn't get punched. You got hit. I'm sorry I hit you like this, but I did not punch you, I did not fucking deck you. I fucking was hitting you."

The story of the recordings went viral. People couldn't square Amber's valiant public image as a domestic-violence survivor and advocate with what they were hearing in the recordings. Two different petitions appeared on Change.org demanding Amber be removed from her position as a L'Oréal Global Ambassador for women. Another petition, to remove Amber from the sequel to *Aquaman*, was started by a Depp fan named Jeanne Larson and signed more than three million times. Amber insisted bots were responsible for the petitions.

An unnamed spokeswoman for Amber was quoted in the *Daily Mail* article. Her words seeded the narrative and jargon around domestic abuse that Amber's team would use during the Fairfax trial: "Anyone familiar with the dynamics of domestic abuse would immediately recognize what is really going on here . . . For Mr. Depp, who lived and lives in an echo chamber of his own making, to try to twist this private conversation to suggest either that he didn't abuse Ms Heard or that she somehow 'deserved it' is nothing more than the latest misogynistic effort at victim-blaming." In the same article, Johnny's lawyer Adam Waldman told the tabloid, "These tapes containing Amber Heard's chilling confessions of violence further expose and destroy her abuse hoax."

A few weeks later, on February 5, another audio recording dropped on the *Daily Mail* website. The thirty-minute recording was taken by Johnny in May 2016, after he and Amber had separated and Amber still had a TRO against him. On the recording, the couple were discussing their impending divorce and Johnny pleaded with Amber to settle their issues privately rather than in open court.

"You can please tell people that it was a fair fight, and see what the jury and judge thinks," Amber said. "Tell the world, Johnny, tell them Johnny Depp, I, Johnny Depp, a man, I'm a victim too of domestic violence."

Johnny simply responded, "Yes."

Later, Adam Waldman testified that he gave the two audio recordings to the *Daily Mail*. The same day that the second leaked audio recording published, he emailed one of Amber's UK lawyers, Louis Charalambous, with a warning: "When we met last, you said 'amber heard would have to be gone girl' for her abuse allegations to be false. One audiotape alone (plus frankly a mountain of other evidence) has shown her to be so. There are more tapes to come. I assume you were blindsided by these tapes, which Ms Heard has admitted she possesses, because she didn't provide them to you. If you would like to discuss a way out of the morass for your client, please call me."

One of Amber's closest allies at the time, who asked to remain anonymous, said the audio recordings signaled the beginning of the end of their friendship. They'd been close friends for more than a decade, and when the recordings leaked they thought, "Why isn't Amber calling me??" If this was a mutually abusive situation, then fuck you for bringing me into this, they recalled thinking at the time. They felt like they'd put their reputation on the line to support Amber, had essentially "fallen on the sword" for her, so she at least owed them a call and an explanation. "I didn't know she, like, hit him," they told their lawyer. When they finally got Amber on the phone, she tried to say the recordings had been manipulated, but the friend was insistent and repeated the words on the recording. "You said you hit him."

"Do you understand the nature of abuse?" Amber responded adamantly. "When someone is dead set on something being true and it isn't, you play into their notion of reality so that you can survive."

Amber was angry with this friend, something they said was typical of what they called the "abusive dynamic" of their friendship. Part of being Amber's friend, they said, was not having personal needs or ever questioning her. The friend decided to pull out of being a live witness in the UK trial. They said "this thing" was ruining their life and eating their time away. It was stressing out their partner. They were worried about getting doxxed.

British socialite, media maven, and photographer Amanda de Cadenet, who'd seen Amber the day after the penthouse fight and was set to appear as a sworn witness for *The Sun*, also withdrew her support for Amber following the audio recordings leak. Amanda had been Amber's longtime friend and was a fellow #MeToo ally. In June 2020, she filed a legal declaration explaining her exit as a witness: "Historically womxn's rights in this area have been chronically undermined and womxn have had their voices silenced," she wrote. "This is one of the reasons why, when Amber told me her version of the conflict between her and Johnny, it was my inclination to believe her and support her." She continued, "I recently acknowledged that I will not testifying (sic) in Johnny Depp's upcoming defamation case against the Sun. I also acknowledged that new facts have come to my attention which has changed my perspective on this matter. When the first audiotape was released and I heard Amber being verbally abusive to Johnny, I was horrified. I texted Robbie Kaplan, Amber's attorney, and let her know I needed to speak with her urgently. When we spoke, I told her I was appalled and shocked to hear how Amber was speaking to Johnny and that it was not ok with me."

Amber told Amanda that the recordings had been edited, though she never pushed this theory in court. According to

Johnny's team, Amber's prevarication about the authenticity of the recordings was more of her "idle winging" about the legal proceedings. But there were at least a couple of damning recordings of Johnny that *he* claimed were inaccurate. Johnny insisted to his team that the audio of him moaning like an animal wasn't from the infamous private jet flight from Boston as Amber claimed, but were recordings from his detox from the drug Roxicodone on his Bahamian island, where he escaped with Amber and Nurse Debbie after filming *Black Mass* in 2014.

"I had hoped Amber would take accountability for her behaviour but she did not," Amanda's statement continued. "I have not spoken with Amber since this exchange and have come to the very painful realisation that someone who I advocated for and believed so wholeheartedly, was not entirely forthcoming with me. I want to emphasise that I have no further personal knowledge of what happened between Johnny and Amber, and no knowledge of the truth of her accusations against him."

She concluded, "I have made this statement in support of due process and upholding the truth."

After the audio recordings were made public, #JusticeForJohnnyDepp trended across Twitter and TikTok. An online community had formed around the hashtag, which had been created by a small internet chat group in early to mid-2016, and it would continue to grow and rally behind Johnny through the upcoming trials. Amber's Instagram comments, meanwhile, were mobbed by angry Johnny supporters. The comment section of every photo was sprayed with vomit, clown, and middle finger emojis and an endless scroll of epithets, name-calling, and threats: "Gone Girl 2," "Psychopath," "Literally filth," "You make me sick," "Take a nap forever," "Too bad you didn't break your neck." On Twitter, she was also getting pummeled with negative comments and harassment: more "YOU DID THIS TO HIM. @realamberheard You poisoned the #MeToo movement for REAL victims & worst of all you painted Johnny as an abuser. Funny that, it was you. you're the VILE. TOXIC. ABUSER. He's innocent!" and "I knew it four years ago. I dont know why #JusticeForJohnnyDepp is just now trending, but I'm not complaining. Amber Heard can go fuck herself with a length of rebar. #AmberHeardIsAnAbuser."

Beneath the many photos Amber had posted to her Instagram page—"candid" selfies gazing lovingly into the camera, hugging a horse on a farm, or bottle feeding her new nephew Hunter—were comment sections full of wrath. Though she could curate an Instagram page that portrayed a rich, happy life of work, travel, friends, family, food, and activism, she couldn't outrun the long shadow of her marriage to Johnny. His online supporters were flexing a new form of power: persecution by social media. Amber's friends and followers weren't spared either. iO Tillett Wright's Instagram was blasted with comments and DMs like, "Abuse apologist. You could go so much further in your career if you drop Amber." And "amber and you are disgusting pieces of shit. how dare you manipulate and fake a domestic abuse story?"

A month after the audio recordings leaked, Amber disabled her Instagram comments. The tides seemed to be shifting online. The internet was starting to take Johnny's side, while Amber was becoming the poster child of #MeToo's overreach.

CHAPTER 16

Bots and Trolls

I t was May 12, 2020, and the midafternoon desert sun blasted outside. Amber was secluded in Joshua Tree preparing for Johnny's defamation trial against *The Sun*. Originally scheduled for March, *Depp vs News Group Newspapers Ltd* had been postponed to July due to the outbreak of the COVID-19 pandemic. Isolating with Amber in Joshua Tree was her new girlfriend of five months, the cinematographer Bianca Butti.

While Amber prepped for trial, Bianca filmed for brief, seemingly random spurts. She took footage of Amber's nephew Hunter, Whitney's one-and-a-half-year-old with husband Gavin. She took footage of Amber trying on various outfits, and of Amber walking through Black Lives Matter protests in downtown LA. And she'd keep filming, on and off, for the next several months, as Amber traveled to London for the trial.

In one of Bianca's recordings, Amber sat in front of the camera while Bianca interviewed her about the online harassment she was receiving, and how estranged she'd become from her friends and support network. Amber was convinced the negative attention online was being secretly coordinated by Johnny and his powerful political connections, aka Adam Waldman. Amber's hair was pulled back messily, her ears adorned with shiny earrings running up each lobe. She was wearing an oversized white oxford shirt half unbuttoned as she pointed at her laptop. "Okay, so this journalist, Rachel Abrams, is writing this—or actually she's just investigating the angle of the online harassment and the bot campaign against me," Amber said. Rachel Abrams was a reporter for the *New York Times*. Amber spoke emphatically about her theory that Adam Waldman had hired bots to harass not just her, but also her friends and witnesses, as well as journalists covering her story. "I mean, the amount of witnesses I have lost along the way . . . As soon as I came forward in public and said something, all of them, one by one, disappeared. They told me they're worried about their career, they're worried about their livelihood, they can't make it in this industry because of what they're facing."

Bianca asked Amber to tell her more about the bots. On social media, the hashtag #AmberHeardIsAnAbuser had trended across posts directed at her: "you are a piece of trash that belongs in a dumpster" one of them wrote; in another: "you're a terrible and rotten human being and deserve nothing but misfortune for the rest of your days."

"Rachel Abrams is investigating what seems to be really unnatural patterns on social media," Amber explained, lightly scratching beneath her eye. "An overwhelming number, way over half, it's in the 70s, 70 something percent, of the activity or the accounts linked to the activity are inauthentic. And many, if not most, of the accounts are created solely with the intent of harassing me or spreading misinformation about me, damning or negative information about me or my case."

"How much do you think this costs to perform?" Bianca asked, referring to the price of the alleged harassment campaign. Amber looked into the distance and thought for a second.

"More than millions . . ." She lifted a thermos and shrugged her shoulders. "Who knows?" Amber's phone chimed on the table, interrupting the recording. "The lawyers, per usual," she said with an ironic smile, lifting a headphone to her ear.

Rachel Abrams did investigate the bot army. She was interested in the idea of a coordinated campaign and did a significant amount of reporting, but a story never materialized. "There wasn't a story because there was nothing to say definitively, despite how assuredly certain people told me there was something going on," Rachel said.

Roberta Kaplan brought in an Internet expert and tech entrepreneur, Christopher Bouzy, to try to help Amber prove that Johnny and Adam were behind the online harassment, in another effort to get the defamation suit against Amber dismissed. Bouzy, who learned coding at the age of nine on a Mattel Aquarius computer and went on to launch a number of tech start-ups including a failed dating app called IfSolo, had created a data analytics service called Bot Sentinel that tracked disinformation, inauthentic behavior, and targeted harassment on Twitter. According to the report it sent to Roberta in March, Bot Sentinel trained its own custom classification model using 800,000 tweets about Amber that they split into two groups, "normal" and "problematic." They identified that two "inauthentic accounts" were responsible for around half of the attacks on Amber. Both Twitter accounts were essentially Johnny Depp fan pages, with tens of thousands of combined followers and tweets. One of them, IFOD_NET, stated in their bio: "Love and support for artist and humanitarian Johnny Depp." IFOD stands for "Italian Fans of Depp." The report ultimately concluded that Amber *was* the target of a smear campaign, noting that it was "highly unusual" that accounts targeting Amber were also praising Adam Waldman.

Johnny's fan base was massive, global, cross-generational, and engaged. Even pre–social media, there were innumerable forums, fan pages, and blogs dedicated to him. Nevertheless, Amber was convinced the negative attention online was being bought and paid for by her ex-husband, who wanted to keep torturing her beyond the divorce.

And public interest in the case was growing by the week. The Depp-Heard legal battle offered the public access to the intimate details of a celebrity marriage on a level not previously seen. It was warping into the ultimate he-said/she-said spectacle, merging two collective fascinations: celebrity and criminality. An interested public could pore over their personal texts, emails, intimate conversations, videos, and photos, showing their bedrooms, their bathrooms, the art they hung on their walls, the type of dishware and glasses they used. It was thrilling to be a voyeur of this world, while also probing whose version of the truth was real. Many people following the story saw traces of their own past or current relationships inside Amber and Johnny's dynamic, sparking heated conversations about toxicity and conflict, the nature of abuse, justice, and due process. At the same time, everyone seemed to want the black-and-white story, turning the legal battle into a global sporting event in which you could pick a hometown hero: Team Johnny vs Team Amber.

It was late June, and the wide terminal at the Los Angeles International Airport was empty. The escalators were abandoned, as were the duty-free shops advertising Sauvage cologne. Amber leaned against the wall outside the security checkpoint before heading to her gate with an airport escort. She wore white-and-black high-heeled boots, a blue scarf as a mask, skinny pants, a black T-shirt, and a large Yves Saint Laurent leather purse. Her carry-on bags spilled over with legal binders. Three months into the global pandemic, travel was still nearly at a standstill, but *Depp vs NGN* was on track to begin on July 7.

Amber and Whitney were flying to London to testify as witnesses in the trial. None of the actual defendants—neither representatives from the tabloid nor Dan Wootton, the author of the article that called Johnny a "wife beater"—would testify in the trial. Amber was the paper's star witness.

While both the US and the UK have defamation laws aimed at protecting individuals from false and damaging statements, the legal frameworks and procedures for pursuing defamation claims differ between the two countries. Compared to the US, UK law is favorable to people trying to protect their reputation. In US courts, the burden of proof lies with the plaintiff bringing a claim of libel, who must show that a false and defamatory statement was made, and that the defendant acted with negligence in publishing the statement. For a public figure like Johnny Depp, there are even higher standards: the plaintiff must prove there was "actual malice" behind a defamatory statement—meaning not only were they defamed, but the defaming party *knew* the statement was false, or didn't care that it was false. It's an incredibly high bar to reach. In UK courts, however, it's the other way around. The burden of proof lies with the defendant. This meant Johnny stood a better chance of winning his case against Dan Wootton and *The Sun* than he did the one he was bringing directly against Amber in the US. And because the UK trial wouldn't be decided by a jury, he had just one person to convince—the judge.

At the airport, Whitney wore all black, her hair split down the middle of her head in two neat braids, her wide-brimmed beige hat squarely atop her head. Amber and Whitney were less than two years apart in age, and though they'd always been close, they'd grown even closer since the start of the pandemic. Amid the fear and stress of COVID and Amber's pending legal battles, in April, their mother, Paige, had suddenly passed away. On May 3, Amber posted a black-and-white picture of her and her mother on Instagram, Paige's arm held lovingly around Amber's shoulder, Amber resting her head against Paige's. "I am heartbroken and devastated beyond belief at the loss of my mom, Paige Heard," Amber wrote in her caption. "She left us too early, clasping onto the memory of her beautiful, gentle soul . . . This has been an unbelievably painful time but in that, I am reminded of what survives us all, love. The kindness, support and generosity my sister Whit and I have received from friends and family has been utterly soul-saving." Amber had always relied on her mother for strength and fortitude. Now she had to handle the emotional battles that lay ahead without her. Subsequent posts showed Amber, Whitney, and their dad David grieving together at home. In one, Amber and David hold open a care package from a friend. In another, Whitney stands behind Amber as she cooks, her arms wrapped around her sister's waist, her head resting on her back.

Whitney was the only witness who'd seen Johnny being violent with Amber during their marriage. Deemed the "marriage counselor" in the relationship, she'd once tried to de-escalate an argument about Johnny's alleged infidelity. This was in March 2015 in the ECB penthouse, where, according to Whitney, she saw Johnny grab Amber by the hair and punch her multiple times in the head. Johnny's security guard Travis McGivern had also been present, but he said Johnny never touched Amber.

Traveling to London with Amber and Whitney was Amber's

girlfriend, Bianca, who was there with her camera. Earlier in the year, Amber had supported Bianca through a surgical procedure after her second bout with breast cancer, delivering flowers, balloons, music, and food to Bianca's hospital room. For Bianca, it made a dire situation seem okay. Now it was Bianca's turn to support Amber, especially after losing Paige. Amber's assistant, Sara Nelson, also came along for the journey. Together, Whitney, Sara, and Bianca made up Amber's support group. After boarding the plane, they sat down comfortably in business class and Whitney took out her knitting supplies while Bianca kept her camera trained on Amber. As the plane slowly taxied down the runway, Bianca began to interview.

"Tell me what we are doing," Bianca said.

"We are going to the UK, a bit outside London, to quarantine for two weeks," Amber replied in a muffled voice, speaking through her mask and over the flight attendant's instructions. "It's going to be six women in a house: two lawyers, myself, my girlfriend, my sister, and my assistant. We are going to prepare for the hardest thing I've ever been through in my life. Nothing has been harder than the four years that have followed my divorce." As she spoke her green eyes grew bigger, mascara painted evenly on every lash.

As they soared through the sky, Bianca took footage of the receding California topography below. Nearly ten hours later, they descended over London, into Heathrow Airport. Bianca continued filming surreptitiously, and the camera captured a sign that read, "Coronavirus just arrived in the UK? Stay Alert." At baggage claim, the turning belts stretched on for what felt like miles. In the distance, Elaine Bredehoft, Amber's new attorney, waved at the approaching group.

Earlier that month, Amber's veteran attorney and legal star

Roberta Kaplan had withdrawn from Amber's legal team. Her team cited complicated travel and logistics amid COVID-19, telling the press, "We believe Amber and we believe in Amber." But the real issue seemed to be money. Amber had taken out insurance to cover her legal bills—which by 2020 had ballooned to $6 million—but Roberta's firm wasn't covered by her policies.

Choosing a new lawyer from a list of Virginia attorneys covered by her insurance, Amber picked out Elaine Bredehoft, a seasoned lawyer who hailed from the Midwest. They were meeting for the first time in London. The UK trial at the Royal Courts of Justice would give Elaine the rare opportunity for a practice run ahead of the US trial. Even though Amber was only a witness in London, not a defendant, Elaine predicted that *Depp vs NGN* would play out similarly to *Depp vs Heard* in the United States, as the same evidence and witnesses would be brought to both trials. "It's ultimately David vs Goliath," Amber had told Elaine. As Elaine and Amber approached each other in Heathrow, they introduced themselves and hugged. Elaine wore a dark green floral-print jacket, black pants, and flat shoes.

Outside of the airport they piled into a white van that was tucked tight with luggage filled with weeks-worth of courtroom attire—a sophisticated below-the-knee black dress, a long skirt ruffled slightly at the bottom, and lots of long-sleeved loose-fitting blouses. Sitting across from Bianca, who was still directing her camera at Amber, Elaine appeared confused about why someone was there filming.

"This is just mine," Amber assured her, referring to the footage. "She's doing this for me, so that I own it."

"Okay, if they discover that, then we waive all of our privilege," Elaine said. "If anyone says have you taped anything with your attorney, you say 'no.'"

In her lap, Amber held a heavily annotated *Media Law and Human Rights* textbook. One of the authors of the book was the British Judge Andrew Nicol—the judge who would preside over *Depp vs NGN*. "I think later what will be interesting for me is capturing this moment which is very unique," Amber said of the footage. "I've been doing it for so long and it's me against this entity." She brushed her hair back against her head.

They arrived at their country cottage, nestled in a field of pink and purple flowers. After settling in, Amber sat at the dining room table next to Elaine drinking iced tea and eating a salad. The doors to the cottage were open and the long floral curtains were pulled back. The view looked out to a swaying cypress and a garden gated with a picket fence. The table was strewn with neon Post-it notes, laptops, iPads, binders, and folders. Amber nervously braided and rebraided her hair as she tried to focus on a Zoom call with *The Sun*'s lawyers, who were discussing the tens of thousands of text messages that Johnny's legal team had accidentally disclosed to them.

In February, Johnny's attorneys at the London office of Brown Rudnick sent an Excel spreadsheet to *The Sun*'s lawyers with what they thought were four hundred text messages, but between the rows of texts, there were thousands more—seventy thousand to be exact—in hidden cells that they hadn't meant to disclose, including about eight hundred they legally *should* have. A paralegal at the firm who'd made the spreadsheet apparently committed what they could only term "a technical error." Before the start of the trial, *The Sun*'s lawyer, Adam Wolanski QC, told the High Court the text messages were "very damaging" to Johnny's libel case. In texts to his friend Paul Bettany in 2013, Johnny said, "Let's burn Amber" and "Let's drown her before we burn her!!! I will fuck her burnt corpse afterward to make sure she is dead."

The Sun had tried to get the lawsuit dismissed on the basis of Johnny's lawyers' failure to disclose key evidence. The judge ruled the omission wasn't enough to strike down the case, but still, the damage was done: hundreds of the "very damaging" texts—which Amber and her team were now combing through on Zoom, looking for new evidence to support her claims of abuse—were admitted as evidence in the trial. Johnny fired his team at Brown Rudnick London for the debacle and brought in another prominent UK law firm called Schillings. (His lawyers at Brown Rudnick's US office weren't affected.)

It was another score for Amber: the damaging audio recordings of her confessing to hitting Johnny hadn't been admitted as evidence, and now, she had tons of terrible and grotesque text messages sent by her ex-husband to back up her case.

Amber and her team fell into a rhythm in the two weeks leading up to the trial. Bianca and Sara ran to town to buy groceries and cook, while Amber, Whitney, and their lawyers worked on the case from 9 a.m. to 9 p.m. They had an agreement: pencils down at 9 p.m. every night. Then they'd do something totally unrelated to the case, like watching *Monty Python* or *Fleabag*.

During the days, the cottage buzzed with adrenaline. Hours passed as highlighters squeaked across page after page, in binder after binder. Amber squatted to add a note to an oversized, two-foot-tall scrapbook on the floor, each page collaged with hundreds of photos, and on the opposite page was a calendar of each month in the year. Each double-page spread represented a different year Johnny and Amber were together. It was a meticulous accounting of a relationship, punctuated with Amber's worst memories.

One morning as they sat around the table, Bianca filming, a question came up about disclosing evidence.

"So I'm saying, 'Ditto on the Toronto tape, we are searching, and if we find it, we will produce.' How about that? Even though we *have* found it," Elaine asked innocently while drafting an email.

"Yeah, we don't have to tell them we've found it yet," Jen Robinson, Amber's UK attorney, said.

"Right, 'If we find it, we will produce,' so in other words, we're being cooperative, we'll look for it."

"We're looking for it," Jen said. "The thing is . . . yeah, we've found *one*, but we don't need to disclose that just yet. Just say we're searching, because then there may well be others."

"Is there anything problematic, or—" Amber asked.

"Just say we're searching for it," Jen said again.

"But within that audio, for me, is there anything problematic?"

"I don't think so," Jen assured her. "Do you want to listen to it again?"

Amber sighed heavily.

"The Toronto tape" was recorded in September 2015, when Johnny's Whitey Bulger film *Black Mass* was premiering at the Toronto Film Festival. On the recording, Amber was upset that Johnny wanted to go to his premiere rather than finish the argument they were in the middle of. Johnny threw his wedding ring on the ground and told Amber he was done, then asked her twice if she wanted to "smack him around the ear again." Amber then told Johnny she loved him, poured him a glass of wine, and offered him a Xanax. Johnny, surprised by the offer, asked her as she poured the wine, "An alcoholic? Are you sure?" According to Amber, drugs and booze are what turned Johnny into a violent monster, yet here she was offering it to him during a heated argument.

Elaine gently patted Amber's shoulder. "So we're not going to be able to *not* disclose things because—"

"I understand that," Amber said. "I understand. I'm just mitigating expectations."

Elaine began to give Amber one of her many pep talks. "The thing is," she said, "you don't have to be ashamed of *anything* that's on those tapes . . . *You* are the victim here. *You* are the one that is being just subjected to absolutely *horrendous, horrible* acts of violence and verbal abuse. The fact that you might scream or you might say something or you might throw things or *anything* is completely rational."

Amber tied her red bandanna around her head. She thought Elaine was perhaps too optimistic. "I just have seen the worst of how . . . readily accepting the public is and how easy it is for our society to absorb that information and process it in that way. And I am so, so conditioned to appreciate that because I have witnesses from the time I filed for a restraining order *with a black eye,* and people were already asking me what I wanted. And yet no one doubted his credibility or his stance when he said, 'She wants something.' No one said, *Is that true?* . . . It didn't really stop him from getting booked on things."

Then Amber asserted what would become her party line throughout the UK and US trials: the courts weren't a place to mete out justice, but a place for abusers to "weaponize the judicial system" in order to enact vengeance on their victims, furthering their abuse through litigation in the courts.

The afternoon passed while Bianca filmed with two different cameras. Sara refilled glass after glass of iced tea with lemon. Snacks filled the table. Banana bread. Chips. Nuts. Charcuterie. Later, red wine.

"I didn't think this through," Amber said. "If I had been thinking . . . not with my heart, I would have filed a police report, but I thought of the likelihood that he would go down for it."

"You're going to get asked, 'Why didn't you file a police report?'" Elaine responded. "It's a beautiful answer and it's true. You're also going to be asked for every single event, why didn't you call the police?" Elaine paused. "[They will ask] 'did you go to a doctor?' And you say, 'No because . . .'"

"Remember, then turn and look at the judge when you do that," Elaine reminded Amber.

Elaine took a sip from her Diet Coke. Her preferred soda, Diet Mountain Dew, wasn't available in the English countryside. She was known to skip lunch, surviving on large quantities of the soda. Originally from Minnesota, she'd been practicing law for nearly four decades. She wore little to no makeup, a basic bob haircut, and oversized skirt suits with sensible heels. After founding her own law firm in 1991 in Fairfax, Virginia, a suburb outside of DC, her first major client was a housing official who resigned because she claimed her boss was verbally abusive toward women. Elaine took the case in front of a federal jury, who awarded the woman $675,000. The *Washington Post* reported the verdict on its front page.

"Do you remember anything about wanting to watch HBO?" Elaine asked Amber during another work session. She squinted as she stared at an Excel spreadsheet of text messages on her laptop. They were sorting out the timeline around an alleged sexual assault by Johnny, the details of which hadn't yet been seen by Johnny's legal team or the public. Amber was now claiming that during the melee in Australia, when Johnny lost a fingertip and the Diamond Head mansion was destroyed, Johnny had raped her violently with a liquor bottle. She'd later have to testify publicly in Virginia about the incident, and that the bottle rape had led her to lose control of her bladder, retch, and bleed, but British law would allow Amber to give this evidence privately before the Judge.

Elaine's voice drifted as she read a text Amber sent to Johnny's sister after the alleged "hostage situation" in Diamond Head, around the time Dr. Kipper arrived on the scene. "'No big deal though,'" Elaine read aloud, quoting Amber, clearly perplexed. "What a strange thing for you to say."

Amber explained that her relationship with Christi had deteriorated, to the point that she wouldn't say anything to Christi that could be "weaponized" against her. "I would've said 'No big deal' no matter what," Amber replied, trying to help Elaine understand her nonchalance. "Also, that doesn't take into account just a very true part of domestic violence [which] is the learned helplessness. You could open the door to a cage; if that animal has been beaten enough, it won't leave. It won't leave the cage. It doesn't think doing anything will make a difference, because nothing you've done has made a difference . . . I could have used a cell phone, I could have called 911. I didn't. That wasn't the point. I wasn't trying to save my life in that moment, I was trying to be in this relationship and preferably not die and not get hit so much. But I wasn't trying to escape it."

Later, Elaine asked about another text, one that Amber sent to Johnny's daughter, Lily-Rose, around 2 a.m. on Sunday, March 8. "So, I'm just trying to piece this together for timing for when the big attack happened. If Lily-Rose is texting you at essentially 12:35 in the morning on the 8th and you text both of them [Lily-Rose and Johnny] two hours later, 'Awww I wish I was there,' that would have been before *the big problem, right*?"

"The worst of it? Yeah. There were lots of moments of down

time," Amber helped clarify. "Lots of moments where it hit a dead end, hit an impasse, whatever, and I'd go back into the bedroom with the chair in front of the door and it locked, and then I'd hear music go off or music go back on . . . And it just deteriorated and deteriorated and deteriorated . . ." Amber made a roller-coaster motion with her arms. "There were a lot of moments where I would have been able to pick up my phone, which is why I really want to see my messages from that specific time."

But, according to Amber and Whitney, critical text messages from that period from Amber's, Whitney's, and other key witnesses' phones had vanished, leaving gaping holes in the timeline.

"You have texts from Stephen [Deuters] in 2015," Amber's assistant Sara said.

"Do you see March?" Amber asked.

Sara searched the records. "You have messages from Stephen Deuters on February 11."

"And no March?" Amber asked.

"Nothing until May 15."

"Can we do an investigation about whether her phone was hacked?" Jen asked. "Because it's so strange that there are no text messages . . . over that particular period."

"All of our phones have something weird like that," Whitney replied. "My messages are scrambled *only* for Johnny's people."

"iO reports the exact same thing," Amber said.

"Very strange . . ." Jen said.

"You don't have the same phone you did then, do you?" Elaine asked Amber.

"No, he threw out my phone on the regular."

Amber shook her head in disbelief, and everyone quietly turned back to their laptops.

CHAPTER 17

The Life Cage

A fter two weeks of quarantine and preparation, on Tuesday, July 7, 2020, it was time for the trial at the Royal Courts of Justice. There, Judge Andrew Nicol would decide if the "wife beater" headline written by Dan Wootton and published by News Group Newspapers was true or defamatory. The day before the start of the trial, Amber had moved out of the cottage and checked into a two-bedroom apartment at the five-star Ham Yard Hotel in London's Soho district. It was a 1,500-square-foot flat with floor-to-ceiling windows, oak floors, designer furniture, and a spacious kitchen filled with Boffi appliances. Fresh flowers sat on the dining room table. Each bedroom had a large en suite bathroom with luxury towels and marble floors. On a regular night, the suite cost around $3,000. Amber would stay for close to four weeks.

During the first day of the trial, held inside a small room tucked down an arched stone hallway of the law courts, Johnny answered a handful of questions from his own legal team but spent most of the day fending off a barrage of questions from Sasha Wass, barrister for *The Sun*. She addressed Johnny's past drug and alcohol use, his habit of damaging hotel rooms, his relationship with Vanessa Paradis, his confrontations with the paparazzi, his readiness for violence under specific circumstances, and his giving Lily-Rose marijuana when she was thirteen. At the end of day one, the ladies—Jen, Elaine, Whitney, and Bianca—got together with Amber at her hotel. They spread out over a round table and couch in the living room, drinking red wine while listening to jazz in the candlelight.

Sitting with her team, Amber insisted she was a bigger star *before* she invited Johnny into her life. "I was photographed twice as much the year before Johnny, had twice as many speaking engagements. Worked twice as much before Johnny. Every year I was with him my income went down half." While there *was* a trend of diminishing film credits during Amber's years with Johnny, it's difficult to say if there was clear cause and effect tied to their relationship. In 2015, the year they were married, Amber had her highest number of credits (tied with 2007, before they met). The types of roles Amber took also changed. Film credits from early in her career are for little-known TV shows and music videos. After she got with Johnny, her work shifted to feature films.

On the second day of trial, Amber and her team pulled up to the Royal Courts of Justice in an armored car and then walked inside the historic halls of justice, where legal challenges such as the investigation into Princess Diana's death and the legality of Brexit have been argued. Bianca had her camera literally up her sleeve, pointing down at Amber's high heels. The High Court of Justice was situated in Westminster, a Victorian Gothic gray stone building with spires that shot up into the sky. The tabloid photographers and journalists who'd gathered there looked like toothpick figures next to its grand scale. Young women gathered with signs that read, "Justice for Johnny." One woman held up a scroll with five colored illustrations of four of Johnny's signature characters—Jack Sparrow, the Mad Hatter, Willy Wonka, and Sweeney Todd—and regular Johnny depicted in the middle. A man dressed as Edward Scissorhands wore felt blades on his hands.

The first day of trial had been a slow start, but today Johnny would continue his testimony and be cross-examined by the lawyers for News Group Newspapers (NGN), the publisher of *The Sun*. During cross-examination, Johnny's text messages to Paul Bettany were brought to light, and he was again extensively questioned about his alcohol and drug use and whether it impaired his behavior and memory, causing him to be violent toward Amber.

As the trial progressed, Bianca continued filming.

"He cannot look at me . . . look at me look at me . . . you shoved a bottle in me while I cried. I'm right here," Amber said one night after trial, her toes pedaling the hotel carpet.

Whitney agreed, holding back tears. ". . . When anybody is speaking the truth, like, there is a conviction, you look that person in the eyes like, NO fucker, you know what you did is wrong, NO fucker. And there's an understanding when you lock eyes . . . And I've had all those conversations with him when he was looping, fucking spiraling out, bending whatever, like, no, Johnny, look at me. Johnny, look at me. And he knew, he knows that that's a moment, right, as any human does, like when you actually have a conversation with somebody, and you're looking at them, you're seeing them. And those like, fucking twenty minutes I was up in the gallery. I'm like, Johnny, fucking look at me, not only because I want you to be accountable for what *you* fucking did and what you put our family through, my sister through, fucking look at me, because deep down, I want to believe that there's a part of you that is good and that like we all loved you, like, please, for the love of God, have that little ounce of humanity in you."

Johnny seemed to be sticking to the promise he made the last time he saw Amber in person, in July 2016, at the Omni Hotel in San Francisco, when he said he wouldn't look at her again.

"Johnny in his world cage of privilege, money, wealth, and power," Amber said. "He decided he had enough of his life cage."

Even though the progressing trial seemed to be going well for her, Amber worried public opinion hadn't shifted in her favor. "What woman has ever benefited from being a victim of domestic violence?" Amber asked one morning on the way to the Royal Courts of Justice. The fan presence for Johnny outside the London courthouse was unnerving. Online, the #JusticeForJohnnyDepp hashtag, born in early 2020 after the audio recordings were leaked to the *Daily Mail*, had been frequently trending across social media, and the r/JusticeForJohnnyDepp Reddit community, created in February, was quickly growing.

She didn't think the mainstream media was on her side either. "Not one person, not one headline points out—not one today— seems to highlight what I think is super fucking important in this #MeToo/Post–#MeToo world we live in, which is that Johnny Depp tried to get me *fired* from my franchise movies for no reason other than having dumped him," Amber said as the camera rolled. Amber was convinced that Johnny had called the Warner Bros. executives and tried to have her fired from *Aquaman*. Her suspicion wasn't entirely unfounded. On June 4, 2016, a couple weeks after Amber took out the temporary restraining order against him, Johnny had texted Christi: "I want her replaced on that WB film!!!" The text came into evidence, and Amber's team used it to corroborate her claim that he was sabotaging her career. Later, on the stand in Virginia, Johnny explained the text he'd sent to Christi: the press had been making him out to be Charles Manson, so he felt responsible to tell Warner Bros. the truth about "exactly what was going on" and warn them that it would "end up ugly." He said it was business, but denied ever asking the Warner Bros. executives to fire Amber from the series.

As Johnny's fans rallied around him throughout the UK trial, Jen Robinson worked behind the scenes doing damage control on Amber's deteriorating public image. As more and more people on social media joined the #JusticeForJohnnyDepp camp, Jen was planning introductions for Amber to some of Britain's top feminist power players, a group that would come to be known as "Amber's Angels." This case was, at times, more of a public relations battle than a legal one, and both sides were working hard to wrest control of their narratives.

On the fourth day of trial, one of the LAPD officers who answered the 911 call from iO Tillett Wright after Johnny allegedly threw a phone at Amber in the penthouses testified over video. Officer Melissa Saenz described what she'd responded to the night of May 21, 2016: "It was a possible domestic incident, and the caller was a third party from out of state, and we were given an address, and the description of the word 'penthouse.'"

A twelve-year veteran of the force, Saenz was a domestic-violence-trained officer, later stating that she'd responded to "hundreds" of domestic-violence calls at that point. Upon arrival, she had spoken to Amber, who was crying, and asked her several questions, but Amber refused to answer her, nor did she make any indication a crime had been committed. Saenz and Officer Tyler Hadden, a trainee who'd been with Saenz that night, then conducted a search of the premises, checking each room. Despite the photo evidence that Amber presented, Saenz said they didn't see any property damage, or anything else to indicate a fight had taken place. "I searched the entire flat and there was no damage and there was no broken glass. There was nothing to report and nothing out of the ordinary." After the sweep, she attempted again to speak to Amber, as well as her friends Rocky Pennington and Josh Drew. No one would cooperate or even give their names. Saenz then asked Josh Drew to step out of the room so she could speak with the two women alone, hoping they'd be more comfortable that way. Again, Amber and Rocky were uncooperative and provided no information to the officers. According to her testimony, at no point during their visit did Saenz or Hadden see any injuries on Amber. Saenz said her examination of Amber's face was "extremely thorough" and that she didn't observe any injuries.

That same night, after the second set of cops who'd been called to the scene had left, Amber started texting her friends and family in detail about the acts of domestic violence committed against her by Johnny that evening. More photos were taken of her reddened face and of the property damage around the apartment. In a statement that would later become part of a defamation counterclaim filed by Amber against Johnny, Adam Waldman suggested Amber and her friends had intentionally "spilled a little wine and roughed the place up, got their stories straight under the direction of a lawyer and then placed a second call to 911." Fifteen minutes after the second set of cops left, Amber texted her nurse that "[Johnny] hit me in the face several times" and texted her parents that Johnny was "hitting her with the phone and then threw her down and hit her in the head." Paige wrote to Amber, "It looks like he used an old fashioned heavy phone. And hit you very very hard. He should be ashamed."

Though Amber refused to speak with four different cops that night, in the following twenty-four hours, she told multiple people about the restraining order she was getting, even telling her ex Tasya van Ree, with whom she was still friendly, that it was filed already. When iO asked Amber why she hadn't made a statement to the cops, Amber replied, "Because it would have gone straight to TMZ, which will happen on Monday anyway," seeming to contradict her claims that her priority was to protect Johnny.

If Amber had given a statement to the cops, or if there had been any indication that an assault had occurred, Johnny would've been arrested on the spot. In fact, it was another celebrity case, nearly three decades earlier, that had changed California's police protocol in response to incidents of domestic violence. During the O. J. Simpson murder trial, the world was confronted with overwhelming evidence of Simpson's abuse of his wife Nicole Brown Simpson over seventeen years in what's been called "a textbook case" of domestic violence. Prosecutors cited sixty-two incidents of abuse, with the police called nine times—but Simpson was only arrested once. Officer Mark Fuhrman declined to arrest Simpson for smashing in the windshield of Nicole's car while she was sitting in the driver's seat. Marcia Clark, the lead prosecutor, wrote that LAPD officers "frequently washed out the charges." Simpson would sign a football for them and he'd walk free.

Nicole had documented her abuse in pictures and in accounts to family and friends. During her murder trial, jurors, as well as Court TV viewers, saw her injuries and heard her frantic voice in several recorded calls to police. They heard testimony from friends and from her sister, Denise Brown, who said on the stand that in one instance Simpson had "grabbed Nicole" and "threw her against a wall." On the one occasion that Simpson *was* arrested, Brown called 911 and told the operator she thought Simpson was going to kill her. When the LAPD arrived, Nicole was hiding in the bushes, badly beaten, covered in mud, wearing just a bra and sweatpants, cold, wet, and shivering. "You guys have been up here eight times before," she told the officer. "All you do is talk to him, you never do anything. He's gonna kill me." Nicole was hospitalized for her injuries.

When Simpson was acquitted for her murder, Nicole Brown became a national symbol for domestic-violence-prevention advocates. According to Clark, before the Simpson trial, people still largely viewed violence between partners as a "family matter," not really even a crime. For many Americans, the televised trial was their first exposure to the issue of domestic violence, an issue that until that point was mostly kept behind closed doors. Nicole's case turned domestic abuse into a public health issue.

Donations to domestic-violence prevention advocacy groups, hotlines, and shelters multiplied in the aftermath of the Simpson verdict. Months after the murders, Congress passed the Violence Against Women Act of 1994 (VAWA) into law and earmarked $1.6 billion for its programs, the largest amount of funding ever allocated to the issue. The bill, championed by then-senator Joe Biden, also included provisions for funding law-enforcement education on abuse and increased criminal penalties, including the mandatory arrests of abusers. Subsequent reauthorizations have changed some of these provisions from state to state, but in California, officers are now all but encouraged to make arrests on domestic-violence calls if they think there's probable cause.

"They didn't go arrest him because I didn't make a statement," Amber texted iO the morning after the alleged penthouse assault. "They said if I did, they would be obligated to go arrest him."

In London, the trial judge suggested that police officers Saenz and Hadden had erred in their response that night. "It is notable that the officers took no contemporaneous notes," Judge Nicol later wrote in his ruling. "While it is not for me to criticise the methods of another police force, the absence of contemporaneous notes means that their evidence does not carry the same weight as it would otherwise." Judge Nicol also noted that the officers "significantly overestimated the length of time that they were in the apartments." Saenz guessed that she had been in the apartment for thirty to sixty minutes whereas the CCTV timer, if accurate, clocked their visit at around fifteen minutes.

The witness testimony was going well for Johnny. On July 17, day nine of the trial, he'd score another win. The actress and #MeToo activist Katherine Kendall—who'd been quoted in *The Sun*'s article as stating, "I don't stand behind hitting people or abusing people. It seems that Amber got hurt. As someone who has been the victim of sexual abuse and a supporter of MeToo and telling my story to help others, I cannot advocate violence"— submitted, in a written witness statement, that in fact she'd been completely misquoted, and that the tabloid had used the #MeToo movement and her words falsely. She clarified that she "wanted to make a comment in general about not being supportive of people being violent with each other," and revealed that, after the article ran, she'd texted the reporter, "I never meant to be in an article that called Johnny Depp a 'wife beater.' I told you that I didn't know that to be true at all!" This development was a terrible look for the defendants, who maintained that the op-ed was important commentary on allegations of public interest. Now it was revealed they'd twisted and misused a #MeToo victim's words, even though this victim had insisted Johnny be given due process.

In the #JusticeForJohnny Twitterverse, users jumped on the news about Katherine Kendall, calling Amber a liar and throwing more support behind Team Depp. But inside the courtroom, the field was still open, and *The Sun*'s star witness was about to take the stand.

Amber testified over four days of trial, beginning on July 20. Part of her testimony, in which she'd describe incidents of sexual assault including the bottle rape in Australia, would take place in private with the judge. On one day of testimony, Amber wore her hair pinned to the top of her head in two long coiled braids. Inside the car on the way to court, Bianca filmed Amber lip-synching to Pat Benatar's "Hit Me with Your Best Shot." As they pulled up to the courthouse, paparazzi scrambled outside the car window, and the song ended right on cue.

During Amber's testimony, Adam Waldman was reprimanded by Judge Nicol for a tweet he posted about trial witness Laura Divenere, an interior decorator to both Amber and Elon Musk. "In memoriam, Elon Musk's decorator Laura Divenere," Adam tweeted. Adam had accused Laura of twice changing her story about Johnny abusing Amber, after Laura told the High Court that Adam pressured her into providing a statement confirming she hadn't seen injuries on Amber's face in the immediate aftermath of the penthouse fight. Amber had also secretly recorded a conversation with Laura that was played to the court, in which Laura called Adam "the biggest asshole under the sun" and said he was accusing her of conspiring against Johnny.

The Sun's lawyers described Adam's "In Memoriam" tweet as ". . . very sinister and macabre. It is threatening." Judge Nicol said the phrase was "unwelcome." Certain sources close to Johnny believe that Adam's bad behavior poisoned the well in the UK trial. In just a few months, Adam would find himself in hot water again with another judge for similar conduct, this time in the United States.

On day sixteen, the final day of trial, Johnny arrived at the courthouse and delivered handwritten notes on COVID facemasks to his adoring fans. Once inside, Johnny's counsel gave closing arguments, emphasizing, once again, that he wasn't a "wife beater." Closing arguments in the UK are radically different than in the US. In the UK, a solicitor gives an overview of the charges and presents evidence while answering questions from the judge, who is often asking for clarification and has been an active participant in the fact-finding process. As sensational as this case was, the conclusion of the trial felt procedural and anticlimactic.

That is, until Amber gave a speech on the courthouse steps.

At the close of the final day of trial, the doors of the Royal Courts of Justice swung open and Jen, Elaine, Amber, Whitney, Sara, and Bianca stepped outside. Amber approached a microphone wearing all black.

"It has been incredibly painful to relive the breakup of my relationship, to have my motives and my truth questioned," Amber read from a statement. She spoke slowly and coherently, adding weight to each word, holding her hand to her heart. Thanking her supporters, she said, "You have given me so much strength and I send it back to you."

Afterward, rewatching the speech back in Amber's hotel room, Whitney called out, "Fuck yeah."

"Beautiful," Sara stated.

Jen and Amber embraced. "You did it," Jen told Amber. "And like I said, top of the news." Jen waved her phone in front of the camera. Amber thanked Jen for coming up with the idea for the speech. "For a case like this, you need to understand how to play the media, and I think that was the right thing to do," Jen said.

She added, shaking her head, "[Johnny's lawyer's] submissions that you are a liar looks ridiculous next to someone who just stood up there and gave that speech with such integrity and dignity."

Amber exhaled loudly, exasperated. "I hope this guy gets a girlfriend soon," she said, speaking about Johnny. "I hope she's made of steel. Maybe one of those Japanese robot ones . . ."

In August, just weeks after testifying in the UK, Amber filed a ninety-three-page counterclaim for $100 million against Johnny in the *Depp vs Heard* case. Inside, she asserted again that Johnny was the aggressor in their relationship and continued to victimize her after she "escaped" their marriage by coordinating a smear campaign, and that he was victimizing her again now by bringing the US defamation lawsuit against her. She singled out several statements made by Adam Waldman in the *Daily Mail* in April and June 2020 that she claimed were defamatory, in which he called her allegations of domestic violence "fake" and a "sexual violence hoax." The counterclaim included numerous text messages sent by Johnny to his friends in which he talked about Amber using vile language: a cum guzzler, a junkie hooker, a disgusting pig, and a sick fucking whore. In a text to their mutual agent, Christian Carino, in August 2016, Johnny said Amber was "begging for total global humiliation." Amber said these texts were "only the tip of the iceberg reflecting Mr. Depp's misogyny" as well as his "deep inner anger and hatred for Ms. Heard."

A large focus of her counterclaim was her theory that Johnny had organized a social-media bot attack against her to ruin her reputation and have her removed from *Aquaman*. She cited the 2016 text to Christi in which Johnny said he wanted her "replaced" on the Warner Bros. film, and the Change.org petition urging the studio to recast her role, which had garnered millions of signatures. Amber believed the signatures were largely fraudulent, but Judge Bruce White of Virginia, who was involved in the pretrial rulings and motions, determined there was a lack of evidence to support this claim and threw out this aspect of her case. "The pleading fails to demonstrate that the social-media accounts communicated obscene language, suggested obscene acts, or threatened illegal or immoral acts," he explained.

He did, however, agree that her counterclaim case would also proceed in Virginia. Now, Johnny and Amber's competing lawsuits would be on trial together. They'd both be responsible for proving their allegations. And this time, they'd do it before a jury of their peers, who would decide whose story they believed.

CHAPTER 18

Judgment Day

As she waited for a verdict in *Depp vs NGN*, Amber settled back into her life in LA with Bianca, moving into a rental home in the Hollywood Hills. But she couldn't shake the court case behind her or the one that lay ahead of her. Though Bianca tried to keep Amber distracted from the lawsuits, the online trolls, and the grief of losing her mother, it was hard to get Amber's mind on anything else. "She had nowhere to put everything," Bianca said. "She didn't know how to cry. She didn't know how to freak out. She didn't know how to break down. She just knew how to keep going. She was completely detached . . . She was shut down."

But Amber had something to lift her spirits: soon, she'd become a mom.

Amber had always wanted to be a mother. When she and Johnny were still newly engaged, he'd told an *Entertainment Tonight* reporter that he loved children and would "make a hundred" more, but he seemed evasive when asked if he actually wanted more kids. "You know what, I, um . . . I just got back from a trip to China, you know, uh, promoting this film and, um I met these little amazing little innocent beautiful perfect little uh Chinese kids and, uh, you know that kind of thing always makes you feel a little broody, you know?" Amber and Johnny's relationship didn't survive long enough to brood, and now, six years later, she'd made arrangements to have a child via surrogacy. A baby girl would arrive in April.

The entertainment industry was still virtually shut down due to the COVID pandemic, but Amber perceived the lack of work she was getting to be a consequence of the negative online noise surrounding her. Her agents tried to find her new parts, but nothing materialized. Amber felt exiled and abandoned. It seemed like the industry had turned against one of its own #MeToo victims.

Finally, Amber would get some relief. Three months after the UK trial, on November 2, 2020, Judge Nicol was ready to publish his judgment on Johnny's libel case against *The Sun*.

It was 1:43 a.m. on a Monday morning in Los Angeles, eight hours behind London, and Amber leaned over her kitchen sink washing dishes. She was wearing a green mechanic's jumpsuit, her hair pulled back with a rolled-up bandanna. "If it doesn't work out for us, it's fine, I just don't deserve to tell my story," she said sarcastically to Bianca, who was filming.

Amber had gathered her close friends and family to cook food and drink wine while nervously awaiting the news. "Vitamin C" by Can played in the background as Amber looked out of her kitchen window at her patio, which was draped in hanging lights.

"Do you still feel positive?" she asked Bianca.

They went outside to join their friends around the patio fireplace. Whitney drank a Red Bull and softly clapped her hands to her face, trying to keep herself awake. "I've had a child and I've never been this anxious about a due date," she said. Her son, Hunter, was asleep inside the house.

Amber held her cell phone in anticipation. They were expecting a call any moment now from the lawyer who'd represented NGN in the UK. When his name appeared on her screen, she picked up the call quickly.

"We won," he said through a muffled connection.

Amber and Whitney were stunned. "We won? . . . WE WON!!"

Screaming erupted, followed by sobs. "I never thought I'd see him be held accountable," Amber said through tears. The lawyer told them Judge Nicol had found Johnny guilty of twelve of the fourteen violent incidents Amber had testified to, and therefore *The Sun* hadn't libeled him when it called him a "wife beater."

Amber left the group to talk privately inside the house. Whitney and Bianca followed shortly after.

"[Judge Nicol] found the sexual assault. He proved that too. I thought that would never happen," she said through tears as Whitney embraced her. "I never thought that would ever happen." A minute later, one of her friends entered the room. "He even found the sexual assault happened. There were only two people in that room. It was just me and Johnny in that room and he said without a doubt it happened. He believed that *even* that happened. I never thought I would ever hear someone validate what happened to me that night. I just never thought anyone would believe how fucked up that was. And he said it happened."

Amber called Jen Robinson in London. "He even ruled on behalf of my evidence about the Australian sexual assault, which is the one I really cared about, you know?" she said incredulously. "The one I thought no one would believe? He even believed that."

"You deserve this vindication so much . . . I am so just beyond delighted," Jen said triumphantly. "Adam Waldman is strangely quiet at the moment."

In another blow to Johnny, Adam Waldman had just been

kicked off the case in Virginia by Judge Bruce White, who was ruling over pretrial motions. Amber had filed for sanctions against
Adam, claiming that he'd leaked information to the press and
social media on "at least two occasions," and that he was dis-
seminating audio recordings, surveillance pictures, and witness
declarations to "websites and Twitter users." Judge White was
persuaded. In October, he ruled that Adam had shared confidential information with the press that had been prohibited under a
protective order, and he was officially barred from working on the
case.

"Eat crow, Adam Waldman. Eat a bag of dicks," Whitney
chimed in, without missing a beat. "Go take a long walk off a very
short bridge, you fucking cunt."

Amber made call after call, pausing in between to talk to the
friends who'd gathered to support her. She was still in shock. "If
you think about where we were four months ago, five months ago.
People had good reason to say when they were backing out of supporting me. The Amanda de Cadenets of the world for instance,
you know, who had to just back out because they saw something
posted . . . or Adam Waldman had said something to them." Amber then redirected her ire to her former makeup artist Mélanie
Inglessis, who'd testified about an incident that occurred in December 2015, the night before Amber appeared as a guest on *The
Late Late Show with James Corden*. "Mélanie covered up a broken
nose, a busted lip, a couple black eyes. She was a hostile witness,
we had to actually subpoena her. She fought it. I had to pay for a
lawyer so that she could fight the subpoena in order to testify for
me . . . When I called her after, she screamed at me, 'How could
I put her in jeopardy like this?'" Amber claimed that during an incident of violence on December 15, Johnny had dragged her by her
hair up and down the penthouse stairs, from one room to another,

then slapped and shoved her, before finally punching her in the head and smothering her on the bed. She also said that he'd violently headbutted her, breaking her nose. In an audio recording made several months later, Johnny admitted he'd headbutted Amber during that fight. "I headbutted you in the fucking . . . forehead. That doesn't break a nose." Explaining himself during the UK trial, Johnny said Amber had been hitting him, so he grabbed her arms to "lock" them, and in the process, their heads knocked. He said it wasn't an act of violence, but an accident.

Other friends and supporters called to tell Amber congratulations. "Cheers to you, Amber, changing the world," her friends said as they toasted with wine and champagne.

As she took a sip of wine, a woman known only by her first name, Victoria, called to congratulate Amber over the phone too. "You are not discredited at all, it's such a complete win," she said.

"Suck it, J.K.," Amber said, referring to J.K. Rowling, the creator behind *Fantastic Beasts*.

Whitney chimed in again with profanities: "Suck it, you fucking old homophobic rag cunt."

"If he hadn't done this, this wouldn't have happened," Amber said, referring to the UK lawsuit. "I hope he sues his lawyer next."

"Dan Wootton is really keen to speak to you," Victoria said on the other end of the line. Amber's eyes darted toward the camera. "Can I send you his number and you give him a call or for him to call you?" Victoria asked.

Amber replied that it was fine if he called her.

Then Sara read aloud a statement from *The Sun*: "'*The Sun* has stood up and campaigned for victims of domestic abuse for over twenty years. Domestic abuse victims must never be silenced . . . and we thank Amber Heard for her courageous efforts in giving evidence to the court.'"

Amber looked at Whitney. "We did it," she said.

"No, YOU did it," Whitney replied.

"I couldn't do it by myself," Amber insisted. "As we know, one woman's word doesn't really matter that much, it takes many."

"This is you," Whitney assured her. "This is your strength, this was your victory, this is your survival." Reveling in the victory, Whitney declared, "Let's go up Sweetzer and spray champagne all over that fucking cul-de-sac."

As the reality of the win settled in, Amber called iO to tell him the news. She expressed her surprise again that the judge had found her account of the sexual assault to be true. "That's the only one . . . not the only one . . . but I really didn't know what to expect . . ."

"You lost your soul over this goddamn thing and you *fucking* won," iO said to Amber. "Do not for a minute discount that. This is huge, not just for you, but for women *everywhere*."

In the background, one of Amber's friends chimed in, "*All over the world.*"

Amber called her acting coach Kristy Sexton, who'd also testified. "You are my hero for doing what you did. You have not backed down and you did not let his fucking money and power win. I am so proud that you are my friend," she told Amber. Kristy was one of Amber's closest friends and had been a key witness. Kristy testified that Amber told her about Johnny's violence on several occasions. She also said he'd control the roles she took on and was jealous and judgmental.

Amber read more of Judge Nicol's judgment on her phone, trying to digest everything, this time grinning ear to ear.

"'Her donation of $7 million to charity is hardly the act one would expect of a gold digger.'" Amber read aloud.

"FINDING OF FACT! Finding. Of. Fact," Bianca exclaimed.

Whitney clapped her hands loudly, using her whole body.

"I'm a very complicated schemer," Amber said.

The clock on the stove read 3:52 a.m. Everyone remained giddy with excitement and buzzed from red wine.

"We won. Go to bed, enough, we won. Go to bed," Sara finally said, giving Amber a tight hug and a kiss on the cheek.

Twelve hours later, inside the dining room, there was a pair of mylar balloons—one in the shape of a champagne bottle, one in the shape of a heart. A princess crown sat atop a bowl of orange marigolds inside a ceramic bowl. In front of the bowl rested a recycled Halloween decoration of a grave that read, "RIP." A banner reading C-E-L-E-B-R-A-T-E in gold letters hung across the window.

"This is huge," Sara said, still buzzing from the verdict.

"Seriously, I have yet to see the real attention being paid to all of the women who actively went against me to hurt me, to throw me under the bus. I was in it entirely alone." Amber was still processing the win. The joy and celebration of the night before had morphed into anger at just how far she'd had to go to defend herself. She scrolled down her phone, checking for headlines and commentary on the verdict. All the major news outlets, from the BBC to *The Guardian* to the *Hollywood Reporter*, were pushing headlines with the news: *Johnny Depp Loses Libel Case*. "I can't believe it," she said, still stunned at her win.

Upstairs, Amber sat at her desk with Jen Robinson on speaker. A sign with the mantra "I'm here, I'm awake, don't push it" sat at the edge of her desk. Prominently jutting out from her bookshelf was *What to Expect When You're Expecting*. Now that Johnny had lost his libel case, she expected him to be fired from the Fantastic Beasts film—immediately. "The thing I want to know, specifically, is J.K. Rowling's response, and the Warner Bros. response," she said to Jen. She believed Johnny had tried to get her fired from *Aquaman*, and now she wanted him off his own fancy franchise.

Jen told Amber her strategy. Once the upcoming trial in Virginia was behind them, she wanted Amber to be a representative for domestic-violence victims everywhere. She wanted her to go on *Oprah*, to speak on behalf of charities. Amber had a platform now, her voice mattered more than ever, and they had laws they needed to change together. "Your stock is so fucking high . . . start thinking quietly now about how to say it, when to say it, and what to say because you have so much to say," Jen told her. "This is it. This is your platform. You have more moral authority now on this subject." Changing laws, changing the world—this was what mattered to Amber.

Winding down their call, Jen speculated about Johnny's own new press strategy now that he'd lost his case. "What I'm interested in is what their PR thing is going forward," Jen said. "I think they are going to start attacking the judge. Like I've said to you, he's been in my chambers, he's friends with [Baroness] Helena [Kennedy] and all these people. I wouldn't be surprised if they start attacking those connections." Amber bit her nails as she listened.

Jen did have close connections to Judge Andrew Nicol. Until 2008, he'd worked at Doughty Street Chambers, where Jen worked as a barrister. Jen had known the firm's founder, Geoffrey Robertson, since her college years. Geoffrey had co-authored the book with Judge Nicol titled *Media Law and Human Rights*, an oft-cited legal text now in its fifth edition, which Amber had been studying in London. Geoffrey had been married to the bestselling Australian-British novelist Kathy Lette for twenty-seven years, and Kathy and Jen Robinson were close friends. Kathy even wrote a blurb for Jen's own book, *How Many More Women?: Exposing How the Law Silences Women*. Kathy Lette was also friends with Judge Nicol's wife, solicitor Camilla Palmer, who specializes in sex discrimination and who founded the Women's Equality Network. During the trial, Kathy Lette hosted a private dinner party for Amber with guests including comedian Sandi Toksvig and Baroness Helena Kennedy. Helena, whom Jen mentioned on her call with Amber, was a fellow human rights lawyer who worked with Jen at Doughty Street Chambers and, apparently, was also a friend of Judge Nicol.

The intimate gathering had been covered by the *Daily Mail* for the Sunday issue. They described the affair as "a low-key party" where Amber "surrounded herself with a stellar cast of powerful, high-profile women." An anonymous source told the paper that the women had become Amber's "secret support network" through the trial and that "Amber's Angels" had become her "solid gang." Photos accompanying the story showed Jen Robinson and Amber standing outside of Kathy Lette's home, Amber clutching two books in her hand. Two additional photos zoomed in on one of the book's covers and boldly circled its title. It was Baroness Kennedy's 1993 book, *Eve Was Framed*, about the unfair treatment of women in the British court system. The close-ups of the book clutched in Amber's hand begged the question: was this an impromptu tabloid sighting or an intentionally placed PR plug for both Helena Kennedy's book and Amber?

Ending the call, Jen told Amber that she'd write to the women who'd been at the dinner party and tell them, "Here's the judgment, we just want to say thank you."

"This is only setting us up with the right weapons that we can then use for actual work," Amber said, just before they hung up. "This is systems takedown, just adding tools to our toolbelt."

On the day the verdict was announced, Johnny was in London, his hair bleached blond for the dark wizard role of Grindelwald, sitting nervously with his lawyers at the kitchen table inside a historic multistoried townhouse. Warner Bros. had rented it for him to live in during the production of *Fantastic Beasts: The Secrets of Dumbledore*. The house was located in a suburb north of London called Highgate known for its Victorian architecture and eclectic character. He'd be staying for a month in the 11,000-square-foot abode complete with swimming pool, gym, and screening room.

Johnny had been filming for only a couple of days when it was announced that the verdict was finally coming down. As they waited inside the townhouse for Judge Nicol's verdict, Stephen and Gina Deuters tried to keep Johnny distracted, while his assistant Nathan Holmes moved about the house. Chef Russell placed Johnny's favorite treat, chocolate-dipped doughnuts, on a serving tray to cool off. Johnny's UK solicitors sat on a bench at the long wooden table across from him, while Stephen and Gina sat on a sofa nearby.

Suddenly, Stephen noticed the lawyers at the table talking in hushed tones. He could tell by their demeanor what it meant. Stephen leaned over and whispered into Gina's ear, "We lost," and her jaw dropped. Johnny, realizing why, looked at her and said, "Fine, just get me a vest that says Wife Beater and I'll wear that for the rest of my life." He went upstairs to his room. On his way back down, he slumped into Chef Russell for a hug on the staircase. Behind tinted glasses, tears streamed down Johnny's face.

Stephen described that morning like a wake, "quiet and muted." Stephen fell asleep for an hour and woke up to "get back to it." "It was a dark day," he said. The lawyers tried to offer hope by talking about the appeal process, but it wasn't enough to lift anyone's mood. One of the lawyers, David Sherborne, an experienced barrister to the stars, was noticeably silent. The lawyers left a few hours later, but Johnny's inner circle stayed behind to support him.

The next few days moved in slow motion as they fielded calls from the press and waited to hear from Warner Bros. A triumphant headline from *The Sun*, now vindicated by the court, spread across the internet. "On behalf of domestic abuse survivors we can now confirm that . . . HE IS A WIFE BEATER." In the weeks and months that followed, Johnny and his team received few calls. Terry Gilliam, Angelina Jolie, and Brad Pitt sent him nice notes, but many of his friends seemed to have abandoned him. Concerned about Johnny's mental health, Stephen had brought in a celebrity therapist named Beechy Colclough, who was plagued with his own past accusations of seducing and having sex with his patients. Beechy was there throughout the trial, and now its aftermath, to try to help Johnny through the difficult time.

Before he could appeal Judge Nicol's decision, Johnny lost his role in the Fantastic Beasts franchise. "No one from Warner Bros. contacted Johnny personally, instead they called me and I had to deliver the news he'd been fired from the film," Stephen said. "The next few months, we had nothing on the calendar for the first time in many years." After he was fired by Warner Bros., Gina recorded a video of Johnny reading a statement for his social media, but they decided to nix it. He looked too "raw," too vulnerable. Instead, he released a typewritten letter on Instagram:

> I wish to let you know that I have been asked to resign
> by Warner Bros. from my role as Grindelwald in
> Fantastic Beasts and I have respected and agreed to
> that request . . . The surreal judgment of the court in
> the U.K. will not change my fight to tell the truth and I
> confirm that I plan to appeal.

Though he'd only shot one scene, Warner Bros. still had to pay Johnny $16 million because there was no "morality clause" in his contract. These clauses, intended to protect a party to a contract in the event that another party to the contract becomes the subject of scandal or contempt, are now included in most film contracts post #MeToo.

Even though the case in the UK had fallen in her favor, Amber was in danger of losing her own big studio job too. Warner Bros. didn't want to rehire Amber for the $215 million *Aquaman* sequel, *Aquaman and the Lost Kingdom,* scheduled to begin filming in the summer of 2021. She claimed it was because of the #MeToo allegations she'd made against her ex-husband, but the former DC Films boss Walter Hamada cited the lack of chemistry between her and the franchise lead, Jason Momoa.

According to *Variety,* in the end it was Amber's ex-boyfriend Elon Musk who got Amber her job back. Elon had one of his lawyers send a "scorched-earth letter to Warner Bros. threatening to burn the house down" if she wasn't brought back for the sequel. Warner Bros. gave in. Amber would be traveling to the UK to prep for the *Aquaman* sequel.

Johnny and Amber could agree on one thing: Warner Bros. was making decisions based on the bottom line. It was just what big studios did. Johnny stated after the loss, "Nobody was man enough to give me the boot based on allegations, but it was still okay to leave the supposed wife-beater on the rides, and it's still okay for them to sell merchandise of the supposed wife-beater, and they can still sell action figures of the supposed wife-beater. So I would say that something's rotten in Denmark."

After the trial loss, Johnny's team also got news that *Minamata,* the Infinitum Nihil film shot in 2019 starring Johnny as intrepid photojournalist W. Eugene Smith, wouldn't be released in the US as planned. *Minamata* told the true story of Smith's final assignment for *Life* magazine, in which he helped expose decades of gross negligence by the Chisso Corporation that resulted in as many as two million Japanese citizens getting mercury poisoning. The film's director, Andrew Levitas, said he was told by MGM acquisitions head Sam Wollman that the film wouldn't be promoted and that MGM had decided to "bury the film" because of Johnny's bad public image.

Andrew wrote a letter to MGM, which included Smith's photos of the suffering and deformities stemming from the mercury poisoning and a link to one of the victims speaking on her experience. He compared MGM's actions to the cover-up done by the Chisso Corporation and described the "deeply pained" voice of a victim's father who described losing their child to mercury poisoning. "Yes, you are legally within your rights to bury their story as so many have done before," he wrote, "but you have a moral obligation to do better than that and at a minimum we implore you to speak directly to Mr. Uemura and the other victims and offer them the dignity of understanding first hand why you think an actor's personal life is more important than their dead children, their siblings, their parents, and all victims of industrial pollution and corporate malfeasance." (MGM ultimately sold the film to another distributor that released it in the US in 2022.)

In March 2021, the Court of Appeal rejected Johnny's application to overturn Judge Nicol's verdict. Judge Nicol had already denied Johnny's appeal, stating, "I do not consider that the proposed grounds of appeal have a reasonable prospect of success," but had given him a window to take his case directly to the higher court. One key theme of Johnny's argument was that the judge had failed to provide careful analysis of the material or an explanation as to *how* he made these findings in Amber's favor. Despite nineteen sworn witnesses and conflicting evidence, they said the judgment showed a "lack of analysis and reasoning which it was incumbent upon the Judge to perform." They argued that the judge should have looked more carefully at how Amber's own evidence damaged her credibility regarding her claims of physical abuse. ". . . the Judge carried out no assessment of Ms Heard's credibility . . . The Judge accepted at the outset that Ms Heard must have been correct in her allegations, and then discounted any evidence to the contrary."

Johnny's lawyers had argued that Amber was an unreliable witness, and as part of their appeal, they offered new proof of her unreliability. They said Amber's promise to donate her $7 million divorce settlement to charity was "a calculated and manipulative lie"; their investigation found that Amber had not made all the promised payments to either the ACLU or the Children's Hospital Los Angeles as she'd claimed. The fresh evidence didn't make a difference—ultimately two High Court judges also refused Johnny's appeal stating, "We conclude that the appeal has no real prospect of success and that there is no other compelling reason for it to be heard."

It seemed Hollywood had reached a similar verdict: insiders predicted Johnny's career would never recover. At a press conference at the San Sebastian Film Festival later that year, Johnny spoke out about cancel culture. "It can be seen as an event in history that lasted for however long it lasted, this cancel culture, this instant rush to judgment based on what essentially amounts to polluted air," he said. "It's so far out of hand now that I can promise you that no one is safe. Not one of you." A month earlier, Johnny had given an interview to the UK newspaper the *Sunday*

Times and said that he was being "boycotted" by Hollywood, describing his industry ostracization as an "absurdity of media mathematics." Soon after, he opened up the sister company to Infinitum Nihil in London, IN.2, which would focus on films with a "European sensibility." Speaking about IN.2 at the San Sebastian Film Festival, Johnny said he spent "many years working inside and outside of the Hollywood system and trying to persuade them that not every outing needs to be a blockbuster, that they don't need to be formulaic, commercial drivel . . . It's ludicrous to play everything safe. Cinema audiences are getting bored." Johnny was leaving his star on Hollywood Boulevard behind for greener, European pastures, where there was less red tape and an openness to scripts that didn't feature comic book superheroes or predictable rom-com characters.

Amber was leaving Hollywood too—if only for a while. "So we are moving . . . some place more quiet . . . with less people to follow me every day," she said, packing up her West Hollywood home for Yucca Valley, a desert town a hundred miles east of LA. "I haven't been able to make this place work for me in a long time now. It's hard to live here, it's lonely and alienating and inhuman in so many ways. It really has to give back to you somehow for it to be worth it and I don't know how it's doing that . . .

"I really hope that the [US] trial will be able to go forward and be finished [soon]. I was really looking forward to the clean slate, a new chapter."

PART IV

CHAPTER 19

The Black Pearl

Back in November 2020, Johnny boarded a private plane for Northern Virginia to begin his pretrial deposition for *Depp vs Heard*. Sitting inside Elaine Bredehoft's office in Reston, Johnny was deposed for three days. On the second day, Elaine asked him if he would've felt vindicated had the UK ruling come down in his favor. Johnny replied that it didn't matter. He lost when Amber made the accusations, the damage was done. "My continuing to demand the truth is not for me to win," he explained, "but it's for the people out there, the women, the victims of this type of thing who are not believed, who are being lied to by your client pretending to be some new messiah of the women's movement. She is a fraud."

The next day, Elaine posed another hypothetical question: Would Johnny validate the Virginia jury's decision should it fall in Amber's favor?

"I can only hope that people will hear the truth and understand it to be the truth," Johnny responded, "but I don't think the young soldiers who were storming the beaches at Normandy—I don't think that they were saying, hey, let's have pizza tonight. I think that they knew what they'd gone into."

Little did Johnny know that the trial wouldn't get under way for well over a year. Originally scheduled to begin in May 2021, the trial was delayed for eleven months due to COVID. While he and Amber waited in limbo, they both went through big life changes. Amber moved to her house in Yucca Valley and, in April 2021, her daughter Oonagh was born by surrogate. In the weeks after Oonagh's birth, she gathered with friends and close family to cook and hang out at home, getting parenting tips from Whitney. She appeared to stay busy with work and activism, posting branded content for L'Oréal on Instagram, along with videos chronicling her intensive diet and exercise regimen for *Aquaman and the Lost Kingdom*, which she'd film over four months in the latter half of 2021. Johnny, meanwhile, unveiled a new vocation: he was a painter. "My paintings surround my life, but I kept them to myself and limited myself. No one should ever limit themselves." In January 2022, his artwork entered the world in the form of an NFT collection titled Never Fear Truth, a collection of Warhol-like portraits of Johnny's family, friends, and heroes on the Ethereum blockchain. He announced he'd donate a portion of what he made to charity.

As anticipation mounted ahead of the trial, scheduled to begin on April 11, 2022, legal experts opined in the media that the odds weren't in Johnny's favor. This time around, he was suing Amber directly, not a tabloid. In order to prove that Amber knowingly made defamatory statements about him, he had to prove a negative—that he never committed domestic violence. It would be a much tougher legal challenge than in the UK, where defamation law should have favored his case, and yet he'd still lost.

On February 25, Amber and Johnny's lawyers appeared in court in Fairfax, Virginia, for a pretrial hearing about televising the trial. The subject of media access had come up several times in the months leading up to the trial, but the question of whether or not cameras would be allowed inside the courthouse had yet to be resolved. How was Judge Penney Azcarate, who'd preside over the trial, going to handle the immense public interest in the case? She couldn't allow any and all media inside the courtroom because there were only a hundred seats. For Judge Azcarate, a former US marine, the chief concern was the safety and decorum of the courtroom.

Every state but Oklahoma has rules about allowing cameras in the courtroom, with the judge generally making the final call. When judges do permit them, it's usually done in the name of "transparency." At a pretrial hearing in Fairfax, Amber's lawyer, Elaine Bredehoft, argued against televising the trial, citing the sensitive nature of the sexual-assault and rape allegations Amber would have to testify to. She emphasized the negative social-media attention Amber was getting from Johnny's die-hard fans, the so-called Deppheads. She warned that filming the trial would put undue pressure on the jury, the witnesses, and even court-room staff.

Johnny's team saw things differently. They wanted the trial proceedings to be witnessed by the world. Johnny's lead attorney, Benjamin Chew of Brown Rudnick, pushed the transparency argument and challenged the existence of "anti-Amber pro networks," as Elaine called them. He pointed out that during Amber's three-day deposition at their offices in Orange County a month earlier, Amber said no one had bothered her at all. The fear was a figment of her and her lawyers imaginations, Ben Chew said. "Mr. Depp has always favored transparency. She's already trashed him in the media. She destroyed his reputation."

Judge Azcarate ultimately sided with Johnny's lawyers. "I don't see any good cause not to do it," she said.

Three months before the defamation trial began in Fairfax, Johnny's lawyers at Brown Rudnick had been thrown a curveball. Johnny had been watching the second season of the Netflix documentary series *Making a Murderer* about the potential wrongful conviction of a man named Steven Avery. He was inspired by Avery's attorney Kathleen Zellner and her tenacity in freeing her wrongfully accused clients. Something powerful that Kathleen said in the Netflix series had lodged in Johnny's mind: that she was "the last person you'd want to hire if you were guilty" because she'd "find out about it."

What if I hire Kathleen to be my lawyer? he thought.

Though Johnny was the one who'd pursued the lawsuit against Amber, he also saw himself as a wrongfully accused person utilizing the justice system to prove his innocence. Johnny had advocated for the wrongfully accused before, specifically for Damien Echols of the "West Memphis Three," who, along with two of his friends, was convicted of a triple murder in the mid-1990s, during the Satanic Panic. (Echols ultimately made an Alford plea, a legal maneuver in which a defendant pleads guilty while maintaining their innocence in order to avoid the risk of going to trial.) Johnny's production company Infinitum Nihil optioned Echols's memoir and planned to make a film about the whole ordeal. The project never materialized, but Echols considers Johnny a great friend. "When I was with Johnny all the stuff that was breaking me didn't matter anymore," Echols said. "We could just focus on the most foolish things like watching Honey Boo Boo, playing guitars and getting matching tattoos." He and Johnny shared two tattoos: an iChing symbol and a crow on the back of their hands.

Johnny left Kathleen a voicemail on her office line. At first, Kathleen couldn't believe Johnny Depp was calling her, asking if she'd be a consultant for him in Fairfax. She'd just learned that the murder case she was prepping for would be continued. Her schedule happened to be open, so she signed on.

Ben Chew and Brown Rudnick associate Camille Vasquez were Johnny's lead counsel on the *Depp vs Heard* case. Ben was a senior partner at Brown Rudnick's DC office and had several years of trial experience. His past clients included Cher, the Dubai government, and two Olympic gold medalists. When Ben built the legal team for Johnny, he knew his young associate Camille was the right person to partner with. He'd worked with young lawyers in his early career and had developed a knack for spotting talent. "When I met Camille, it was pretty obvious. I mean, you don't have to be a lawyer to see her talent that I saw right away. I wanted her to be on our team." Camille Vasquez, who was thirty-seven, was the daughter of immigrants, her mom from Cuba, her dad from Colombia. She grew up in a middle-class tract home in Buena Park, California, near Disneyland. Her mom worked for the school she and her sister attended on scholarship, and her dad was in management at Hilton Hotels. She was given two choices for a career: doctor or lawyer. Her sister became a doctor, and Camille became a lawyer. But up until this lawsuit, she'd only taken part in one trial, a slip-and-fall case, which they'd lost.

Before the defamation suit, which Ben and Camille had been building for three years, they also represented Johnny, alongside Adam Waldman, in the lawsuits against his former business managers at The Management Group and against his ex-entertainment lawyer Jake Bloom, winning him a massive multi-million-dollar settlement in the latter case. Now, with the arrival of Kathleen Zellner just a few months before the Fairfax trial, Johnny was abruptly bringing an outsider into the fold.

While Johnny was upending his legal team, Amber was still trying to make the whole trial go away. Three weeks before opening statements, Amber requested a mediation to settle. This was her third and final attempt to get the case dismissed.

The mediation was held in March 2022 at an office in downtown Los Angeles, where Kathleen, Ben, and Camille gathered with Johnny, who wore an oversized tan-colored suit with a navy newsboy cap and aviator sunglasses. Amber and her counsel participated by telephone. This was unusual for a mediation, which is designed to bring together the disputing parties in person to come to an agreement, but the judge allowed it. "There was never any face-to-face interaction with them," Ben said of the mediation.

"You *will* lose this case, you should settle it," the judge said, looking Johnny squarely in the face.

This was not the message Johnny was expecting—but settling also seemed impossible. According to a source close to the lawsuit, Amber was demanding north of $10 million, and the mediation failed.

The trial would move ahead as scheduled in Fairfax.

By now, thirteen years had passed since Johnny and Amber had met when she was twenty-three and he forty-six, and five years since #MeToo had sparked a global reckoning. But the world had changed since the zealous, hardline early days of the #MeToo movement. The refrains of "Believe Women" or "Believe All Women," the slogans put forth to entreat people to not automatically dismiss a woman's story of abuse or harassment, were no longer at a fever pitch. Now, almost everyone knew someone who'd been canceled or de-platformed. To some, distinctions between inappropriate comments, harassment, and assault no longer seemed clear, or even relevant. To others, frustrations with "cancel culture," the erosion of due process, and #MeToo's perceived excesses simmered. People seemed more willing to acknowledge the gray areas: a relationship simply not working out isn't the same as an abusive one.

Of course, a court of law differs from the court of public opinion. Even though these public-facing cancelations of men like Aziz Ansari and Harvey Weinstein put varied offenses on equal footing—an awkward hookup and a sexual assault—it wasn't so easy when it came to the law. For many people who were canceled, they never got that far; they were lost in the noise of the accusations before the claims against them could be substantiated or unsubstantiated through legal channels. Finding themselves, rightly or wrongly, inside the maelstrom, some chose to stay in the shadows and fade away, some even committed suicide, and some fought back.

Johnny was taking Amber to court in Fairfax to argue that her *Washington Post* op-ed, though it hadn't named him, *implied* he was an abuser, damaging his reputation and career. Amber was countersuing Johnny for defamation: his insistence that her abuse allegations were a hoax were damaging *her* reputation and career. Little did they know—little did anyone know—that over the course of the trial, *Depp vs Heard* would come to represent something much greater than two celebrities fighting to correct the record and salvage their careers. It would become the ultimate he-said/she-said—with only two direct witnesses (Whitney and Johnny's security guard Travis McGivern)—unfolding amid the shifting winds of #MeToo. Amber and Johnny would transform into symbols of the larger contentions around the accuser and the accused, sparking a new social phenomenon, a world sporting event, and an inflection point for the state of sexual politics in America and around the world.

The French sociologist Jean Baudrillard wrote about celebrities as media constructs, who exist in a glitchy, hyperreal, manufactured version of reality. He spoke about their mediated images being preferred over their real selves, their projected reality being more authentic than their actual reality. Johnny and Amber had public facades, public *faces*, prescribed roles: she the beautiful and intelligent actress-activist, he the bohemian Disney darling. Underneath these facades, who were they really? The trial would broadcast something more raw, and even though they could put on their own performances, if one stared long and hard enough at the livestream, between the blips of internet connectivity, another truth would emerge.

This was a trial about words and their meaning. Did Amber purposefully harm Johnny's reputation when she wrote the op-ed calling herself "a public figure representing domestic abuse," and did she knowingly make a false statement? In order to prove defamation to the jury, the former couple would parse the truth of their domestic-violence claims in court. As plaintiff, Johnny had to prove that Amber's statements were false, had caused him reputational harm, and were made with "actual malice." Though he faced the more challenging legal battle, he did have two advantages in the Fairfax trial that he hadn't had in the UK: the leaked audio recordings of Amber admitting to hitting him had been deemed admissible as evidence, while the text from Stephen Deuters apologizing to Amber for Johnny kicking her on the drunken flight from Boston to LAX had not.

Both parties would claim innocence: Johnny by fashioning himself as a Kentucky gentleman who'd never hit a woman in his life and was himself a victim of Amber's violence. Johnny's team would assert that Amber lied, pathologically, and enacted a battered woman. They'd argue there was overwhelming evidence to show that the stories she'd told about Johnny weren't her own. Domestic violence was an unfortunate common experience for many women, but the narrative didn't belong to Amber, they'd insist. They believed she was acting out a film role, and this insulted and disempowered *actual* victims of domestic violence. Her stories, they claimed, were false, defamatory, and caused harm—not just to Johnny, but to DV victims everywhere.

Amber's team, on the other hand, would continue to argue that she was the victim of a controlling husband with severe addiction issues who'd dominated her career choices and subjected her to a pattern of emotional, physical, and verbal abuse. She was *never* the aggressor, rather a caged animal who occasionally lashed out in self-defense. His addiction was so severe he often blacked out and didn't remember how savagely he behaved. She'd claim her ex-husband was still abusing her through the legal system, and she simply wanted to move on with her life. She insisted that her coming out against Johnny had harmed her career and reputation, like so many other women who had come out against powerful men.

Any civil or criminal case rests on believability. Nowhere is this more resonant than in cases of sexual assault or domestic violence, when crimes are typically committed behind closed doors and it becomes one person's word against the other. These cases face particularly difficult challenges if evidence isn't collected and preserved, or if significant time has passed, placing pressure on the memories of victims, perpetrators, and witnesses. On paper, Amber's case was solid. She had a restraining order, pictures of her injuries, text messages, and a direct witness in her sister, Whitney. How could anyone argue that she wasn't a victim?

But a second (and third) take revealed more to the evidence than was initially understood: the audio recordings and photos often didn't align with Amber's telling of what had transpired. Johnny's story, too, was hard to rationalize. He had to prove that he never abused Amber in any form, yet his text messages alone seemed to imply that he did. He called her abhorrent names and texted his friends about killing her and desecrating her corpse. Amber and others close to her and Johnny claimed he acted differently while under the influence, and that he often blacked out. How could he argue about what he couldn't remember?

To have any shot at victory, Johnny would have to carefully distract the narrative away from these volatile moments, and from his addiction to alcohol and drugs, telling the jury and the world that these substances only made him more docile and helpless. He'd have to paint Amber as the aggressor and craft a picture of a troubled, calculating woman—one who cruelly abused Johnny throughout their relationship. This wasn't a story people were familiar with. And given the fractured social milieu, it was going to be one hell of a story to sell.

On March 28, two weeks before the start of the trial, Ben Chew, Camille Vasquez, and the rest of Johnny's legal team assembled in the Georgetown neighborhood of DC to prepare for the journey ahead of them. For reasons that were never made public, Kathleen Zellner had already stepped back from the case (though she'd continue to support him on social media). *Depp vs Heard* was back in Ben and Camille's hands.

Five days before the trial began, the team checked into the Ritz-Carlton, Tysons Corner, in McLean, Virginia. At first, the trial was only scheduled to last two weeks, but ultimately both parties conferred and decided on six weeks, with a week-long break in the middle, so that Judge Azcarate could attend a pre-scheduled judicial conference. Johnny and his team would live out of the hotel for the duration of the trial. They called themselves "The Black Pearl," after the ship from the Pirates of the Caribbean films, captained by Johnny's Jack Sparrow and said to be "nigh uncatchable."

Despite being recently renovated, the Ritz-Carlton, Tysons Corner, was shabbier than your standard Ritz, but it was attached to the Galleria, a luxury mall with a Gucci and a Louis Vuitton, and was the nicest hotel close to the Fairfax courthouse. The surrounding neighborhood of the twenty-four-floor hotel was made up of corporate parks, defense contractor buildings, and highway construction. For dinner, the legal team would eat catered meals in the War Room as they worked into the night, or they'd travel a few yards to the the Palm Restaurant next door for steaks and chicken parmesan. During their time in Fairfax, they could often be spotted decompressing in the hotel bar, sipping cocktails, snacking on free pretzels and nuts, and sometimes dancing to whatever local band had booked the lounge for the evening.

In addition to his legal team, Johnny's closest associates would live and work out of the hotel too. Jason Forman, Johnny's executive and friend who'd worked for him on and off for seventeen years, checked into Johnny's suite ahead of the trial. He arranged Johnny's four guitars along the wall and organized his recording equipment. Jason also shipped Johnny's vintage manual typewriter and all his art supplies. He ordered a black baby grand piano so Johnny could rehearse for his tour with Jeff Beck, scheduled to begin as soon as the trial ended. Throughout their stint in Fairfax, Johnny and Jason would stay up late inside the suite, with Johnny playing music in the bathroom, setting up a microphone in the hollow shower and an amp just outside of it. It was a nice distraction but sometimes too much of one. Often

Jason had to coax Johnny to bed so that he'd get some rest before a long day.

Jason also coordinated with Johnny's hair and makeup artist, Kenny. If they were going to be in this depressing slice of Northern Virginia for six weeks, Johnny would need to escape the confines of the hotel—but they'd have to get creative if he wanted to fly under the radar. Jason suggested a disguise. They purchased a latex "Old Grandpa" mask found on the Immortal Masks website, a prominent mask house in the Valley back in LA. Then they customized it, making the hair a little thinner, and took to Amazon to shop for old man attire: a wooden cane, orthopedic sneakers, and a T-shirt that said "Florida." Now he could walk around undisturbed, even if he had to act like a geriatric.

One night soon after arriving in Fairfax, Johnny pulled the "Old Grandpa" mask over his head, put on a vintage checkered jacket, and hobbled out of his hotel suite holding a stick of Old Spice deodorant in one hand and a worn-out teddy bear in the other. He took a few steps down the hall and knocked on the door of the War Room. One of the young lawyers on his team, Sam Moniz, opened the door and looked at the decrepit old man in front of him, utterly confused. As the grandpa barged into the room holding out the stick of Old Spice, a junior attorney jumped from her chair and screamed. "Oh my god, oh my god, you can just leave!" she exclaimed, thinking he might be an unhinged Johnny fan. Then she looked closer at the tattoos covering the old man's hands and realized it was her client. They howled as Johnny shuffled old-man-like toward the television in the living room. He grabbed a bag of Starburst and scooted back to the door and down the hall, never breaking character.

Ben Chew was a local—he lived in a DC townhouse just thirty minutes from Fairfax—but most of Johnny's ten-person legal team were transplanted from across the country. The Black Pearl all had nicknames based on Winnie-the-Pooh characters: Camille Vasquez was Tigger; Sam Moniz, a thirty-two-year-old junior attorney from the same Orange County office as Camille, was Eeyore; Ben Chew was Winnie; and thirty-four-year-old calm and mild-mannered Jess Meyers, who'd conduct Johnny's direct exam during the trial, was Owl. Ben's other nickname was "Golden Retriever" because he was so friendly and excitable.

Most of the attorneys on the team were under thirty-five and were ready to pull as many all-nighters as needed. "Obviously we wanted to do the opposite of what Johnny's counsel did in London," Ben said, referring to the trial strategy for the case against *The Sun*, which had failed miserably. They calculated Amber's lawyer, Elaine Bredehoft, would pull her script pretty much straight from the UK trial. But to Ben, things were different this time. "It isn't a bench trial in front of an old man; it's a jury trial. It's a totally different audience, different evidence standards, different laws. Amber's legal team weren't that imaginative."

A week before the trial began, both legal teams were in court arguing over which parts of various prerecorded depositions they wanted to play for the jury. Many of Amber's witnesses didn't testify live, so both legal teams relied on the depositions from these subpoenaed witnesses to argue their case. Amber's team wanted Judge Azcarate to grant evidence of something she'd once told their couple's therapist, Dr. Laurel Anderson, but Jess Meyers objected. "No, that's hearsay, they don't get to put that in," she told Judge Azcarate, who agreed. Jess clocked the look on the opposing legal team's faces. It was clear to Johnny's team that Amber's lawyers weren't prepared for the numerous hearsay objections they were bumping up against. The UK courts had accepted all of Amber's hearsay evidence, but now, items like her own diary entries,

email drafts to herself, therapy notes, and texts to friends, for example, weren't being permitted into trial. "They're like, 'Oh, my
God, *none* of this stuff is coming in,'" Jess recalled. Jess explained
that these were basic evidence rules, and that if the tables were
turned and this had happened to her a week before trial, she'd
have gotten together with her team and rethought their strategy.

On April 10, the eve of the first day of trial proceedings, Camille rode the elevator up to the twenty-third floor to have a chat
with Johnny and make sure he was feeling okay. Before his marriage to Amber, Johnny, despite his superstardom, had been able
to maintain a modicum of privacy around his personal life. No one
knew much about the inner workings of his long union with Vanessa. That privacy was now a distant memory. Starting the next
day, his character and brief marriage to Amber would be prod-
ded at, pried into, and dissected by a team of lawyers before not
only a panel of jurors, but also millions of gawkers on live television. Even his medical records would be made public; a judge had
ordered he sign a HIPAA waiver in order to evaluate his claims
that Amber cut his finger off. Camille remembered asking Johnny
months earlier if he was sure he wanted to go to trial. "Have you
ever been accused of doing something you didn't do?" Johnny had
asked her. "Talk to me when you have."

After checking in on Johnny in his suite, Camille wished him
good night. Before she left, he turned to her with an impish smile
and said, "Just remember, there's no reason why this can't be fun."

The following morning, Johnny's personal therapist, Beechy
Colclough, who lived with Johnny on and off and traveled with
him everywhere, woke him up with a cup of coffee and a calm conversation. Jason picked out a navy three-piece Tom Ford suit. Suits
with a waistcoat would become a uniform for Johnny throughout
the trial. Jason said that Johnny's favorite was a $100 Amazon Ba-

sics suit he had overnighted to the hotel in a pinch. Johnny took a few deep breaths before riding the service elevator down with his security detail, then ducked into a black Cadillac Escalade SUV with tinted windows. Once Johnny's crew was also loaded inside, Mark, his driver and security guard, gunned it down the highway to the Fairfax County Circuit Courthouse, a twenty-minute drive away.

It was a morning routine that Johnny would repeat dozens of times over the next six weeks. Unlike on movie sets, Johnny would always be on time and ready for court in the morning. But this was like no on-camera performance he'd done before. Rather than portraying someone else's story, Johnny was flinging open the doors of his private life in the pursuit of the truth.

CHAPTER 20

Courtroom 5J

It was an overcast morning in Fairfax on Chain Bridge Road, and the satellite on top of the Court TV broadcast van shook as the engineer slammed the heavy door shut. Their logo was italicized above a blood-red fingerprint with the words "Your front row seat to justice." Overhead, a cable line was elaborately jerry-rigged to stretch several hundred yards like a zip line running from the van in the back "press lot" all the way to the brick and columned courthouse in the distance. An electric-green Sunbelt generator hummed over two Court TV employees' banal banter about their hotel breakfast. Over the next six weeks, this parking lot would be their domain, where they'd smoke cigarettes and idle in camp chairs while trial proceedings unfolded each day. It was just another day at the office, traveling the country covering high-profile trials. A posted sign read, "Court TV POOL: All connections and changes must be made by Court TV engineers." In small letters beneath, a warning: "You don't want the blame for taking the pool off the air, do you?"

On April 11, the first day of proceedings, the front lawn of the Fairfax County Circuit Courthouse was eerily quiet. In the lead-up to the trial, there had been anticipation in the press, mostly news articles about the potential for A-list witnesses appearing to testify, but nothing like the wall-to-wall coverage to come. The Fairfax courthouse had made the witness list, along with most other court filings in the case, public on their website. Amber's witness list included names like Elon Musk and James Franco, but ultimately neither would appear. The case was brought in Virginia; non-Virginian citizens weren't compelled to give live testimony unless they volunteered to. If the lawyers couldn't subpoena someone, that was that. Amber's only in-person witness who was not a paid expert would be her sister, Whitney. Johnny would have at least ten nonexpert in-person witnesses appear, which Amber's camp claimed were all on his payroll.

The headlines on day one predicted the trial would become a "mudslinging soap opera," but for now, all was still calm, and only a few curious spectators were on the scene. Courthouse visitors taking care of parking fines trickled in and out of the front doors, seemingly oblivious to the small press presence gathered out front and to the celebrity trial getting underway inside. A smattering of reporters, engrossed in their phone screens, sat in folding chairs behind a handful of tripods set up to catch any action that unfolded at the courthouse entrance. No one had informed them that all the action was happening in the back of the courthouse, where Johnny and Amber would enter and exit through iron security gates flanked by Fairfax County Sheriff's officers.

Near the front doors, Molly Golightly, a life coach and YouTuber from Hershey, Pennsylvania, explained to two men exiting the courthouse on a mundane errand what was happening inside. "That courtroom is LIT!" she said, her hands swinging around, baby pink acrylic nails accented by a large diamond wedding ring. She resembled Anna Nicole Smith with her teased platinum blond hair, full glossy lips, and deep cleavage squeezed into a Lululemon athletic zip-up top. The unassuming men were listening. "Captain Jack Sparrow is inside getting sued and he's suing her," she told them.

"Can we go in?" they asked innocently.

"Yes, you can get a wristband. There aren't that many spectators," she told them. "I actually couldn't take it, the emotions were all over the place. I even got teary-eyed at one point. I realize that Johnny Depp is a very gentle soul."

Courtroom 5J was as drab and unembellished as any modern utilitarian courtroom, with rows of benches on either side—one side for Amber, one side for Johnny—wood-paneled walls, and a brown carpeted aisle where deputies paced back and forth watching the gallery for cell phone usage, which was banned inside the court. Staid historic paintings of Fairfax County judges adorned in robes hung on the walls. A minute before 10 a.m. on day two of the trial, two stern-faced cops closed the doors to the back of the courthouse and reminded everyone to turn off their phones.

"Johnny Depp is coming!"

Whispers spread around the gallery as Johnny and Amber entered from opposite side doors and walked to their corresponding tables. Then the jury entered, and Ben Chew took to the podium to begin opening statements.

The opening and closing statements of a trial are the only opportunities the legal teams have to narrate their clients' cases—creating characters, playing on emotion, and exploiting the theatricality of the trial. In Ben's opening, he explained that Johnny's name was no longer associated with box office success but with false statements made by his ex-wife, Amber Heard. Words matter, Ben emphasized, and this case was about the impact of

Amber's words on Johnny's reputation, specifically the words she used in the op-ed published in the *Washington Post* in 2018. "Ms. Heard did not use Mr. Depp's name in the op-ed. She didn't have to," he said. "A false allegation can devastate a career and it can devastate a family." A pivotal line early in Amber's op-ed—"Two years ago, I became a public figure representing domestic abuse"—implied the abuser was Johnny. Everyone knew it was him because of her very public TRO two years prior in which she *did* name Johnny as her abuser.

Camille Vasquez was up next, and she began by painting a jarring portrait of Amber and Johnny's relationship dynamic: "The evidence will show that Mr. Depp started coping with Ms. Heard in the same way he did as a child. He would try to get away, avoiding the conflict. But his trying to leave enraged Ms. Heard. She would resort to physical violence, throwing things at him, hitting him. She would tell him he was a coward. She would tell him he wasn't man enough because he wouldn't stay and fight with her." Throughout the course of the trial, Johnny's team would return to this portrait of the couple over and over again, portraying Amber as relentlessly needy and overly controlling. She demanded Johnny's full emotional attention, and when she didn't get it, she snapped. Johnny was a classic avoidant, his lawyers said; he'd conditioned himself to escape from conflict as a kid living with an abusive mother.

Johnny's team highlighted what they saw as Amber's calculating behavior from the start of the relationship. "She pursued him. She wooed him. The evidence will show that Ms. Heard went to great lengths to win him over by playing the doting girlfriend," Camille said. Johnny's lawyers went on to explain that in the early days of their relationship, Amber would treat Johnny like a king, kneeling before him every night when he got home, removing his boots and pouring him a glass of wine. One time, Johnny kicked off his boots himself and Amber told him, "No. That's my job."

They didn't shy away from calling Amber a liar, but they also recast her "hoax" as Amber taking on a new theatrical role. Portraying Amber as a #MeToo opportunist emerged as a core tenet of the Black Pearl's legal strategy. It also sparked fervent public debate over the idea that someone could capitalize on the movement for personal gain. "She presented herself as the face of the #MeToo movement, the virtuous representative of innocent women across the country and the world who have truly suffered abuse," Camille said in her opening. "Ms. Heard, as you know, is an actress. When she accused Mr. Depp of abuse . . . Ms. Heard took on the role of a lifetime."

It was no coincidence that in Camille Vasquez, Brown Rudnick was deploying a young, charismatic female attorney who would offer the world a fresh, if provocative, take on #MeToo—that feminism could be exploited for personal gain—and do it all with a perfect blowout and 100-watt smile. A few spectators in the courtroom cried as Ben and Camille delivered their opening statements. Amber looked on stoically as Johnny's lawyers painted her as a lying and deceptive seductress.

After Camille finished, it was time for Amber's side to make their opening statement. Amber needed her lawyer Elaine Bredehoft to craft an emotionally compelling story of her case and of her character for the jury, the way Johnny's team just had for him.

"The evidence in this case, simply put, is overwhelming and compelling," Elaine began, addressing the jury and speaking in a harried tone. "In the six weeks, we're going to try to show you as much as we possibly can. There are many, many, many photographs." She explained that Johnny's team would allege the photos of Amber's injuries were edited, and then conceded that perhaps they were: "Well, all iPhones have the photo editing where you can make it a little lighter, a little darker, move it to the center or not. That doesn't discredit the photographs," she said. "They're all very legitimate photographs. And listen carefully to the evidence from the experts and you will find every single piece is authenticated and is true." Then she teased the Cabinet Video, showing Johnny yelling and slamming stuff in his kitchen. "That's going to be a pretty graphic one for you to see."

Elaine moved on from describing the evidence to introducing her client, Amber. Elaine told the jury that Amber grew up very poor in a ranch area outside of Austin and that her late mother, Paige, dropped out of medical school to marry her father. She shared a vivid story from Amber's childhood: Amber broke her arm several times as a child helping her father tame wild horses, but she wasn't deterred by the pain and learned how to never show fear. Amber's attorneys promised to show Johnny as an "obsessed ex-husband hellbent on revenge." They agreed that Johnny's career was in crisis but that this wasn't Amber's fault, it was his own, because of the choices *he* had made.

The horse-breaking story was compelling, but Elaine aborted it and pivoted to the allegations of violence and abuse. She portrayed Amber as similar to other victims of domestic violence: she'd married a monster she only wanted to rescue. "Amber made the mistake that millions before her and millions after her have who are victims of domestic abuse: she chose to stay and try to fix the problem, thinking that she could do that."

Elaine's delivery seemed rushed and disorganized, and at times nearly incoherent. "Now, you'll see a video from them of the Bahamas place that they stayed in on his island, and the video just conveniently leaves out the wardrobe in the bathroom where he committed the assault. It just goes around and makes it look like it's one room, and his kids were there, and there's no way they could have done that. But you'll hear the testimony, and you'll see the pictures." Throughout her opening, Elaine spoke as if the jury already knew the details of these alleged incidents. Her statement unfolded like a haphazard highlight reel of her case.

She ended by arguing that Amber had lost out on numerous film and commercial opportunities because of Johnny and Adam's claims that Amber had devised an abuse hoax. "Nobody will touch her. She's a pariah.

"Enough is enough," Elaine continued. "But we're also going to ask you to hold him responsible and try to fully and fairly compensate Amber for what he has done to her."

Elaine was representing Amber alongside another lawyer, Benjamin Rottenborn. Rottenborn had joined the case early in Roberta Kaplan's tenure, before they knew it would proceed to trial. He'd met Roberta on a case against white nationalists who marched on the University of Virginia for the Unite the Right Rally, in which one of the participants drove his car into a crowd and killed one person and injured thirty-five others. Rottenborn, who was trim with salt-and-pepper hair in his mid-forties, was quick on his feet and self-possessed. He had his own brand of lawyerly charisma and a passionate way of speaking.

Rottenborn later said that there were people who used Amber's trial to get famous, but "I'm not one of them." He rented his own Airbnb near the courthouse, and on the weekends he'd drive more than three hours home to Roanoke to spend time with his family.

The strategy of his opening statement was to give a dry and formal discussion of the legal technicalities of the First Amendment. He read aloud the nearly eight-hundred-word *Washington Post* op-ed, displaying it on the courtroom screens. The article's headline in the paper's print edition had been much less provocative: "A Transformative Moment for Women" versus the digital headline that read, "I spoke up against sexual violence—and faced our culture's wrath. That has to change." Amber asserted that she hadn't written the headline and that she didn't even notice it until the recent litigation. But she'd linked to the online edition of her op-ed in a tweet she posted at the time of publication. She'd later tell the courtroom that when she tweeted the op-ed, she hadn't noticed the title of the article. That title, plus two other statements in the op-ed—"Then two years ago, I became a public figure representing domestic abuse" and "I had the rare vantage point of seeing, in real time, how institutions protect men accused of abuse"—made Johnny's entire case for defamation.

A few lines into Rottenborn's reading of the op-ed, the mood in the courtroom shifted. People stared at the ceiling and glanced around at one other. Wrapping up his opening statement, Rottenborn said, "I know that was a lot, but that is the central issue in this case . . . The article isn't about Johnny Depp. The article is about the social change for which [Amber] is advocating and that the First Amendment protects . . . It's about the freedom of speech. It's not about the soap opera that Depp will turn this case into. It's not about who you like better. It's not even about whether you agree with the words she wrote. It's about her right to speak them."

A clinical discussion about the First Amendment, while warranted, fell emotionally flat next to the intrigue that had been laid out by Camille Vasquez and Ben Chew. Only two days into the trial, there were already whispers that it might go in a different direction than the one against *The Sun*.

The first five days of trial included opening statements, testimonies from Johnny's employees, and fact witnesses who challenged

Amber's assertions that Johnny was an abuser and who instead cast her as the aggressor. Johnny's sister, Christi Dembrowski, testified about their turbulent childhood and described moments in which she'd witnessed Amber bullying her brother. Johnny's longtime friend Isaac Baruch, whose art career he bankrolled and whom he let live in one of the ECB penthouses rent-free, described Johnny as a kind and gentle human. He became emotional as he described the hurt Amber's allegations had inflicted on their inner circle. He also had the courtroom chuckling as he commented on Amber's "great teeth" in his thick New York accent.

On day six, Johnny's sound technician, Keenan Wyatt, who'd been with Johnny and Amber during one altercation on a private jet, said the fight hadn't happened the way Amber described it. On day ten, Johnny's estate manager for the property in the Bahamas, Tara Roberts, told the jury via live video that she once witnessed Johnny trying to leave a violent situation with Amber. As more witnesses were called by Johnny's lawyers, the jury heard testimony from Sean Bett, Johnny's bodyguard, who testified that Amber would argue about money with Johnny and that he once heard her say, "Am I going to be taken care of if you die?" when asking about his life insurance policy. Sean said Johnny told him Amber would "slap him on the side of the face" or "push him" if he was late or didn't get back to her. The jury also viewed photos of Johnny's alleged injuries caused by Amber, showing bruises and blackened eyes, a cut on his nose, and the infamous photos of his severed finger.

One running theme presented by Johnny's team was that he was an addict, but it didn't make him a violent person. They seemed to want to get ahead of his substance use and have Johnny speak openly about his struggles with pills and booze, because they knew Amber's side would emphasize his raging addictions and blackouts over and over as proof that he was a violent person, and if he says he wasn't, then he doesn't remember.

In the early days of the trial, the thinly veiled metaphor Amber used in her op-ed, alluding to Johnny as a "ship that is a huge enterprise," began to surface as truth: Johnny was a one-man institution. This was central to Amber's defense strategy. Because his witnesses were his paid employees and their lives depended on him and his bankable star power, they couldn't be objective. "When [the ship] strikes an iceberg," she wrote "there are a lot of people on board desperate to patch up holes—not because they believe in or even care about the ship, but because their own fates depend on the enterprise." But Johnny's witnesses were unified: he was imperfect, but Amber was Machiavellian.

When Johnny first took the stand, on the sixth day of trial, he wore a dark gray three-piece suit with a brown shirt and paisley tie. His hair was slicked back into a ponytail and his facial hair trimmed into a neat goatee. That day he'd be answering questions from his lawyer Jess Meyers. Her mane of brown curly hair was worn down and she looked out from behind circular, clear-framed glasses. The camel-colored suit she had on blended into the paneled wood, beige walls, and podium she held on to. She later said the outfit was intentional; the point was for her to disappear. This was about Johnny, not her.

Johnny's four days of direct testimony proceeded nearly uninterrupted, by neither his attorneys nor the defense. When answering Jess Meyers's third question, "Can you please tell the jury in your own words about your childhood upbringing?" he monologued for eight minutes without objection. Johnny said that Amber was like his mother Betty Sue, and he employed the same defensive strategies with Amber as he had with his mom. In this narrative, Johnny was his dad, and like his dad, Johnny was an escapist—he ditched the situation when things got violent. Throughout Johnny's childhood, his dad had kept to himself, but Betty Sue's dark moods took away any semblance of peace. Like his ex-wife, Johnny's mother threw stuff at him: an ashtray at his head, a high-heel shoe. She whipped her kids with green switches—limbs that were still fresh so that they wouldn't break and it'd hurt more. One day, when Johnny came home from school, he found his father's stuff was gone. His dad couldn't stand the insults and violence from Betty Sue anymore.

Here was Johnny weaving a painful tale about his childhood that the jury and the public could sympathize with. "You start to slowly realize that you are in a relationship with your mother, in a sense. And I know that that sounds perverse and obtuse, but the fact is that some people search for weaknesses in people, and that is to say sensitivities, and when you've told that person your life and what you've lived through, what you've been through, just as happens in relationships, the more that became ammunition for Ms. Heard to either verbally decimate me or to send me into a kind of a tailspin of confusion and depression, and well, it's not a happy day, it's not a happy week, it's not a happy month when you're constantly being told how wrong you are about this or that, what an idiot you are, or anything. It just—then it increased, increased and became an endless—it became endless, that endless circle."

Hours into Johnny's direct examination, Benjamin Rottenborn offered one of his first objections. When the objection was sustained by Judge Azcarate, Johnny hit back with, "Good one." This small yet tense interaction would set the tone for the strained back-and-forth between Rottenborn and Johnny throughout the trial.

Johnny endeared himself to the jury and the world while giving what was essentially the longest, deepest on-camera interview of his career. He was an imperfect Hollywood star, admitting his deficiencies and addictions, while coming across as charming, poetic, and funny. Almost in real time, online clips of his testimony were being pushed by the algorithm across sites like TikTok, YouTube, and Instagram, power-boosting his counternarrative to Amber's across the farthest reaches of the internet.

During the cross-examination, Rottenborn introduced Johnny's text messages as evidence, reading them aloud. Reading the texts himself, rather than asking Johnny to, was strategic. "I knew that if Johnny read them, he would do some kind of self-serving performance. He'd mumble or editorialize his way through them." The contrast between a buttoned-up Rottenborn reading the jumbled, obscene prose from Johnny was jarring.

"'For the idiot cow. I'll smack the ugly cunt around before I let her in. Did that worthless hooker arrive?'" Rottenborn read.

Johnny looked grim as he acknowledged this was a text he sent about his then-girlfriend Amber. But other texts were comically inane and the internet went wild with the footage of Rottenborn speaking as Johnny. Innumerable remixes were made on TikTok. "You text her," Rottenborn asked, "'Rears, uhh, tears, beers, sheers, sapphires, leers, jeers, peers, queers, here's, faquirs, mouseketeers ears. I can go all night, DJ Maxipad! The old vintage motherfucker you went for . . . Dumbass'?"

Johnny leaned into his microphone to correct him. "I was signing off as Dumbass."

"Let's go to the next one," Rottenborn continued. "'You sicken me . . . Leave me fuckin' be, Officer square head . . . Your display of guilt and matronliness as a lesbian camp councllor was plenty . . . Your future is on display. Best [of] luck . . .'" Rottenborn wanted to show Johnny in a bad light through his texts, but the courtroom gallery could barely stifle its laughter.

In addition to lurid texts, Rottenborn presented inconsistencies in Johnny's own account of what happened to his finger in Australia. At one point, Johnny told Dr. Kipper that he smashed his finger in a large accordion door. But later, he said the injury was caused by Amber throwing a vodka bottle at him, severing the tip clean off. Johnny testified that he'd lied to Kipper about the accordion door. Rottenborn also wanted to underscore that Johnny's memories of what happened were generally unreliable because of his heavy substance use. On this matter, Johnny didn't do himself any favors. During his pretrial deposition with Elaine, which was referenced in his cross-examination, Johnny was asked how booze and drugs affected his memory. "My memory is actually very good," he answered. "I don't think anything has been affected by an overabundance of foreign chemicals in my brain. It's been played out in every act of this sort of Chekhovian kind of puppet show that, you know, every incident starts with—I'm sorry. What What? I don't even know what I'm talking about now."

Finally, Rottenborn drilled into the idea that Johnny sabotaged his own career by being constantly late to set and unprepared to shoot. According to Rottenborn, his financial troubles started *before* Amber entered the picture and worsened as he started suing everyone around him. The last few movies he starred in had flopped, and he simply wasn't the bankable star he once was.

To Johnny's fans, however, this argument didn't resonate. Johnny was Captain Jack Sparrow, Edward Scissorhands, Willy

Wonka. If a movie he starred in was a failure, it was *in spite of* Johnny, not because of him.

It remained to be seen if the jury felt the same.

Back at the Ritz-Carlton, on day nine of the trial, and after his testimony had concluded, Johnny sat cross-legged on the carpeted floor of his penthouse suite assembling a spliff of hash, rolled with his preferred Rizla Liquorice papers. He smelled like patchouli, his left arm covered wrist to elbow with bracelets. He flipped through a book of inspirational quotes and photos that, like the bracelets on his wrist, had been gifted by fans. Around 10 p.m., Johnny's assistant Jason poured glasses of red wine, and Johnny snacked from plates of chicken fingers, fries, tacos, and grilled cheese sandwiches.

The Black Pearl, still in their courtroom attire, gathered around a large coffee table, decompressing after the day of proceedings. The cold air from the AC unit stirred the smoke from Johnny's spliffs. He'd made the penthouse his temporary home, and had even taped one of his own paintings—a lanky rabbit figure rendered against a splashy red abstract background—over a piece of generic hotel artwork. The rabbit was a figure he called The Bunnyman that he saw in a recurring dream, and he'd come to frequently use it in his art. Johnny's website NeverFearTruth.com, where he sold, among other products, original art, merch, and NFTs, described the figure as appearing "like a guardian who stands with a sword of truth, protects the heart and, when needed, a shapeshifter who evolves into whomever the artist needs him to be."

The fireplace mantel in Johnny's suite was dotted with plush toys, trinkets, and greeting cards, all gifts from fans. A large clothing rack stuffed with his three-piece suits had been rolled in front of the oversized hotel windows. His bedspread, a plain white duvet, had also become a canvas: on it he'd painted a giant cartoon image of a turd, above which he wrote his nickname for his ex-wife: "Scamber." Johnny was still disturbed, or maybe just obsessed, by the poop. He kept a color-corrected picture of it on his phone. If you zoomed in, you could see what he claimed were corn and beans, which he said was entirely incriminating since they were part of Josh Drew's Mexican meal for Amber's thirtieth birthday celebration.

Joelle Rich, a British lawyer and Johnny's crisis reputation manager, was huddled alone in the corner of his hotel suite, sitting cross-legged and swiping on her phone. Each day in court, Joelle sat behind Johnny, analyzing the jury's body language and facial reactions. She cut a formidable figure in the courtroom, dressed impeccably in designer suits and carrying expensive handbags. Tonight, though, she wore leggings and a sweatshirt, cradling a glass of wine in one hand, her phone in the other.

Johnny had nicknames for nearly everyone on the opposing side: Elaine Bredehoft was "Breadsticks"; Benjamin Rottenborn was "Rotten Egg"; Adam Nadelhaft, another lawyer on Amber's team, was "Nadelcock"; and Elon Musk was "Mollusk." Inside the suite, the conversation turned to the viral social-media remixes of the trial on TikTok. Jason pulled up the team's favorite—there were already hundreds to choose from—on the flat-screen TV above the mantel. The video featured a catchy pop song with heavy reverb mixed with clips from Johnny's testimony. A clip of Rottenborn reading aloud the mocking text Johnny sent to Amber—"Leave me fuckin' be, Officer square head"—had everyone bursting out laughing.

As he rolled another spliff, Johnny explained that, more than once, he'd tried to settle with Amber privately, but she'd refused. He knew the odds were stacked against him, and that pretty much every legal expert weighing in on the case was predicting he'd lose, but he didn't care, he had to keep fighting. He couldn't let his kids think these things about him.

Around midnight, the lawyers got up to say good night and retreated to their hotel rooms. Joelle stayed behind, clicking through endless TikToks and taking notes.

"I know what's happened to me, all of this, this is not normal. And I've accepted that," he said. "Now I just have to get through it and move on with my life."

CHAPTER 21

Ren Faire on Crack

The view outside Johnny's tall hotel room windows stretched all the way to Fairfax, where, over the course of the first week of the trial, the energy in the small Virginia suburb had begun to shift. By day six of the trial, Johnny supporters, curious spectators, and members of the press had started forming lines to get inside the courthouse. Once Johnny took the stand, online viewership of the trial multiplied by 4.5 times; his testimony alone would later be tallied at 2.7 million hours watched. The mainstream media attention surrounding the case was also picking up, as was the social-media punditry, complete with hashtags and memes on TikTok, Reddit, and Twitter. Depp fans from around the country had even taken up residence at the hotel, having sleuthed out the Ritz-Carlton as Johnny's base camp. Anyone who worked for Johnny—his lawyers, his security team, his drivers—suddenly held cult status too. Just by passing Johnny's people in the lobby, the fame-seekers felt famous by extension. They knew Jack Sparrow himself was several floors above them. They were breathing his same air, and it was intoxicating.

In the first days of *Depp vs Heard,* Courtroom 5J had been barely half-full and the media presence was scant. Angenette

Levy of the Law&Crime Network was one of the few reporters there from day one. Law&Crime, or "Court TV 2.0," was founded by Dan Abrams of ABC News, who started his career at Court TV and gained a profile covering the O. J. Simpson trial. During *Depp vs Heard*, the network offered the public an uninterrupted livestream of the trial online—ultimately tallying more than 138 hours of footage—with an interactive chat box of rowdy commentary on the side. They quickly became the most-watched coverage of the trial and would hit nearly a billion views on its content related to the case from the start of the trial to the verdict.

Court TV, which ran the televised trial feed, couldn't keep up with those numbers with its anchor commentary and commercial breaks, something many viewers could choose to go without. "People caught wind of our feed and started tuning in. It became like a compulsion," Angenette said. She kept hearing, "I don't want to watch a news story or read somebody else's article and have it filtered." People following the trial wanted to watch it live and uninterrupted and decide for themselves what to think.

Many trial followers were determined to witness the action with their own eyes. One morning on the Fairfax County courthouse lawn, trial spectators Robin and Randy walked the grounds with Donald and Danny, their two freshly groomed collies dressed in white-and-blue-striped ties. The couple had driven from Cincinnati, Ohio, where celebrity sightings were as rare as UFOs. For divorcé Randy, this case hit close to home. He said when he divorced his ex-wife and mother of his kids, she filed ninety-six accusations of abuse against him and, suddenly and without questions, he wasn't allowed to see his children. According to Randy, he battled his ex in the court system for six years and eventually won full custody of his kids. His ex-wife ultimately landed in jail.

"Something's really got to change," Randy said. "Just because someone said you did something, doesn't mean you're guilty."

His wife, Robin, agreed. "It seems too easy to accuse," she said. In her mind, people lie all the time—man or woman, it didn't matter.

"Just 'cause you say something, doesn't mean it's true," Randy said.

During another day of trial proceedings, YouTuber Molly Golightly ran across the road when she spotted witness Isaac Baruch, who'd been the second witness to testify. Molly's impulse to approach Isaac wasn't surprising, as she liked to insert herself in the action of high-profile cases. Before the Fairfax trial, she'd gone viral in 2021 for a stunt related to the Gabby Petito murder case. Gabby's boyfriend and prime suspect Brian Laundrie was still a fugitive when Molly went to his parents' home in Florida and placed a laundry basket and a sign reading "Dirty Laundrie come clean" next to a memorial constructed for Gabby on their front lawn.

Over the course of a few weeks, Captain Justin Sherwood and Lieutenant Charles Taggart of the Fairfax County Sheriff's Office watched as their suburban courthouse transformed into a freaky festival: there was a pair of stinky alpacas wearing rainbow pom-pom necklaces, countless Jack Sparrow impersonators, and a lady, in a nod to Poopgate, "dressed like a turd" who arrived holding a cane and wearing a fuzzy poop emoji hat, a brown crop top, and a brown tutu. Someone even managed to get a full-scale pirate ship on the courthouse grounds. "It was kind of like a Ren Faire on crack," Lieutenant Taggart commented. The sheriff's office tracked the IDs of every spectator that waited in line to get a wristband for entry to the courtroom; they logged driver's licenses from forty-one different states and passports from fifteen different countries. One woman named Jacinta traveled all the way from Australia and used her entire four weeks of earned vacation time to be at the trial.

Most of them were there for Johnny. During the hour-long lunch breaks, figures from the Johnny Depp trial Twitterverse, which first sprung up during his lawsuit against *The Sun*, milled about the cafeteria tucked in the basement of the courthouse. There were Johnny supporters like "Laura B," aka "TheRealLauraB," a whip-smart self-taught legal researcher, sitting with Jax, aka "TheNamesQ," a wealthy Hollywood hipster with a designer backpack and oversized glasses. There was Brooke, aka "Depply-Hallows," petite but passionate, with a major crush on Johnny, and also "ThatBrianFella," a blond, muscled Kansas boy-next-door bro. Through Twitter, they'd all become friends and formed a community.

One day, a Johnny supporter wearing a top hat, white T-shirt, and black Converse sneakers walked by under an overcast sky holding a sign on white poster board scrawled in permanent marker: "We believe you, Johnny, have faith." Another young woman in pigtails and a purple velour fedora held a tiny black pirate flag and wore a red *Cry Baby* T-shirt with Johnny's juvenile face emblazoned on it. She pulled out a ukulele and strummed softly as she sat on the courthouse lawn. A woman wearing a white beanie and big silver rings similar to Johnny's held a poster that read, "JOHNNY IS INNOCENT." Local hairstylist SanDee Edwards, a self-proclaimed "celebrity chaser," was there to support Johnny, and thrilled a celebrity trial had landed on her doorstep. It wasn't her first—after Michael Jackson's trial in 2005, she and some of his fans followed him to Neverland Ranch, where he took her hand inside his and thanked her for her support. "The softest hand I've ever felt," she said. SanDee tragically lost her husband—her soulmate and best friend—only months before the trial in Fairfax, and she found the trial to be a needed distraction. Waiting in line for a wristband one night at 4 a.m., she and her neighbor Dusty speculated that Amber's bruises could have been from Botox.

Almost every day of the trial, a few minutes before the courthouse opened, Johnny's Escalade pulled up blaring Bob Marley. As his car slowed, Johnny rolled down his window and leaned out of the car, his arms outstretched to receive the drawings, books, and jewelry being thrust at him by fans. As the electronic gate opened, he smiled and clasped his fist in front of his chest in gratitude. Then his SUV drove through the gate, and Johnny stepped out of the car along with his security team and support crew: his reputation manager, Joelle Rich; his therapist, Beechy; his sister, Christi; and his longtime friend and avid supporter, Josh Richman. Fans yelled out, "JOHNNY! JOHNNY!" Then the courthouse door closed behind him, leaving his supporters, mostly women aged eighteen to sixty-five, screaming and jumping up and down. One of them, Rebecca, a young woman in jeans and a ponytail, said she took time off from her job at an Applebee's a several-hours' drive away to show her support for Johnny. She said she grew up with domestic violence—her dad abused her mom—but she wanted to support men who've been abused too.

In order to get a seat inside the courtroom, visitors needed to obtain a brightly colored wristband (they changed color day to day) from the Fairfax County Sheriff's Office, which had set up a folding table outside of the courthouse. When the first hundred wristbands ran out, they'd hand out fifty more designated for the overflow courtroom, where the trial proceedings would be broadcast on a TV. The hundred wristbands quickly became a coveted commodity, and diehards started lining up for them outside the courthouse the night before trial, sleeping on the ground and ordering food via Grubhub. There were rumors of counterfeit wristbands, paid line holders hired by journalists, fake sob stories to cut the line, and one wristband that sold for $4,000. Some supporters' names were being mentioned in court by Elaine Bredehoft, who alleged Johnny's fans were working with Adam Waldman to amplify the hoax claims. The fans felt intimately involved in the unfolding drama, even celebrated.

At the courthouse, the legal teams had to use the same restroom as the trial spectators, and during breaks, Camille Vasquez was often mobbed inside the women's bathroom. Spectators were also seen intermingling with jurors. Jury sequestration is sometimes used in high-profile trials to avoid exposing jurors to community pressures and media bias. They're put up in a hotel for the duration of the trial and live in isolation without newspapers, phones, wi-fi, or television. Sequestration is rare (it's expensive, and the isolation is hard on jurors) but still invoked for media-frenzied trials. Jurors were fully sequestered during the Bill Cosby trial in 2017, and partially sequestered in 2021 for Derek Chauvin's trial. But those were criminal cases; *Depp vs Heard* was a civil trial, where sequestration is almost unheard of. The jurors hadn't been sequestered in Fairfax, and surely they'd noticed the throngs of fans wearing Johnny Depp T-shirts and Jack Sparrow costumes inside the cafeteria. Were they also aware of the twenty-four-hour line to get into the trial, or the masses of Depp supporters with posters and megaphones that gathered each morning and evening in the back of the courthouse chanting that Amber was a liar and her story a #MeToo hoax? Would this affect their view of her and her testimony?

The trial became daily and nightly entertainment. Like the O. J. Simpson and Menendez brothers trials before it, *Depp vs*

Heard was spoofed on *Saturday Night Live,* where jokes were made about poop in the bed and Johnny's severed fingertip. It wasn't just Amber and Johnny being spoofed and parodied; both sets of lawyers became fodder for content and caricature, especially on the Internet. A TikTok video showing Ben Chew looking impressed with one of Johnny's doodles quickly exceeded five million views. Many videos focused on Elaine's difficulties in court, offering compilations of her struggling with words, mispronouncing others, and mixing up people's names.

During the trial, Johnny gained 9.56 million new followers on Instagram—a hundred times more than Amber, who gained 91,511. Factions of loyal fans, often referred to as "Deppheads," formed around Johnny, and they were willing to get their hands dirty, playing armchair detective with whatever public information they could find in order to defend his personal and professional reputation. Dozens of YouTubers and Twitch streamers became full-time Amber Heard smear machines. #AmberHeardIs-APsychopath trended on Twitter for weeks straight. On TikTok, #JusticeForJohnnyDepp would ultimately tally more than 15 billion views.

These fan websites and social-media accounts differed from other heartthrob celebrity fandoms in the intensity of the parasocial behavior on display. Johnny's fans felt like they knew him—and Johnny had always reciprocated the intimacy, freely kissing them, hugging them, and receiving their gifts. Johnny appeared to be as loyal to his fans as they were to him, always willing to stay and sign autographs, do meet-and-greets and take photos, often to the chagrin of his security team. One fan, Yvonne de Boer, an ex–costume designer from Los Angeles with jet-black hair who carried a tote bag printed with a photo of her and Johnny hugging at a 2016 Hollywood Vampires concert, described herself as

Johnny's fan for decades. She fell in love with him when she saw *Edward Scissorhands* and, ever since, she's followed him to red carpets, music shows, premieres, and now the Fairfax County Circuit Courthouse—anything she can do to spend time with him. According to Yvonne, she and Johnny share "a very special loving bond and connection" and she claims Johnny knows her and will come to her first when he sees her in a pack of fans. She used up her entire vacation time to be in Fairfax for the duration of the trial and to sit in the seats behind him.

Throughout the trial, Paul Barresi, the PI hired by Amber's former legal team, became a hero among Johnny's supporters after he started tweeting tidbits from "the Barresi files," the "treasure trove" of research he'd dug up about Johnny back in 2019. (Later, Paul would self-publish a book about his investigation: *Johnny Depp's Accidental Fixer: How a Hollywood Sleuth Saved a Pirate's Honor.*) Paul learned quickly that pro-Depp content fared much better online than even neutral content he shared about Amber, which garnered hateful tirades and DMs. He went on to trace Johnny's entire family tree to his seventeenth-century great-grandfather eight generations back and posted several photos to Twitter of their ancient crumbling gravestones, to the delight of Johnny's fans. "With $100,000 thanks to Elon Musk," Paul posted, "I found no evidence Johnny abused women. I challenge anyone to provide proof to the contrary. I'll put 1000 pages of my factual reports & equal measure of notes against your findings any day. Got anything, bring it on or SHUT THE FUCK UP!" According to Paul, he even became buds with Adam Waldman. "I told him he wasn't a lawyer, he was Johnny's consigliere. Adam loved that."

Leading up to and during the trial, a new wave of internet journalists worked around the clock on YouTube, Instagram, Twitter, TikTok, and Substack to create a counternarrative to the mainstream, liberal media reporting, which they felt was squarely on Amber's side. In the middle of the trial, *Vox* published a story with the headline, "Why the Depp-Heard trial is so much worse than you realize: Amber Heard is just the first target of a new extremist playbook." A *New Yorker* piece by Jessica Winter, also published midtrial, urged readers to empathize with Amber even if they didn't "trust" her, and offered a laundry list of Amber's evidence, then cited and refuted two pieces of Johnny's evidence of being abused by Amber and compared the entire trial to "a high-budget, general-admission form of revenge porn." Winter assured readers the "core matter" of the trial was simple and rested on half a sentence in the op-ed which didn't name Johnny.

The internet journalists became their own investigators and lawyers, crowdsourcing evidence and poking holes in the stories—mostly Amber's. Before the trial even started, they'd begun to highlight the issues in her story, including her previous arrest for domestic violence against Tasya Van Ree, and clips from the never-aired reality show in which Whitney's friends seemed to suggest Amber had beaten Whitney up. The motivation to investigate was as much about the thrill of internet sleuthing as it was a response to a liberal media they believed wouldn't report a #MeToo story without bias. The media wrote about Johnny's fans like Hillary's "deplorables." "Bots, shitposters, men's-rights activists, women who were in middle school when 'Edward Scissorhands' came out" is how Winter described Johnny's supporters.

While the trial was a massive and complicated undertaking for the Fairfax County Sheriff's Office, it was also comical in its absurdity—like a rollicking county fair in a sleepy meat-and-potatoes community. With a range of Johnny Depp–inspired costumes, rambunctious children, and older women with intense celebrity crushes, the trial had a uniquely modern sense of triviality, more like Judge Judy than O. J. Simpson, even though the subject of the trial was darkly serious. On one occasion, the sheriff's office had to kick a trial spectator out of the courtroom who was doing blowjob gestures for the pool cameras and making other obscene hand signals on live television. "They knew where to position themselves, and they knew right where the camera was pointing," the Captain of the Fairfax County Sheriff's Office said with a laugh. During another day at trial, Johnny's security guard Mark Gibbs farted loudly. Everyone who heard it erupted in laughter.

Most mornings, by the time Amber arrived in her black Dodge Ram truck, the majority of the spectators had dispersed, but some remained to heckle her. She pulled into the gate to boos and jeers from the small crowd, who hurled hateful and vitriolic slurs—"blonde devil" and "whore." One shook a poster reading "Scamber Turd." On any given day, Amber had only one to three of her own supporters. One of them, Dan Kim, held a simple white poster board written in black marker: #IStandWithAmber. He emphasized free speech and wanting to listen to all views and talk about it in a considerate manner. Another young woman in a brown cardigan held back tears and said, "She leaves court every day and people shout, 'I don't believe you.' People made it into a funny TikTok trend to dance and act out her sexual-assault testimony. It's just sick. It's become a trend to hate her." The woman explained that there had been a power imbalance in Amber and Johnny's relationship, and therefore mutual abuse couldn't have occurred. Because, as she explained, "He's older than her, richer than her, more famous than her," it wasn't possible that she could have abused him.

Another woman in a large black fedora hat traveled sixteen

hours from New Hampshire, taking a series of buses and trains to get to Fairfax. She held up a sign that referenced a text Stephen Deuters sent to Amber after the infamous flight from Boston: "'When I told him he kicked you, he cried. It was disgusting . . .' —One of Depp's enablers, to Amber Heard before she ever fought back." She said this was a witch hunt against a woman who'd already proven her case over many years. This supporter was forty-eight and had recently found herself in an abusive relationship for the first time in her life. In her ex, she saw so many of the same characteristics as Johnny.

One morning, Amber exited her car followed by her personal assistant, Jacquelyn, and Pamela Johnson, a representative from Travelers Insurance, one of the insurers covering Amber's legal bills. Someone heckled her through the gate, waving a sign that read, "BOO Amber Turd!" with a poop emoji drawn on it. Someone else yelled, "Get fucked!" before Amber disappeared into the courthouse.

This cruelty was nothing compared to the online mob, where people were attacking Amber in droves with obscenities and accusations, and gleefully fantasizing about doing violence to her. Days before she was set to testify, Amber fired her PR team, Precision Strategies, led by Obama's former deputy campaign manager Stephanie Cutter. According to sources, Amber was fed up with the intense social-media backlash against her and decided she needed to start fresh.

It was an unorthodox move to adopt an entirely new PR strategy in the midst of a high-profile trial. But her chosen replacement was even more perplexing: David Shane of Shane Communications, who was notorious for allegations about his own #MeToo transgressions.

Almost as soon as David Shane landed in Fairfax, he started

getting his own bad press. "Why Amber Heard's Spin Doctor Is Facing His Own PR Nightmare," a *Newsweek* headline read. A *Daily Mail* headline was less subtle: "Amber Heard's new PR guru hired to paint Johnny Depp as an alcohol-bingeing abuser has two DUI arrests, left two jobs after sexual harassment claims and is known as 'the walking #MeToo case' in industry circles." In the article, David's former colleagues said he was investigated by two different HR departments for "a slew of complaints." A woman named Hollie Doker said she met David on the invite-only dating-app Raya. After two fancy dates in limousines, she alleged he forced her head down into his crotch, insinuating she owed him a hookup for taking her out. She refused, and David became angry, allegedly telling her, "I'll call you a fucking Uber." Afterward, Hollie warned other women about him in a private LA Facebook group and reported him to Raya, which, according to Hollie, kicked him off the app. David firmly denied the allegations.

David's past allegations didn't seem to deter Amber from "Hurricane Shane," his nickname in PR circles, perhaps because he'd squared off with Johnny before, when he was hired by The Management Group during the lawsuit with Johnny. But as a champion of #MeToo and sexual-assault survivors, it was a bold move to team up with a man whose alleged history of sexual impropriety seemed to be an open secret.

CHAPTER 22

Breaking Horses

On day fourteen of the trial, Amber walked up to the stand wearing a baby-blue collared shirt and suit jacket, her blond hair swept elegantly to one side. She told the jury why she was there: her ex-husband had sued her for an op-ed she wrote. Elaine asked her how she felt, and Amber stumbled over her words, looking straight at the jury: "This is the most painful thing I've ever gone through."

From the start, Amber and Elaine crafted a version of Amber as the "everywoman." Amber described for the jury her humble beginnings growing up in a small town outside of Austin with her younger sister, "Whit." Elaine asked what her parents did, and Amber picked up the narrative Elaine had begun for the jury in her opening statement. "My father broke horses," Amber replied.

"Can you tell the jury what is involved in breaking horses?" Elaine asked.

"Just got to stay on," she said with a sideways smile. "It's a wild animal, it doesn't necessarily like to be ridden."

"Did you learn from your father about how to react to the horses?"

"The key things are to not show fear, not get intimidated," she said. "Be tough and calm." Amber and Elaine were constructing a metaphor for Johnny as an erratic and uncontrollable wild horse that doesn't like to be ridden and is nearly impossible to train. The key was to demonstrate Amber's willingness to stay with an abuser in the face of repeated physical pain and failed attempts at reconciliation.

Amber detailed her early home life, emphasizing that she wanted to leave home from an early age. Her testimony elided any mention of her parents' issues with substance use or her father's physical abuse, though her sister would testify to it, stating that their father was rough with them and used heavy discipline, hitting them in the face or on the bottom with his hands or a belt. In meetings before the trial, Amber told her expert psychologist in the case, Dawn Hughes, that she'd been raised in a climate of violence, that her father was "explosive," and that she learned early on how to "caretake" and cope in an abusive environment. Dawn's own testimony stated that Amber had grown up with opiate-addicted parents and had witnessed intimate partner violence in the household.

But Amber chose to focus on the favorable aspects of her childhood on the stand, namely her own diligence and drive. She described to the jury that she'd been a "scholarship kid" at her upscale Catholic high school, volunteered daily at a soup kitchen before school, learned sign language as a preteen by auditing college courses, worked several different part-time jobs, and hustled to modeling and acting auditions. She explained how she broke into the movie business by getting a small role in *Friday Night Lights*, where she met an important film agent who asked Amber to come to Los Angeles. She recalled how she played bit parts in big studio films and a couple of leading roles in indies until she got an audition for a Johnny Depp–produced film called *The*

Rum Diary. When Johnny called her to give her the part, he said, "You're it, kid. You're the dream."

A year later, in Puerto Rico, they kissed on set and their kiss felt real. "When I was around Johnny I felt like the most beautiful person in the whole world," she said on the stand, her voice breaking. "[He] made me feel seen, made me feel like a million dollars." She recalled how, when they finally got together on the press tour for the film a year later, he took the foil from a bottle and put it around her ring finger after just a few weeks of dating. "It felt like a dream. It felt like absolute magic," she said of falling in love with Johnny.

Amber described to the jury how Johnny enamored her friends and family. He paid for extravagant trips for everyone and bought her dad knives and guns. He even fulfilled her childhood wish to have a white horse, the one she named Arrow. When she was with Johnny, she said, she felt electricity in her body, butterflies, she couldn't see straight. "I was head over heels in love," she explained. "I felt at the time there wasn't any other love like that, you know?"

But as their relationship developed, Johnny became unhappy with her approach to her career, Amber explained. He told her she was fame hungry, complained about her "ambition" and how she'd take any role that was offered to her. Johnny was painted as a controlling, possessive partner who abused drugs and alcohol and didn't want his woman to work or fraternize with other men, even professionally. She told the jury how after spending romantic days together in a "little bubble of secrecy" reading poetry, sharing music, professing their love, Johnny would disappear for days. He'd go off grid and become unreachable, only to show up later without an explanation for his whereabouts.

Her testimony took a dark turn as she described the first incident of violence. Amber said that, after asking about his Wino Forever tattoo, Johnny slapped her in the face so forcefully that she flew off the couch. She remembered lying on the ground and looking at the dirty carpet. But Amber stayed, just like other women do, because she wanted to make it work. Johnny would apologize, get sober, and "put the monster away," only to let it out again. She reiterated that she did her best to deal with a monster she loved, and that she only tried to help him quit booze and drugs.

As Amber and Elaine weaved through the thirteen incidents of violence, some details were vivid and specific, while other recollections felt more detached, like she was speaking about someone else's relationship. None of this was unusual for someone living in an abusive dynamic, but the internet interpreted it to mean she was less credible. Instead of sympathy, Amber's traumatic accounting of events was inspiring mass skepticism. Amber's supporters pointed to internalized misogyny as the reason for people's incredulity, but much of the public's disbelief seemed to be instinctual, their own gut-level distrust of someone they believed to be an unreliable narrator. Camille Vasquez said in their War Room during the trial, "With Amber . . . there's a disconnect between the words you are receiving and the feelings you feel like you should be feeling . . . you can't help but think, oh God, I really should be feeling sympathy and empathy for this person, but there's just something that doesn't make sense."

Amber winced when she described one particularly vicious fight. She said it had happened around the same time "My dog stepped on a bee." The statement instantly went viral, with TikTok users making poems, rhymes, remixes, and memes of the seemingly random remark that racked up millions of views. "My dad has to pee," "I forgot my house key," "My child spilt my tea."

Two days later, detailed clinical notes from Erin Falati, Amber's former personal nurse, were presented that referenced her emotional instability, codependence, jealousy, past cocaine addiction, and MDMA use. When the notes were introduced by her own lawyer, Amber disregarded them, saying, "There's a lot of mistakes in here." One of Erin's notes read: *Client laughed and also reported using illicit drugs (mushrooms and MDMA) on 5/9/16 at home with a high-profile male acquaintance. Client reported that her husband was not aware of the male visitor, nor her illicit drug use.* Amber told the jury she didn't remember being in LA at that time and thought she'd been in London. "It seems like the wrong date," she said. Throughout her testimony, she presented herself as someone who seldom overindulged or lost control; to admit to taking drugs or getting drunk would complicate her claims about Johnny. And if she was violent, it had been reactive or in defense of herself or Whitney. Perhaps, faced with contradictory evidence, she simply chose denial.

Like Johnny, Amber was on the stand for four days, but her testimony didn't seem to be going as smoothly. On social media, people following the trial criticized her, saying it seemed like she was acting, that her emotions didn't seem genuine, that she was reciting lines from movies. While Johnny was deemed more credible for displaying his downsides—living in excess and having a temper—Amber was judged to be less credible for crying or for being overly emotive in her gestures. People made TikToks mocking moments of her testimony that they perceived as overly dramatic. One moment that received particular ridicule online was Amber wiping her nose with a tissue. People slowed it down and analyzed the footage second by second, insisting she was taking a bump of coke on the stand.

"People unfairly criticized her for sounding rehearsed when, in fact, she was just taking her case seriously," Benjamin Rottenborn said. "There wasn't an exhibit or case file she didn't review." Rottenborn explained that in Amber's own War Room, inside a house in Northern Virginia she'd rented with her family, there were binders full of exhibits and timelines. He saw how much she'd prepared. "It didn't seem like Johnny was as prepared to answer specific factual questions. He was asked about seven (factual) questions in his direct examination and was allowed to riff in generalities."

Rottenborn said Amber looked at every facet of her case clinically, like a forensic researcher. "I would venture to say that there wasn't a court filing in the case that she didn't put her eyes on and prepare with, and I'm confident that she reviewed every single exhibit." In Rottenborn's opinion, Amber's testimony on the stand demonstrated her bravery, and he found her to be genuine. "Some people said she didn't cry when she was on the stand, that there were no tears," he said. "I saw her right after she gave some of the most harrowing testimony in the case, just bawling." He didn't understand why Amber would be criticized for the level of knowledge and detail of what she testified to, while Johnny didn't get criticized for rambling for hours during his direct testimony, with little specific recall. "I never understood that," Rottenborn said. "It was her life. Amber listened to every word and took notes about the witnesses, while Johnny colored in his coloring book." Rottenborn was referring to Johnny's frequent pen doodling during proceedings.

Bianca Butti, who was no longer dating Amber but still a close friend, was by Amber's side for the entire ordeal. She watched Amber testify and could tell that she was in a total PTSD disconnect.

"It almost sounded like someone else was talking," she said. Amber had reviewed her case over and over again, told her story to lawyers multiple times, made timelines and witness statements, and had already testified in another trial. "By the time you tell it a million times you remove yourself from emotional content . . . I believe all of it," Bianca said. "Especially as someone who was her intimate partner. If I made a sudden move during an argument, she would recoil. It was clear to me that she was in a very violent relationship." She described Amber as feisty, someone who doesn't take no for an answer. Someone strong-willed and opinionated and who doesn't work well with those who want to dominate or run things. "Their dynamic didn't allow them to express themselves in a proper way . . . She was trying to stand her own ground and he just wasn't having it. He was blacked out and drinking, a lot of drug doing, alcohol, and that is always a recipe for disaster."

Amber kept her attention fixed on the jury almost the entire time she was on the stand. Every time she answered a question, she talked and motioned directly to the concealed jury box to her right, eyes moving back and forth down the line of jurors. She was trying to establish a conversational intimacy with them. But to some, her one-sided heart-to-heart with the jury began to feel unnatural and forced. In interviews after the trial, an anonymous juror said that her constant engagement with them made them uncomfortable.

The last day in court before the midtrial break ended on a stunning cliffhanger. During Amber's direct testimony, she claimed that when she and Johnny were on the private island in the Bahamas in 2015, Johnny shoved her into a closet and jammed his fingers inside her, asking her, "You think you're tough?" before chasing her out of the house. It was a distressing scene to end on as the trial went on a ten-day hiatus. Now there'd be a long, agonizing commercial break for the trial's avid followers.

During the ten-day break, Johnny's and Amber's legal teams caught up on sleep and prepared for the final two-week push, in which Amber would be cross-examined, and the jury would hear the largely prerecorded testimony of her witnesses. Johnny flew to England to rehearse for his upcoming tour with Jeff Beck. He stayed with Jeff and his wife, Sandra, trying to maintain a sense of normalcy, while rehearsing at a space in Kent. Amber is believed by someone close to the case to have mostly stuck around northern Virginia. Because she was still in the middle of her direct examination, she was on strict orders by Judge Azcarate not to discuss her testimony with anyone.

On the last night of the break, Ben Chew zipped across the lobby of the Ritz-Carlton carrying a tall Starbucks coffee and a shopping bag. He wasn't wearing his usual conservative courtroom attire but a burgundy plaid blazer and crisp white shirt, red leather shoes, and torn-up jeans. The words "Hollywood Vampires" were emblazoned down the left leg—custom merch from Johnny's rock band. He was Virginia lawyer from the neck up, flamboyant rocker from the neck down. Ben rode the wood-paneled elevator twenty-three flights up to the penthouse floor and entered the War Room through an inconspicuous door. A Post-it note outside read, "DO NOT RING BELL."

Inside, Camille Vasquez was preparing to perform a mock cross-examination of Amber. It was a Sunday night, and Camille wore blue jeans, a white button-up shirt, and Chanel flats. She grabbed Ben by the arm and pulled him inside. In front of a flat-screen television in the living room sat piles of brightly colored candy packages: Starburst, Sour Patch Kids, Twizzlers, a lot of gummy bears. Fans of the Black Pearl had started sending candy when they saw the legal team tossing back sweets on TV. "Now we've got to eat them, we can't let it go to waste," Ben said, eyeing the formidable bounty.

Ben and Camille took their seats across from each other in the living room, flanked by associates ready to listen and take notes.

"Start at the top?" she asked.

Ben nodded, ready to begin.

"Good morning, Ms. Heard," Camille said, launching into the mock cross-examination. "Mr. Depp hasn't looked at you once this entire trial, has he?"

"No, he hasn't, and I think he does that because he's guilty," Ben answered as Amber.

"But you've looked at him many times, haven't you?"

"I have no choice, Ms. Vasquez, he's right in front of me."

"Let's please pull up Plaintiff's Exhibit 346."

One of the associates played a piece of video evidence from a laptop, a 2018 clip from a Dutch late-night talk show in which Amber discussed the money she'd donated to charity from her divorce settlement. Amber is wearing red lipstick and a red blouse, her blond hair gelled back, her eye shadow sparkling. You can faintly hear her Texas drawl as she tells the television host that "$7 million in total was donated; I split it between the ACLU and Children's Hospital Los Angeles. I wanted nothing."

"Yes, I wanted nothing, that's right," Ben said after the clip ended, still playing Amber.

"You say in this interview that you quote 'donated' your entire divorce settlement to charity, right, and you say this because you quote 'wanted nothing,'" Camille shot back at Ben. "But you hadn't donated your $7 million divorce settlement to charity at this point, had you?"

"You're playing games," Ben replied curtly. "It was my intention, I pledged it over time, and I still intend to honor my commitment if your client stops hounding me."

"You would agree with me that you still haven't donated the $7 million divorce settlement to charity?"

"Not all of it, but I've donated everything I could afford."

"It's because you did want something," Camille insisted. "You wanted Mr. Depp's money? You wanted good press. You wanted to seem altruistic publicly, didn't you?"

"I am altruistic. Publicly and privately."

"You wanted to be seen as a noble victim of domestic violence?"

"I AM A NOBLE VICTIM!" Ben shouted in mock frustration, and the Black Pearl broke into laughter.

The Black Pearl's strategy was not just to catch Amber in a web of lies, but to show all the variations of her responses—or "personalities," as they said—on the stand. Showing this range of behavior would help the jury discern when she may be flubbing, telling the truth, or flat-out lying. They were deliberately constructing a complicated picture of Amber, but showing that inside this picture there was consistency, a pattern, which might reveal something dishonest about the larger story she was telling.

At this stage in the trial, the Black Pearl's legal strategy seemed to have the advantage—at least in the court of public opinion. But even though many people found Amber's stories hard to believe, before the break, she'd told the jury, in explicit detail, about multiple incidents of violence and sexual assault at the hands of her ex-husband. For ten days, her words had rung unchallenged in the jurors' minds.

During cross-examination over the next two days, Camille would have the difficult and unpleasant task of poking holes in these accounts of violence. She couldn't have known after the mock cross-examination inside the War Room that the real cross-examination would play out in court like déjà vu.

The following morning, inside Courtroom 5J, Camille stepped up to the podium in an all-black suit while Amber took the stand wearing a dark gray button-up jacket.

Camille started her cross-examination of Amber by confronting her with her own photo evidence. She asked Amber about an incident in March 2013, in which she said Johnny hit her in the face so many times she lost count, while he was wearing several heavy metal rings on his fingers. The photo Amber produced as evidence was displayed on the screen and showed Amber taking a selfie with a bruise on her upper arm. Her face was unblemished.

Next Camille asked about another incident from March 2013, in which Amber claimed Johnny hit her so hard in the mouth that her teeth went through her lip and blood sprayed on the wall. "There isn't a picture of you with injuries after that alleged incident, is there?" Camille inquired.

"I don't know if I've seen one. I can't recall, there are a lot of pictures," Amber said. "I don't believe I've seen that picture admitted."

"That picture doesn't exist," Camille shot back.

Camille moved on to a 2013 trip to Russia, in which Amber claimed Johnny whacked her in the face so hard while wearing his heavy rings that her nose bled. She claimed that Johnny's bodyguard Jerry Judge, who'd passed away in 2019, and whose face Johnny had tattooed on his arm next to the text "jj," had witnessed her bloody nose. But when clear and well-lit tabloid photos from the Russia trip were displayed on the courthouse's TV screens, showing Amber and Johnny dressed up on their way to a press dinner, Amber's face appeared flawless. (Stephen Deuters had once said of Jerry Judge, speaking about the UK trial, "Nothing he would have enjoyed more than telling what he knew. Wild horses couldn't have stopped him from testifying [on Johnny's behalf]." Jerry had witnessed a lot of Amber's alleged abuse. Had he taken the stand in the UK, Stephen said, "he would've raised the roof.") Camille pulled up another photo showing Amber and Johnny sitting side by side at an All-Star Comedy Tribute to Don Rickles in 2014. Again, Amber was smiling and her face looked pristine. "This is a picture of you and Mr. Depp at the event the night after Mr. Depp allegedly whacked you in the face so hard you thought he had broken your nose?" Amber confirmed that it was. She explained that she was wearing makeup. "I have a picture of it underneath the makeup. That's how I know how to reference it."

Several hours into her cross, Amber implied that the most graphic photos of her injuries hadn't made it into evidence and that it wasn't her "job" to get them in. But after so many of her own alleged injury photos had been leaked to the media by her own team, it was hard to believe she wouldn't produce the more egregious photos to prove her claims. If she had them, where were they now, when she needed them most? Elaine's own opening statement had emphasized the "many, many" photographs they had as proof and said that Amber provided "all of her different devices" over the years. Elaine had told the jury, "Ms. Heard took all kinds of photographs, and her friends took photographs, and all of those remained on the Cloud." But Camille hammered on, pulling up photo after photo that appeared to contradict Amber's version of events.

As the gallery stared at photos of Amber's unmarked face and body while Camille described the graphic violence Amber had allegedly been subjected to at the time they were taken, a cognitive dissonance seemed to set in. Camille asked Amber why she hadn't taken photos or sought medical attention after the alleged assault in Australia, when she was covered in bloody gashes and had been sexually assaulted with a glass liquor bottle. Amber's reasoning was simple: she didn't want to tell anyone. Camille brought up an incident from December 2015, in which Amber claimed to have had a broken nose, hair ripped out of her scalp, and probably a concussion; she said that there'd been "blood everywhere." Amber produced photo evidence from the incident that showed discoloration under her eyes and a lesion on her lower lip. It was one of these photos that had made it onto the cover of *People*.

"You gave these pictures to *People* magazine after you publicly accused Mr. Depp of domestic abuse, didn't you?" Camille asked.

Amber told Camille that she gave the photos to her lawyers and representatives at the time.

"So, it's your testimony, Ms. Heard, that your lawyers and representatives gave these pictures of their client to *People* magazine in the middle of a contentious divorce?"

"I certainly did not personally give it, no," Amber replied.

The cross-examination continued as a downhill slide for Amber, and Elaine did little to stop it.

Next Camille questioned Amber about the charitable donation of her divorce settlement, a point Judge Andrew Nicol had noted in his ruling in the UK. "I recognise that there were other elements to the divorce settlement as well, but her donation of the $7 million to charity is hardly the act one would expect of a gold-digger," Judge Nicol had stated. Camille asked her about a statement she released in 2016 in which she stated she'd be donating the entire $7 million to charity: half to the ACLU and half to Children's Hospital Los Angeles. Camille read the statement aloud. "As described in the restraining order and divorce settlement, money played no role for me personally and never has, except to the extent that I could donate it to charity, and in doing so, hopefully help those less able to defend themselves. As reported in the media, the amount received in the divorce was $7 million and $7 million is being donated. This is over and above any funds that I have given away in the past and will continue to give away in the future."

Camille then pulled up the video clip of Amber being interviewed on the Dutch late-night talk show. During the program, the host asked Amber about being called a "gold-digger."

"You got $7 million and people were saying this is all about the money. But then you did something that twisted that whole argument. What did you do with that money?"

Amber responded, "Seven million in total was donated to—I split it between the ACLU and Children's Hospital Los Angeles. I wanted *nothing*."

The video ended, and the courtroom was dead quiet.

"The $7 million divorce settlement was paid to you in full by February of 2018, right?" Camille asked.

"That's correct," Amber answered.

"Sitting here today, Ms. Heard, you still haven't donated the $7 million divorce settlement to charity; isn't that right?"

"Incorrect," Amber quickly responded. "I pledged the entirety of the $7 million to charity."

Amber *had* donated money: she gave $350,000 to the ACLU. Children's Hospital Los Angeles never received any payments directly from her. Other payments were made from a donor-advised fund at Vanguard, the largest investor in Tesla. Regardless, Benjamin Rottenborn said the charity evidence should never have been allowed into the trial, because it had nothing to do with whether abuse had occurred. To get the evidence into court had been a battle for Johnny's legal team. They'd sent subpoenas to the ACLU and multiple staff members before seeking intervention from a New York court to compel them to turn over a cache of documents.

Camille continued pressing Amber over whether she'd donated, *not* pledged, the money, as Amber kept using the two terms synonymously.

"Sitting here today, you have not donated the $7 million, *donated*, not pledged, *donated*, the $7 million divorce settlement to charity?" Camille asked again, growing irritated.

"I use pledge and donation synonymous with one another," Amber said. She wasn't budging.

Camille furrowed her brows. "But I don't. Ms. Heard, I don't use it synonymously . . . You didn't donate it? It's a yes or no."

"I made the pledge. I want to be very clear. I pledged the entirety. I haven't been able to fulfill those pledges because I've been sued," Amber said.

"You had all of the $7 million for 13 months before Mr. Depp sued you and you chose not to pay it to the charities you pledged it to; is that correct?"

"I disagree with your characterization of that," Amber replied.

Camille ended day one of her cross-examination. The gallery was stunned.

The leaked audio recordings came back to bite Amber in court during the second day of her cross-examination. Camille had played what became known as the "Suck My Dick Tape," in which the jury heard Amber use choice words in a tense fight with Johnny. "You lonely shallow insulting fucking cocksucker," she said. "Fucking cock-sucking demon fucking child. Go fucking eat a dick. I came here for fucking nothing. You're a parasite." She told Johnny over and over again to "go fucking suck my dick" and then ridiculed him about his career, calling him a sellout and a "washed-up piece of shit." She used a fake, cooing baby voice to taunt him about his unfinished book project and sarcastically called him the "fucking master of fucking cinema" and "sensei." "I hope to God Jack's stepfather teaches him more about being a man than your fucking, your fucking left nut," Amber said, referring to Johnny's son with Vanessa. Johnny lobbed insults back at her in a detached tone, describing her as a "filthy whore." "Your jealousy is so tragic," Johnny told her.

The courtroom was rigid after the recording was played. Spectators, mostly Johnny Depp fans, looked at each other wide-eyed, some shaking their heads in disapproval. To many, this recording was evidence that Amber was not the person she portrayed herself to be. She was being verbally abusive to Johnny, deploying crass, misandrist language against him, the same type of language she'd condemned him for using against her. People wondered, *Who would so cruelly taunt their spouse this way?* Especially if that spouse had a latent personality called "the monster" that beat them. To some domestic-violence-prevention advocates, this sounded like an abuser speaking. Amber's continuous verbal assaults on Johnny were combative and goading—as if she *wanted* to trigger his anger and escalate the fight.

The person on the recording was not the one Amber presented publicly, as a salt-of-the-earth, virtuous woman who'd been savagely abused and then unjustly persecuted by her ex-husband, the system, and the world. A committed #MeToo activist who specialized in gender-based violence issues and human rights. Responding to the recording in which she said, "I hit you, I didn't punch you," she used the words "self-defense" and said Johnny was "proactively punching" her and she was "reactively hitting" him. She continued, "I took on as much as I could. I had, the whole relationship, been blamed for everything: for his drinking, for him hitting me, no matter what I did, I couldn't change the senseless nature of the violence."

The day after Amber's cross-examination ended, on May 18, Whitney took the stand. Her sister was Amber's only live witness, a shocking sign of how much Amber's world had changed since 2016. Her close former allies—Amanda de Cadenet, her BFFs Rocky and iO—were done. Former flames James Franco and Elon Musk, who spent time with her in the direct aftermath of the alleged violence, had dodged their subpoenas. iO and Rocky filmed their compulsory video depositions and left it at that. The optics of this didn't help Amber's credibility.

Still, Whitney was convincing on the stand, and her testimony directly corroborated Amber's story. She spoke about Johnny allegedly assaulting Amber on the stairs of the penthouse apartment. Whitney also said she saw Johnny being verbally abusive to her sister and that she'd observed the aftermath of domestic violence in the form of bruises and cuts on Amber's body. On cross-examination, Whitney said that she'd had "suspicions" Johnny was hitting her sister in 2013. She testified that after witnessing Johnny's alleged assault of Amber on the stairs, she continued to support their relationship and play the "marriage counselor" because she wanted to support her sister. "They wanted to be together, it seemed like, so I just helped as best as I could."

In his prerecorded video deposition, iO testified to Johnny's intense jealousy and possessiveness and described what he'd heard on the phone with Amber and Johnny the night he called 911 from New York in May 2016, mimicking a smacking sound with his hands. He detailed how cruel Johnny became toward Amber while under the influence, ridiculing her body and telling her she had no talent. In Rocky's deposition, she claimed that Amber had confided in her about the abusive relationship and that she personally witnessed the aftermath of several alleged violent incidents. She testified to seeing injuries on Amber's body and face on various occasions, including bruises, cuts, and a swollen nose. Notably, she referred to "deep cuts" on the back of Amber's forearms after the disastrous Australia trip—the same injuries that members of Johnny's team observed and described as thin, self-inflicted hash marks. Rocky also related a story in which she and Amber got into a physical fight one Thanksgiving in Los Angeles. Rocky had pushed Amber, and Amber hit Rocky in the face. Rocky stated in the deposition that they no longer spoke, but aren't enemies.

On the final day of witness testimony on May 26, the day before closing arguments, Amber took the stand once more, in the trial's rebuttal phase—a stage in which one party can counter the evidence and/or arguments of another party. During her rebuttal, Amber offered a powerful statement to the jury and to the world.

"I am harassed, humiliated, and threatened every single day. Even just walking into this courtroom, sitting here in front of the world, having the worst parts of my life, things I have lived through, used to humiliate me. People want to kill me, and they tell me so every day. People want to put my baby in the microwave.

"I'm not sitting in this courtroom snickering," she continued, seemingly alluding to Johnny at the table in front of her. "I'm not sitting in this courtroom laughing, smiling, making snide jokes.

I'm not . . . and even though Johnny promised that I deserved this, and promised he'd do this, I don't deserve this."

The night before the last day of trial, Camille sat with the Black Pearl inside the War Room discussing what to cover in their closing arguments: how to emphasize that #MeToo was not applicable to Johnny in this case and the inconsistencies in Amber's story. Dr Pepper cans and half-full water bottles littered the tables. A beautiful bouquet of soft pink roses slowly wilted inside a vase. Behind Camille and Sam Moniz were stacks of candy that were torn through but far from finished: jelly beans, Starburst, gummy bears, Red Vines, and Life Savers. More gifts from their fans.

"Guess how many emails I have?" Camille said to one of the other lawyers. "Two thousand six hundred and twenty-five. It all happened right after the cross." Internet sleuths from all over the world had emailed the team uncovering new "evidence" and inconsistencies, and providing their thoughts on the case.

The final day of trial drew the largest crowd of spectators yet. As the lawyers were inside making their closing statements, the entire block behind the courthouse was cordoned off with barriers, and cop cars and motorcycles lined the street. Spectators stood four- and five-people deep by the side of the road, waiting for Johnny to exit through the gates so they could say a final farewell. Unsurprisingly, there were several more Jack Sparrows in the crowd, but also someone dressed as George Jung from *Blow* and another as *Fear and Loathing in Las Vegas*'s Raoul Duke, in yellow aviators and a cigarette dangling from his lip. The alpacas came to pay their respects and were wearing tricorn pirate hats as they patiently posed for selfie after selfie. Robin and Randy returned too, and they brought their twin collies, Donald and Danny, both wearing "Depp Legal Team" T-shirts. There were several kids up on their dad's shoulders, wagons full of golden retriever puppies, and life-size cardboard cutouts of Johnny and Amber.

When Johnny's Escalade SUV finally pulled out of the gate, resounding screams poured out from the crowd, and everyone's arms shot up in the air, primed to film the moment with their phones. Fans were ringing cowbells and shouting into megaphones, and someone buzzed loudly on a kazoo. Johnny drove away slowly with the window down and gave his usual head nod and hand-to-heart in thanks to the adoring crowd.

CHAPTER 23

Crocodile Tears

For the millions of people around the world who'd been following *Depp vs Heard*, by the end of the six-week trial, you were either Team Johnny or Team Amber, or you were disgusted by the entire spectacle. Starbucks and Dunkin' Donuts across the country had tip cups for either side, with Team Johnny's often decorated with hearts, and more often full. Rock City Cakes in Charleston, West Virginia, had started selling poop-shaped pastries called Amber Turds, with Amber's face on them. Even the side of a building in Spain was covered in graffiti of Amber's face, her nose long like Pinocchio's. On the internet, the trial had gone so viral that it was amassing more attention than Russia's war in Ukraine, COVID-19, and even abortion rights—and this was just weeks after the leaked Supreme Court decision that would overturn *Roe vs Wade*.

Johnny was undeniably the people's favorite, at the courthouse and on social media. Twitter users reposted their favorite evidence from the trial, Amber's worst moments from the audio recordings, and photos of Johnny's severed fingertip and his bruises paired with #JusticeForJohnnyDepp and #JohnnyDeppIsInnocent. A few celebrities went public in their support for

Johnny, some more overtly than others. Jennifer Aniston quietly started following Johnny on Instagram after the trial started. His *Dark Shadows* costar Eva Green posted a photo of the two of them on the red carpet and wrote, "I have no doubt Johnny will emerge with his good name . . ." During a stand-up performance, Chris Rock told the crowd, "Believe all women, believe all women . . . except Amber Heard."

Support for Amber came mostly from establishment media op-eds, who condemned the trial and the events around it as a misogynistic circus that was reversing the advancements of #MeToo as well as triggering domestic-violence victims. *New York Times* columnist Michelle Goldberg wrote that because the "volatile actress" was "very far from a perfect victim," it made her "the perfect object of a #MeToo backlash." *Vogue* columnist Raven Smith asked, "Are we not witnessing a modern-day witch trial?" He urged readers, "It's time to believe women—all women. It's time to believe Heard." Even the famously conservative *New York Post* published an op-ed decrying the "unfair vilification of Amber Heard."

Amber also had her own social-media support camps, and though they were much smaller than Johnny's, they were passionately posting in her defense—especially her friends Eve Barlow, a music journalist, and Stanford law professor Michele Dauber. In one of Dauber's tweets, she said, "In a society that strips women of real power, some women have learned to seek male approval in the hopes they won't be raped or abused or humiliated. Sucking up to power might feel good to you but it won't work. You will be next."

After closing arguments on Friday, May 27, as the jury began their deliberations, Johnny departed rainy Virginia on a private jet for the UK, where he'd join guitarist Jeff Beck on a European tour. He and Johnny had recorded an album in 2020, with the release scheduled for a few weeks after the trial's end. One song he wrote seemed to speak to his struggles with Amber. "You're sitting there like a dog with a seven-year itch, and I think you've said enough for one motherfucking night."

Amber remained in Fairfax, waiting with her team for the jury's verdict. Several days passed before it came down, on June 1, 2022.

It was a typical late-spring morning in Virginia: hot, sunny, humid. White tents, tripods, tangled wires, long-lens cameras, and microphones dominated the scene in front of the courthouse. Curious onlookers and fans gathered on the courthouse lawn, staring down at the livestream on their phones, broadcast from five floors up. Cameramen braced to capture their reactions.

As the jury foreman brought out an envelope with their decision, Amber, present in the courtroom, looked nervously at her lawyers. Judge Azcarate asked, "Mr. Foreperson, is this the decision of the jury? Is this unanimous?"

"Yes," he replied.

The clerk began to read. "One: As to the statement appearing in the online op-ed entitled, 'I spoke up against sexual violence and faced our culture's wrath, that has to change.' Do you find that Mr. Depp has proven all the elements of defamation? Answer: Yes."

Outside, the crowd chanted. *Johnny! Johnny! Johnny!*

"Two: As to the statement, 'Then two years ago, I became a public figure representing domestic abuse and I felt the full force of our culture's wrath for women who speak out.' Do you find that Mr. Depp has proven all the elements of defamation. Answer: Yes."

"JOHNNY!" Fans continued to scream, jumping up and down.

"Three: 'I had the rare vantage point of seeing in real time how institutions protect men accused of abuse.' Do you find that Mr. Depp has proven all the elements of defamation. Answer: Yes."

Amber held back tears. Whitney scowled. Elaine jotted down notes. The color drained from Benjamin Rottenborn's face.

Johnny won the case.

The jury found unanimously that Johnny had proven defamation for all three statements in Amber's 2018 op-ed, including that the statements were false and that Amber had defamed him with "actual malice." They awarded him $10 million in compensatory damages and $5 million in punitive damages. The punitive damages would later be reduced to $350,000 due to a limit imposed by Virginia state law.

Ruling on Amber's $100 million defamation counterclaim, the jury found just one of the three statements made by Adam Waldman in the *Daily Mail* to be defamatory and false and made with "actual malice." She was awarded $2 million in compensatory damages from Johnny but no punitive damages.

Amber hugged her lawyers tight before exiting the courthouse through the back doors. The livestream felt muted as it captured her and her sister's shocked expressions. Across the room, Johnny's lawyers grinned quietly, vigorously shaking one another's hands in congratulations, in awe of the unbelievable verdict.

Johnny had been in his hotel suite in England, joined by his assistant Nathan Holmes and his security guard Malcolm Connolly. They sat quietly in front of the TV as the verdict was read. Then they burst into tears.

Later that day, back at the Ritz-Carlton, the youngest members of the Black Pearl gathered in the hotel lounge. Camille Face-Timed her family, with her boyfriend by her side. The associates stood around a table in their courtroom attire, giddily sipping champagne and discussing their near-inconceivable victory. Some on the team had been sure they'd lose.

"It really was, as we argued, all or nothing," Camille reflected. "You either had to believe she was an abuse victim or she wasn't. And this jury came back and said, 'We don't believe her.'"

"Every single one of us believed him," Camille continued. "He's not perfect, we are the first to admit it, we know. But he did not do this and this team knew that."

It seemed the internet believed him too. By the end of the day, Johnny had nearly 2 million new followers on Instagram.

Before, during, and after the trial, it was clear that *Depp vs Heard* had become a vehicle for myriad divergent political and personal causes. The world wanted a black-and-white story: villain vs hero, abuser vs victim, liar vs truth-teller. These binaries carried over into conversations around domestic violence and #MeToo, with each side of the debate cherry-picking favorable evidence and ignoring anything contradictory to their beliefs. The mainstream media played into these binaries, some declaring the verdict the end of #MeToo. "The Me Too Backlash Is Here" (*Vox*); "Depp-Heard verdict will have chilling impact on #MeToo, advocates fear" (*Washington Post*). Some outlets framed the lawsuit as a new legal strategy that would discourage women from coming forward publicly with accusations for fear they'd be sued for defamation, just as Johnny had done to Amber. The *Washington Post* wrote that "the Depp-Heard verdict is a gag order for women." An op-ed in *The Atlantic* argued the opposite: "The majority of defamation lawsuits arising out of #MeToo have been filed by *victims* suing abusers for calling them liars, not vice versa . . . First Amendment advocates need not view this as an insurmountable blow to free speech."

More headlines poured in: "The Johnny Depp-Amber Heard Verdict Is Chilling," "And the Winner of the Johnny Depp v. Amber Heard Trial Is . . . Men," "'Men Always Win': Survivors 'Sickened' by the Amber Heard Verdict," "Depp-Heard verdict is the defeat of the toxic #MeToo Movement," "Is the #MeToo Movement Dying?"

Among a handful of more nuanced viewpoints in the mainstream media, *The Guardian* published a series of letters featuring four readers' takes on why the trial didn't mean the end of #MeToo. "'All women really ask of men—and, arguably, vice versa—is the chance to be heard without prejudice.' Heard was. The jury gave up six weeks of their lives to painstakingly comb through the evidence in detail. It indicated that Heard was not telling the truth. This should not create a challenge for the #MeToo movement, if it cares about the truth, and not condoning the egregious defamation of an innocent person, who happens to be a man." Sunny Hostin, a host on *The View*, stated on the show, "I don't think it's the death of the #MeToo movement. Because if you really look at the stats, one in three women certainly are physically abused, one in four men are physically abused. So, the notion that the #MeToo movement only applies to women is really a misnomer."

Months after the trial, the Deppheads banded together online to crowdfund thousands of dollars to pay for unsealed trial documents. They viewed the post-trial reportage as too positive for Amber and hoped to root out more damning evidence against her in the unsealed materials. They watermarked the documents, published them to a website, and immediately their efforts backfired. Headlines started to fly about certain salacious tidbits in the tranche of materials, but they were all about Johnny—his possible erectile dysfunction, and his unsavory, misogynist texts about Amber exchanged with Marilyn Manson. Nevertheless, the

Deppheads, who'd stood valiantly by Johnny's side for two years, couldn't seem to let go of the case. It will be an enduring irony of this story that the inquisition among Deppheads to prove Amber wasn't a victim of abuse ultimately made her a victim of unimaginable harassment, online bullying, and even death threats.

Kat Tenbarge, a tech and culture reporter for NBC News, compared Johnny's supporters to the QAnon community, referring to their beliefs as a "mass delusion." Kat didn't feign objectivity—she believed Amber was telling the truth, while also disclosing that she only watched certain parts of Amber and Johnny's testimony. She described the "Depp-Heard effect," the framework through which "huge populations of people online now view any allegation of sexual assault or domestic violence, or both"—that framework consisting of victim-blaming, regressive takes on women's credibility, and what Kat called the "reverse witch-hunt dichotomy," wherein the witch hunt takes place against the accuser, not the accused. For Kat—and others in legacy media—Amber's loss was symbolic. Here was an exemplary female victim who society had failed. Over and over, the verdict was tied to partisan politics and the perception that our society was regressing to barbarism, fueled in part by Trump and TikTok.

The verdict had come at a chilling moment for women. On May 2, during week four of the trial, a draft majority opinion from the Supreme Court that would overturn *Roe vs Wade* and *Planned Parenthood vs Casey* was leaked to the press. A smattering of activists took to the Supreme Court steps to protest, a mere thirty minutes from the mobbed Fairfax courthouse, where the sordid details of Johnny and Amber's marriage were being dissected for the world. The leak amplified the sense of fear and paranoia about the state of women's rights in this country. Less than a month after the *Depp vs Heard* verdict, *Roe vs Wade* was successfully overturned.

For feminists following the trial, the SCOTUS ruling, combined with Amber's loss and the unbridled misogyny leveled against her on social media, signaled a true danger to women's liberty. Conflating her story with other women's stories, Amber was made a martyr of the #MeToo movement. Mainstream media called the trial an "orgy of misogyny." Amber was all women, and all women should be scared. Fanning the flames of these anxieties were controversial figures like Kyle Rittenhouse and Donald Trump Jr., who celebrated Johnny's win, exploiting the moment to galvanize their bases and connect with their tribes. The day of the verdict, Rittenhouse tweeted congratulations to Johnny and his team. "Johnny Depp trial is just fueling me, you can fight back against the lies in the media, and you should!" Trump Jr. posted a photo of Johnny holding his fist in the air triumphantly, the caption reading, "Johnny Depp will always be remembered as the first man to win an argument with a woman."

But for Katha Blackwell, CEO of Partnership Against Domestic Violence (PADV), the largest nonprofit domestic-violence organization in Georgia, *Depp vs Heard* was not so cut and dried. PADV has been serving the metro-Atlanta area for more than forty-four years and sees more than ten thousand domestic-violence survivors (and their children) a year for services like emergency shelter, support groups, legal advocacy, career guidance, and transitional housing. Katha said that for some of her colleagues in the domestic-violence space, the trial was confusing, and not everyone reached the same conclusion. When her organization was asked to sign an open letter in support of Amber, Katha declined. She thought at the time, "We can't jump on board with this. We are seeing signs that Amber is abusive. The lines are gray." Katha saw the trial as a missed opportunity to educate people about toxic relationships instead of encouraging people to pick a side. "On TV you don't see healthy relationships. On reality shows people are disrespect-ful to each other. The next generation coming up and seeing this are thinking, this is love," Katha explained. "It's setting a bad ex-ample. The same for Johnny and Amber. Amber's behavior in the relationship was abusive and toxic, she is not a martyr."

Neither was Amber an "everywoman." She was a Hollywood celebrity with money, an armored truck and driver, a revolving door of lawyers, PR wizards, and media connections at the ready. Her ex-istence was totally alien from the day-to-day lives of most domestic-violence victims. This doesn't mean she couldn't also be a victim of abuse—but she wasn't a stand-in for other survivors. Society tends to use celebrities as vessels to carry every social examination, ev-ery social problem, every social ill. But celebrities aren't the norm; they aren't representative of anything except celebrity.

Amber said time and time again that she chose to speak up about Johnny's abuse for those who don't have a voice. But Am-ber hadn't assumed a central role in the #MeToo movement on her own; she was aided and encouraged by powerful institutions like the ACLU and the *Washington Post*, which viewed her as an apt representative for the latest cause célèbre, betraying their own detachment from everyday victims. Throughout the trial and its aftermath, many sectors of the media held the line on this narra-tive, trumpeting Amber as a martyr for the movement and selling her experience as exemplary and relatable. In their analyses of the trial as a systemic failure and "the death of #MeToo," they failed to see their own complicity in constructing a myopic, unrelatable notion of social justice.

Katha Blackwell acknowledges there's an upside to celebrity activism around domestic violence: more people pay attention, thus there's more opportunity to change perspectives. But she said there's little thought given to the support needed on the ground.

Every day, women are being urged to speak up, speak out, come out from behind their walls of silence and face their abusers—but then what? If they don't have support services around them, who is going to be their pro bono lawyer? Who is going to give them a job when they leave? What happens to their kids?

Fifty-three-year-old Tom Nugen served on the jury in Fairfax. Before retiring, he worked as a defense contractor and was an executive at Booz Allen & Hamilton working in intelligence. He's lived in the Fairfax area for forty years and had served on several juries in the county before *Depp vs Heard*. Tom said that before the trial, he hadn't been aware of the underlying story. "I knew nothing, really. You watch the news and you only watch the things that are important to you." He continued, "I pay attention to world news and the economy but never really entertainment, except watching a movie." He knew who Johnny Depp was, and remembered some of Johnny's characters and films. "I hadn't been living under a rock." But he had no idea who Amber Heard was. He said 90 percent of the jury didn't know who she was either until the trial. The weeks-long trial was difficult for him, he said. He missed his daughter's high school graduation. "Eight hours a day was pretty tough for most of us."

Legal pundits, journalists, and Amber's lawyers insinuated that the social-media coverage of the trial, primarily pro-Johnny, had an outsized influence on the verdict. They suggested that even though jurors swore not to view social media, it was impossible to avoid it because they weren't sequestered. But Tom said it was the opposite. "I don't use Facebook or Twitter or TikTok or Instagram. I'm not on any social media. I used to have a Facebook when it first came out, but I've never updated it. I have no clue about the noise around the case . . . A few of the other jurors didn't use social media at all either."

Tom said when it came to deliberating the verdict, the jurors were all pretty much on the same page. They didn't believe Amber. They also couldn't rely on her photos of the abuse, which they said varied drastically depending on the lighting and angle of the photo. Also, they liked watching Johnny testify. "For me, I enjoyed his testimony," Tom said. "He was pretty entertaining going back and forth with Heard's lawyers. We were sitting there for eight hours a day, and having him on the stand was a breath of fresh air."

The compensation question was where they had to deliberate the most. "Probably took three or four hours to just settle on a number," Tom said. Some of the jurors wanted to give Johnny more, and others wanted to give him less. "Some people felt sorry that she probably wouldn't have enough to pay him. Others said he probably won't make her pay it all anyways. So let's just make it what we think it should be, and not based on pity, right? We settled in the middle."

In terms of the one defamatory Adam Waldman statement awarded to Amber, in which he called her abuse allegations a "hoax," Tom said they understood it was a contradictory verdict. "We talked about that a lot. We looked at the time that he made those statements versus after the fact knowing everything." Tom said they thought Adam making those statements at that time, without true knowledge or evidence of a hoax, was defamatory.

"We didn't believe a lot of what she was saying," Tom said, explaining that Amber's believability wasn't necessarily tied to her delivery during her testimony, though he did say she sounded rehearsed. "They're all actors, they can put on a different face if you pay them enough." He said more than anything, it was that her story and the evidence didn't match up. "The evidence provided, even by her side, didn't support what she said." Tom summarized her case succinctly: "Too carefully planned . . . but with lots of holes in it."

Amber's account of the sexual-assault allegations from Australia were difficult for Tom and the other jurors to listen to. "But at the end of the day we looked at it like this: if you are beaten that badly, why didn't you go to the emergency room? If you were cut up, you're barefoot, walking on glass, bleeding all over the place. You didn't go to the doctor, you actually got on the plane the next day to go home?"

Another major turning point for them concerned the events of May 27, 2016, when Amber obtained the TRO at the downtown LA courthouse, augmented by the testimony from former TMZ employee Morgan Tremaine. At that point, he said, they'd heard several times from Amber and Elaine that Amber never left the house without makeup on, which they said explained why several witnesses didn't see her injuries. Tom didn't understand why she'd then show up to the courthouse "with no makeup on—supposedly—with her publicist and all this press is there." He hung on Amber's own words that she wanted the allegations to stay private to protect Johnny, whom she loved, and that she wasn't in it for any financial gain. "Then why all the circus?" The courthouse appearance seemed like a "setup" to make Johnny seem like the monster in the divorce. "This was what put the proverbial nail in the coffin," Tom stated.

He said the jury noted these kinds of contradictions throughout Amber's case—contradictions that accumulated week after week. They decided her story wasn't just not believable, it was *unbelievable*, he said. "There are so many inconsistencies between what she said, what the pictures told and the story that was being prosecuted. There were so many holes in the story, it was hard for us to believe any of it." The jury was made up of two women and five men. Tom said the women on the jury were tougher on Amber than the men.

One male juror, whose name and juror number are unknown, spoke to *Good Morning America* soon after the verdict. He said Amber's emotional testimony didn't add up and they believed her to be the aggressor. "All of us were very uncomfortable . . . she would answer one question and she would be crying and two seconds later she would turn ice cold . . . some of us used the expression 'crocodile tears.'"

"She didn't help the #MeToo movement at all, she probably set it back a decade," Tom stated. "But it also brings light to this idea that not every case of abuse is from the man. Every incident like this needs to be looked at before you make a judgment. I agree, in a lot of cases in the past, it probably was the man. But you can't just jump to that conclusion.

"For someone like Johnny Depp, he can weather the storm," Tom continued. "He's got money, fame, connections. But an ordinary guy like me could lose his job and livelihood. There's just no way of coming back from that. Before people start to put a scarlet letter on you, you have to let them have their day in court, or at least allow them to defend themselves without any prejudged ideas."

Amber's legal team maintains the jury got it wrong. "I think when you listen to some of the tapes, or read some of the text messages, or you see the kitchen cabinet video, you could argue that many of those communications constituted verbal or emotional abuse," Rottenborn said. "A lot of the trial devolved into, what did Amber do wrong? But that's not what the trial should have been about. It should have been about the words that Amber wrote in that op-ed. Were those words protected under the First

Amendment? I believe the overwhelming weight of the evidence showed that they were." To the end, Rottenborn emphasized Amber's First Amendment rights.

The day after the verdict was announced, Elaine went on the *Today* show to explain why she thought the jury hadn't believed Amber. "A number of things were allowed in this court that shouldn't have been allowed and it caused the jury to be confused." She said the jury were influenced by social media and the cameras in the courtroom. "There's no way they couldn't have been influenced by it, and it was horrible," Elaine said. "It really, really was lopsided.

"It's like the Roman Colosseum how they view this whole case," she continued. "I was against cameras in the courtroom, and I went on record with that and had argued against it because of the sensitive nature of this, but it made it a zoo."

Elaine said she believed that Amber had excellent grounds for an appeal.

After her loss, Amber released a statement on Instagram.

"The disappointment I feel today is beyond words. I am heartbroken that the mountain of evidence still was not enough to stand up to the disproportionate power, influence, and sway of my ex-husband." Amber then described the verdict as a setback for women. "It sets back the clock to a time when a woman who spoke up and spoke out could be publicly shamed and humiliated."

Within weeks, she sold her house in Yucca Valley, California, for a little over a million dollars, and, like Johnny, took off to an island. On the Spanish island of Majorca, she hid out for a couple of months and sunk into a sweet domestic routine with her daughter. She lived under the moniker "Martha Jane Cannary," the legal name of American frontierswoman Calamity Jane. Bianca said Amber loved living in Spain, where she finally had the space to be a mom. "She met all the people who lived in the village, and Oonagh made friends with the village kids. They'd go to the square at 5 p.m. No one was weird about her or said anything," Bianca said.

Then, someone in town tipped off the newspaper, and suddenly she had helicopters circling her house. So she left for Madrid, where she could be more anonymous. There, she bought a nearly $2 million villa in a suburban barrio of Madrid, the exclusive neighborhood of El Viso. She was occasionally snapped by paparazzi going with her nanny and daughter to the local playground, but mostly she seemed to live a quiet, uninterrupted life. Close family and friends remained a priority.

On December 22, 2023, a year and a half after the trial, *Aquaman and the Lost Kingdom* came out. Her role had been drastically edited down to eleven one-liners, a few grunts, and some laughs. Entertainment media said the twenty minutes of screen time appeared purely contractual. Though she'd been the dynamic lead in the 2018 *Aquaman*, in the sequel her role was reduced to a stock character: the doting wife and mother to a newborn baby (fathered by the Aquaman himself, Jason Momoa). As one entertainment journalist described in *Business Insider*, "Like Ariel in Disney's 'The Little Mermaid,' whom Mera resembles with her red hair and green outfit, it's like someone stole her voice."

Before the US trial, Amber spoke candidly on her time in Hollywood. "Fame, in general, it's all fake. It's ephemeral and illusory . . . we have the perception of what it is and it's so inaccurate and it's constantly enforcing an illusion that just takes from, not just the people it centers itself on, but it takes from all of us. It creates this culture that prizes it and values it, and obsesses over it and strives for it, and we trade it like a social commodity. It is a disease. It doesn't mean anything—only to the effect that you can do something with it, that really affects change. That's the only thing I can see this being worth."

Johnny may seem like the victor in this case, but there are no real winners. Johnny and Amber were both victims of the same Hollywood machine, a singular ecosystem built on the projection of our dreams and desires, and fueled by the rise and fall of its stars. What began as a love story gone bad turned into a merciless publicity war meted out by a spectrum of characters who relied on figures like Johnny and Amber in order to thrive: the lawyers, agents, publicists, media corporations, social-media influencers—and even writers like us.

Hollywood has a short attention span, skimming the top off important societal issues and then moving on to the next hot topic before enacting real change. As quickly as establishment Hollywood adopted #MeToo, they dropped it. Within just a few years, the white ribbons tied around celebrities' wrists on the red carpets signifying solidarity with #MeToo were gone, as were the sentimental #MeToo montages played at the Oscars, and the slate of #MeToo-related feature films after the fall of Weinstein. Sure, film sets now have intimacy coordinators, and film contracts now include morality clauses. This protects actors and film workers from unsafe work conditions. But it also protects studios from liability.

While the awards shows moved on from #MeToo and Time's Up to DEI (Diversity, Equity, and Inclusion), the perfunctory speeches no longer revolved around justice and equality for women, but in casting and hiring LGBTQ+ folk, disabled people, and minorities. Ricky Gervais, as host of the 2020 Golden Globes, mocked the Hollywood elite for going so political: "Well, you say you're woke, but the companies you work for, I mean, unbelievable: Apple, Amazon, Disney. If ISIS started a streaming service, you'd call your agent, wouldn't you? If you do win an award tonight, don't use it as a platform to make a political speech, all right? You're in no position to lecture the public about anything. You know nothing about the real world, most of you spent less time in school than Greta Thunberg."

Roberta Kaplan's Time's Up imploded after the New York attorney general released a report revealing that she was giving Governor Andrew Cuomo legal advice on how to confront allegations of sexual harassment against him. At least one client of Roberta's law firm, Kaplan Hecker & Fink, who apparently remained a client, spoke to the New York Times anonymously and pointed to the hypocrisy and opportunism that had embroiled the Time's Up organization. "Most distressing is the realization that Kaplan Hecker may be using pro bono cases like mine, and in particular cases representing sexual violence victims, in order to launder the firm's reputation and purchase credibility with which they can more effectively market themselves as paid representatives for perpetrators and enablers."

The industry, since its inception, has been built on mythologizing and spin, supposedly rooted in American ideals and righteous moralism dictated by the mores of the moment. But its efforts are largely hollow and faithless, with every decision driven by profit, growth, and self-preservation. Do the women and their children seeking safe harbor inside Katha Blackwell's shelter in Atlanta cite the movie She Said as helpful, meaningful, or even relatable? Who was that film made for? Or was it simply a purification ritual for Hollywood in the form of a $32 million maudlin social issue film?

There's no question that there's more awareness around the issues plaguing women than there was before October 2017, when Weinstein and the wider film industry were outed as hostile, exploitative, and abusive to women. But income inequality, access to basic healthcare, including reproductive rights, and gender-based violence remain the largest factors impacting women's freedom.

"Hollywood ran [Amber] over, put the car in reverse, then ran her over again, and did it one more time," Bianca Butti said. "If it helps their reputation and popularity, then they'll have an opinion." Bianca insisted Amber wasn't trying to hurt Johnny by writing her op-ed—she was trying to be an advocate for other people. "I wish she wouldn't have written that."

Dan Wootton, the author of the UK tabloid piece calling Johnny a "wife beater," wishes he wouldn't have written his article either.

"I don't know what happened between Johnny and Amber . . . and, frankly, it was not my business to interfere," he said in 2024. "I greatly regret that I ever did."

CHAPTER 24

Leaving Los Angeles

T his story is like mutton," Johnny said, sipping a margarita from a mason jar on the patio of his Little Halls Pond Cay bungalow in the Bahamas. "The more you chew on it, the bigger it grows. Then, you choke." Almost a year had passed since the verdict in Fairfax. Three months earlier, Johnny's best friend and bandmate Jeff Beck had died suddenly from bacterial meningitis. The crystal-blue water stretched endlessly behind him, and the salty island wind blew the tall palm trees above.

His home was dark compared to the sun-blasted exterior, and his bed was covered in stacks of books, painting supplies, and papers. A TV he called "the glass tit" hung next to a shelf by the bed with green novelty street signs that read "420" and "Bourbon Street." One of his paintings showed a cartoonish stoner man with one hand formed into Christ's two-fingered Hand of Benediction; the other held up an Apple TV remote.

On the patio, his personal therapist Beechy Colclough reclined behind Johnny in a lounge chair wearing a tight purple T-shirt, his hands resting atop his round belly as he stared into the distance. Beechy, now seventy-six, said Johnny had been "running the block" with psychiatrists, doctors, and therapists when they were first introduced to each other in 2018 by rock photographer Ross Halfin, who photographed the Hollywood Vampires. At first, Johnny ignored Beechy. "Nah, they're all the same," Johnny said, referring to the litany of therapists he'd already seen. But, eventually, he warmed up to Beechy and his unorthodox style of therapy.

"I'm mad as a box of frogs. I don't give a fuck what I have to do to help someone," Beechy said in a thick Irish accent. He shunned the titles of counselor or therapist, and described his work as "encounters." When Beechy started working with Johnny, he could see how damaged he was by Amber's accusations. "The colors had gone out of the pictures in his mind. Everything was gray. If he does something, it isn't the street he lives on that knows about it. It's the whole fucking planet."

Johnny introduced Beechy to others as his "wife" because they were together all the time. They spent six months quarantined on the island during the pandemic. "It was like Robinson Crusoe, you know, on the island with his Man Friday. I was fucking calling myself Wednesday." Beechy said they've never had an argument or a dispute. "Fundamentally, the reason for that is because I tell him the truth," he said.

He started his treatment career as the director of a rehab facility, and from there he became a therapist to A-listers like Kate Moss, Robbie Williams, Michael Jackson, and Sir Elton John, who still credits Beechy with saving his life. Elton even wrote the preface to Beechy's book *The Effective Way to Stop Drinking*, writing, "I am now convinced that those of us too proud, too arrogant or too frightened to ask for help need people like Beechy to nourish us and help us claw our way back into existence. I would personally like to thank him for his love, kindness, compassion and honesty. It has helped me so much." As with Johnny, to Elton, Beechy was more than a therapist: he was a soulmate and close friend.

Beechy had been by Johnny's side throughout the US trial and was filmed and photographed coming into court with him every day. But during the UK trial, he'd been absent from public view. Beechy would wait at the hotel for Johnny to return, he said, and then together they'd process the day. He was afraid to be photographed by the British media because of his own controversial history. In 2006, Beechy was accused of having inappropriate sexual affairs with three female patients at his London office. One woman said that after six months as his patient, Beechy offered massages, which eventually turned into sex. Once their affair began they had sex during most of her sessions.

At the time, he was Britain's most famous therapist, known as "the Rock 'n' Roll Therapist," making regular TV and radio appearances. When the women's stories came to light, he was banned from practicing under the banner of the British Association for Counselling and Psychotherapy. Beechy said he was "set up" by the British media. He said the *News of the World* tabloid sent women to his office wearing cameras and recording devices to take him down.

Until Johnny's US trial, Beechy hadn't been photographed in over a decade. For a while, he wore a mask in court to evade detection. But then someone told him he was being overly cautious—he didn't have to worry about it anymore—so he dropped the mask. Within a week, the *Daily Mail* published a story making the connection.

Beechy struggled with alcoholism from the age of fourteen. When he was thirty-four, he decided to stop drinking after he woke up slumped under a lamppost and a dog was pissing on him. "Addiction is a very simple process for supposedly complicated people," he said. Laughing together was key to Johnny and Beechy's dynamic. "We will laugh from morning until night." But some days they'd also sit in silence. "We've sat together for a few hours with not a word between us."

"One of the best ways of connecting with somebody for me is just to enter into their world," Beechy said.

Beechy worked with Michael Jackson in November and December 1993, for thirty-one days, taking Michael off painkillers during the time of the child-abuse allegations. One day, Beechy suggested an outing to Kentucky Fried Chicken in one of London's busiest neighborhoods. Michael was hesitant. He was at the height of his fame (and infamy) and there was no way he could venture out without being recognized and swarmed. But Beechy wasn't worried. No one would believe Michael Jackson was casually rolling up to a busy KFC joint without security detail. "If you're presented with something surreal, you'll go, nah." Beechy convinced Michael to put on a jacket and hat and make the trip. "I ordered, he was standing behind me. It was one of the most exciting things Michael ever did. God help him."

Beechy said that like Michael Jackson, Johnny pays a "very, very high price" for his talents. "For lack of a better expression, he's become a victim of his ability. He can't go out. He's too famous." Stephen Deuters echoed this and stressed that, like Michael Jackson when he was alive, Johnny has to fly privately and pay for security, there's really no other option.

On one ordinary weekday in London in 2023, Beechy pushed a disguised Johnny in a wheelchair down the cobblestoned streets to a local bookstore. Beechy yelled out in a singsong, "We don't give a fuck!" As the old grandpa, hidden underneath half an inch of rubber makeup, Johnny was free.

"He's treated like a product, and that's not right," Beechy said. "If I can protect him from idiots and fuckwits, I will." Johnny was turning sixty the following month. "I'd rather he fucking sold a lot of things and had the peace and quiet and live the life that he wants," Beechy said. "And to find someone to make him laugh every morning, like we do. That'd be great."

One Russian woman in her late twenties, Yulia Vlasova, helped Johnny laugh. She posed in the Bahamas with Johnny's arms wrapped around her at the Cafe Cabrones bar he had built for Amber. According to a source, their conversations took place through Google Translate because she didn't speak English. He tried to relate to her through the old cartoon Rocky and Bullwinkle, telling her about the two Russian spy characters, Boris and Natasha. Tall with long blond hair and high cheekbones, she had an uncanny resemblance to Amber.

Johnny will be Beechy's last client before Beechy returns to his life at home amid the French Alps in Chamonix-Mont-Blanc. He resides there with his wife, Josephine, their two bichons frises, Louis and Gigi, and their African gray parrot, Pippa. But as of this writing, he's still living with Johnny, these days inside his nineteenth-century rental townhouse in London, far from the preying paparazzi and red carpets of Los Angeles. Johnny's other homes have tunnels, back doors, and secret egress passageways, but in London, he only has the front door.

"I want to eat Hollywood alive while they watch," Johnny said one afternoon at the townhouse. But Hollywood still feasts on Johnny. It's a vampiric symbiosis. A large painting of a cock-eyed skeleton with the stenciled word "DEATH" written above it hung on the wall behind him, one of a series he'd been working on for decades titled "Death by Confetti." The concept was based on the idea of being falsely celebrated in a "factory of movement with no intention, nothing true or real."

In September 2024, the painting was included in an immersive art experience titled "A Bunch of Stuff" in Manhattan's Chelsea neighborhood. The exhibition featured a series of rooms with paintings, animated projections, and re-creations of Johnny's private spaces, like his typewriter and desk. In an accompanying film, he described the painting to the public: "The business celebrates you . . . they build you up to this great height, but you're choking on that. I think the skeletons understand that."

Johnny was still attempting to channel Hunter S. Thompson: the show opened with a hand-scrawled text recalling the illustrations of Ralph Steadman and quoting a famous line from *Fear and Loathing in Las Vegas*: "Buy the ticket, take the ride." As Johnny pushed away Hollywood and retreated into making music and art, it seemed he was finally trying to get off the ride he'd bought the ticket for when he arrived there in 1983. He was making something uniquely *him*.

Still, he couldn't help but remain a product, albeit a *Johnny Depp* product. His Never Fear Truth brand could be found in the exhibition gift shop in the form of sweatshirts and T-shirts marked in his handwriting, and famously preworn by him. Visitors to the exhibition could buy a stuffed animal of Johnny's now-deceased pit bull terrier Mooh, or iron-on patches, tumblers, and totes. The intellectual property of his own *self* proved irresistible. But at least now Johnny was defining his own character through work that was born from within and unencumbered by the machinations of Hollywood. For Johnny, it was a step in the right direction.

"I've been more people than most people have been," Johnny confided in a voiceover at the end of the exhibition. "The question becomes, is there anything that I can offer? Is there anything uniquely me that I can add?"

Except for a select few in his inner circle, in the years immediately following the Fairfax trial, no one knew Johnny was hiding in plain sight in the middle of Soho in London. His temporary townhouse was three stories tall and, despite its modern fixtures and clear plexiglass floors, retained its historical character, including rickety wooden stairs, upon which Johnny tripped and broke his foot. Through the glass floors, Johnny could see his security guard Malcolm sitting at the kitchen table two stories down chain-smoking cigarettes.

Upon entering the townhouse, visitors were greeted with a cannon, a worn leather couch, and candles burning inside mason jars. In the living room was a bull dick shaped like a whip and a portrait painted by Johnny of his departed friend Marlon Brando. Johnny liked *stuff* with character and a story—a vintage roulette table, a tattered wind-up monkey, a statuette of a cherub holding its own skull. At one point, Johnny hobbled downstairs, a cast on his broken foot, and came back with a massive femur bone from an unnamed animal.

He has rarely returned to his Sweetzer compound in West Hollywood, preferring a secluded life in the middle of one of London's busiest neighborhoods. A fortress from the inside, windows with one-way glass have been installed for privacy. At night, drunken tourists yell and laugh on the street outside as they stumble from bar to bar. Johnny looks out from the townhouse at the lively world below and raises a glass to the revelry. He likes being in the middle of the action, even if he has to watch from behind the glass.

Acknowledgments

Hollywood Vampires would not be possible without the care and attention of our literary agent Allison Devereux. Without her guidance and advice as well as her hand in editing and fact-checking, we wouldn't be here. We would also like to thank Samantha Culp and Matthew Specktor, who generously connected us to Allison, making this book possible. At Dey Street, Carrie Thornton and our editor, Stuart Roberts, supported us and believed in our vision for this book. Along with Bill Adams, Trina Hunn, and Anna Montague, they helped us tell this complicated story with gracious edits and pertinent insights. We are indebted to Hilary McClellen, our fastidious fact-checker, who worked nights and weekends to double- and triple-check every single detail and correct our mistakes.

Thank you to Carson Mell, who gave writing advice, good jokes, and encouragement. We'd also like to thank Jarett Kobek for his research, i.e., insane sleuthing skills, and "Laura B," who covered the *Depp vs Heard* trial in Fairfax and had encyclopedic knowledge of the case, which she always shared with us. To Jackie Zimmerman and Enna Wholey, for their support and feedback throughout our writing process; we are so grateful. Makiko thanks KS and DG for always being there. Kelly thanks Chrissy

Stuart and Christina Burchard. We want to thank our parents for their love and advice.

We are also appreciative of Roberto Sheinberg, Susan Barbour, and Hannah Fidell and her family for offering us quiet spaces to write. Kelly would like to thank her daughters, especially her youngest, who patiently waited for more of her mom's attention as she was born right at the book deadline. And to Mischa Schuman, Katha Blackwell, Lucas Leyva, Pamela Colloff, and Aya Gruber for their research and writing, and for talking us through some of the big ideas and themes we worked to articulate in the book.